The Story of Golf
in Fifty Holes

A FIREFLY BOOK

First published by Firefly Books Ltd. 2015
This paperback edition published by Firefly Books Ltd. 2023

First printing

Library of Congress Control Number: 2022934922

Library and Archives Canada Cataloguing in Publication

Title: The story of golf in fifty holes / written by Tony Dear.
Names: Dear, Tony, author.
Description: Previously published in 2015. | Includes bibliographical
references and index.
Identifiers: Canadiana 20220199914 | ISBN 9780228103486 (softcover)
Subjects: LCSH: Golf—History. | LCSH: Golf courses—History.
Classification: LCC GV963 .D43 2022 | DDC 796.352—dc23

Published in the United States by
Firefly Books (U.S.) Inc.
P.O. Box 1338, Ellicott Station
Buffalo, New York 14205

Published in Canada by
Firefly Books Ltd.
50 Staples Avenue, Unit 1
Richmond Hill, Ontario L4B 0A7

Conceived, designed, and produced by
The Bright Press, an imprint of The Quarto Group
1 Triptych Place, London,
SE1 9SH, United Kingdom
T (0)20 7700 6700 www.quarto.com

Cover and interior design: Lindsey Johns
Printed in Malaysia

The Story of Golf
in Fifty Holes

written by Tony Dear

FIREFLY BOOKS

Contents

Introduction   6

11th St. Andrews (Old Course)   8

8th Ratho Farm   12

17th Prestwick   14

17th St. Andrews (Old Course)   16

15th North Berwick   22

1st Prestwick   28

8th Royal Troon   34

5th Royal St. George's   36

3rd Biarritz Le Phare   38

16th Askernish   44

18th Muirfield   48

10th Atlantic City   54

16th Royal Lytham & St. Annes   56

17th The Country Club   60

16th Glen Echo   64

18th Oakmont   68

17th Pinehurst (No. 2)   74

11th Merion (East)   82

18th Merion (East)   90

13th Pine Valley   98

18th The Lido   108

4th Baltusrol (Lower)   110

1st Cherry Hills   114

18th Royal Birkdale   118

11th Thornhill   124

16th The Olympic Club (Lake)   126

3rd Philadelphia   128

16th Cypress Point   132

2nd Royal Pedreña   136

10th Kasumigaseki (East)   138

18th Carnoustie (Championship)   144

6th Royal Melbourne (West)   150

5th Hirono   156

10th Augusta National   158

15th Augusta National   162

17th Augusta National   170

10th Colonial   174

18th Turnberry (Ailsa)   178

7th Torrey Pines (South)   184

18th Falconhead   186

9th Colonial   188

1st The Woodlands (Oaks)   190

18th Glen Abbey   192

10th The Belfry (Brabazon)   194

17th TPC Sawgrass (Stadium)   198

18th Kiawah Island (Ocean)   202

10th Mission Hills (World Cup Course)   206

16th Bandon Dunes   208

2nd Fancourt (Links)   212

18th Trump National Los Angeles   216

Further Reading   218

Index   220

Credits   224

Introduction

This book chronicles 50 holes, past and present, where significant events in golf's illustrious history have taken place. Essentially, it's a personal, albeit carefully considered, list—and what do lists do but divide and separate those with some interest in the subject matter? As a rule, golfers hold some strong opinions about the sport they love, so the typical reader will naturally be shaking their head in disapproval before long, thinking the author a complete fool for having left out X, and for not even mentioning Y. That's fine; it's to be expected—healthy discussion is fun and a tremendous excuse to stay at the 19th hole a little longer (as if you needed one). You may even agree with some of the entries. How, for instance, could one write a history of golf (full-length or otherwise) without mentioning the treacherous 17th on the Old Course at St. Andrews—the famous Road Hole—where some of the British Open's most memorable moments have taken place? Or the seductive 15th at Augusta National where, in 1935, Gene Sarazen hit the shot that helped the Augusta National Invitational become the Masters? These indispensable entries, along with holes and courses throughout Australia, China, Europe, Japan and South Africa, are featured in this book.

GRAND SLAM
Gene Sarazen, born Eugenio Saraceni, became the first player to complete professional golf's career Grand Slam when he won the 1935 Masters.

GLORIOUS PAST

Over the last 500 years, give or take, golf has become far too big a subject to condense easily into one book. The world's most comprehensive golf libraries possess several thousand volumes, and though you'll find titles like "The Ultimate Golf Book," "The Complete Golf Book," "Everything Golf," "Total Golf" and "Absolutely and Unequivocally the Most Important Golf Book Ever Written" (OK, I made the last one up), none of them can hope to say it all. This book doesn't seek to answer every question and curiosity you have; it might even stimulate more questions than it gives answers. If, however, in the seasoned golfer it sparks a hitherto untapped interest in the game's past (and perhaps motivates that golfer to go out and play more golf), then it will have met its purpose. If it inspires one person who has never played golf in their life to at least locate the nearest driving range or pitch and putt to hit a few balls into the distance one afternoon, then it will have gone above and beyond.

HOME OF GOLF
Oh, the history members
of the Royal and Ancient
Golf Club have witnessed
through the Big Room
windows that look out
onto the 1st and 18th
holes of the Old Course
at St. Andrews, Fife.

There is much to be inspired by in the story of golf. The focus here is not on constructing a perfect timeline (though the holes are listed chronologically, not in the year when the significant events happened but when the hole opened) so much as capturing the reader's interest by presenting some important dates, places and people any fan or player should be aware of before entering into a conversation about the game's eventful history. Along with the hole and documented incidents that made it famous, you will find some elaboration on the course, the designer and anything else of note.

GOLF FOR EVERYONE

The scorecard at Augusta National is wonderfully simple as there are just two sets of tees—one for the members (6,365 yards) and one for the Masters Tournament (7,435 yards) played in April every year just before the club shuts down for the summer. Nowadays, in order to accommodate as many skill levels as possible, golf holes at public-access courses often have four, sometimes five, even six sets of tees, making for messy scorecards.

In this book only one yardage is given for each hole—the longest distance the hole has ever played. It's true few readers will ever play the 17th on the Old Course from the very back-est of back tees, installed prior to the 2010 British Open and extending the hole to 495 yards, but, again, it just made things simpler.

A number of the holes appear at courses so private the closest you might ever get to them is by looking at the picture. But I estimate that, by paying the green fee or with a well-written letter to the club secretary, you could play well over three-quarters of them.

11th St. Andrews (Old Course)

Location: St. Andrews, Fife, Scotland

Distance: 174 yards, par 3

Original course designer: The Good Lord

Subsequent alterations: Daw Anderson (1832), Allan Robertson (1848), Tom Morris Sr. (1869), Martin Hawtree (2012)*

*NB: This is by no means an exhaustive list. Since the days of Anderson, Robertson and Morris, the Old Course has continued to evolve, being lengthened at various stages to accommodate "improvements" to the golf ball and increasing popularity of the course.

HOME OF GOLF The Old Course at St. Andrews dates back over 600 years. The Swilcan Bridge, which crosses the Swilcan Burn on the home hole, is thought to be even older.

In *The Spirit of St. Andrews* (written in 1933 but lost and eventually published in 1995), course architect Alister MacKenzie wrote that the 11th on the Old Course at St. Andrews may be "considered one of the ideal holes of the world." He went on to recite a story about a friend of his putting his tee shot into the Strath bunker, short and right of the green, during the Amateur Championship one year. His opponent, meanwhile, went into Hill bunker, short and left. Both hit their recovery shots over the back of the green, into the Eden Estuary, then played back toward the flag down the sharp slope that distinguishes the hole. After each had taken 14 strokes they were back in the bunkers where they started, but in each other's, so to speak. They eventually halved the hole in 17. That's the beauty of "High"—it can be played in four relatively easily by the mediocre golfer taking no risks, but it can be a nightmare for the good golfer seeking a birdie. In 2012, course designer Martin Hawtree was commissioned to make changes to the Old Course, one of the more significant being the very controversial flattening of the back left portion of the green at the 11th to accommodate a new pin position.

CARD-WRECKER

Given the humble, accomplished, upright man he would become, and the respect and admiration he would most certainly earn, it's surprising to discover that Bobby Jones was prone to petulant temper tantrums and club-throwing in his youth. Actually, the outbursts and colorful language continued as he grew into a young man. "I was full of pie, ice cream and inexperience," he would say years later. "To me, golf was just a game to beat someone. I didn't know that someone was me."

At the 1921 U.S. Amateur Championship at St. Louis Country Club, the 19-year-old Jones was 1-down to (British) Amateur Champion Willie

Hunter after 34 holes of their third-round match. Needing to hit a good approach to the 17th hole to put some pressure on his opponent, Jones instead skimmed his shot across the green and, in a fit of pique, threw his club to the ground. It bounced into the gallery and struck a woman on the leg (she wasn't hurt). The following week, Jones received a letter from George Walker, President of the United States Golf Association (USGA), saying he would never play in a USGA event again unless he learned to control his rage.

It was by no means the only time Jones let himself down that year. Four months earlier he had come to the 11th hole at the Old Course at St. Andrews during the third round of the British Open, and left it with his scorecard torn in pieces and, if one account is to be believed, thrown to the bottom of the River Eden.

He had traveled to the U.K. in May as part of a U.S. team that played against Great Britain in an informal team competition at Royal Liverpool Golf Club. It was the forerunner to the Walker Cup, the first official match between the two countries' best amateur golfers being held the following year at National Golf Links of America. The day after the team competition at Hoylake, the American players competed in the Amateur Championship. Jones reached the fourth round, where he was beaten by the host club's Allan Graham.

A few weeks later, Jones was at St. Andrews for the British Open and, after 36 holes, was low amateur following rounds of 78 and 74. He began the third round in contention for the title, but it was a very windy day and Jones probably wasn't used to the conditions. He struggled on the outward nine, reaching the turn in 46, though some reports said it was actually 43.

He made a double-bogey 6 at the 10th, and then hit his tee shot into the savagely deep Hill bunker at the 11th. Or was it Shell bunker, short of the intersecting 7th hole?

Publications carrying the story of Jones' trials couldn't agree on his front nine score or the bunker into which he hit his tee shot at High. But it is here where details get really foggy. There are some that say Jones took to 4 to get out of the bunker, missed his putt for a 5, then picked his ball up before completing the hole. Others said he did finish the hole in 6, while others, including Jones himself, though his memory of the incident didn't always appear trustworthy, said the ball was already in his pocket when he emerged from the bunker.

"It was the most inglorious failure of my golfing life."

Bobby Jones, 40 years after he picked up on the 11th at the 1921 British Open

(In his 1927 biography *Down the Fairway*, Jones said he picked his ball up on the green when he "had a short putt left for a horrid 6." In *Golf is My Game*, published 33 years later, however, he wrote the ball had only come out of the bunker "in my pocket.")

Whatever score he made or didn't make, and however he made it, virtually everyone that ever commented on what happened said Jones then tore up his scorecard … except Jones. In *Down the Fairway*, published just six years after what happened, remember, Jones used the phrase "tearing up my scorecard" but then said, "that is a figurative term, by the way."

ROCKY START
His introduction to the Old Course might have ended in humiliation, but it wouldn't take long for Jones to fall for the course, and the Scottish galleries to fall for him.

Adding to the confusion, golf writer Bernard Darwin later said Jones might well have angrily teed up a ball and hit it into the estuary. "If he did, it was a gesture deserving of sympathy and if he did not, I am very sure he wanted to," added Darwin.

What happened next is well known to anyone who has read the record books, but the facts clearly haven't got in the way of those wishing to

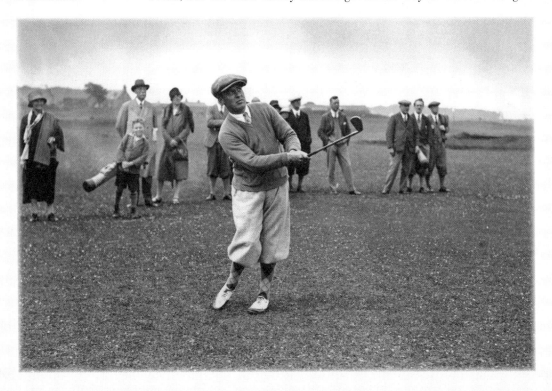

emphasize the seriousness of the situation, who will tell you Jones then stormed off the course to the horror of the galleries. Actually, Jones regained his composure, played out the rest of the round and shot an even-par 72 the next day. Had he not disqualified himself on the 11th hole in the third round by picking up his ball/ tearing up his card/dropping his card into the river/walking off the course (delete where appropriate), he might have been a serious threat down the stretch.

Jones would have to wait until 1926 for his first British Open victory—at Royal Lytham & St. Annes (see p.56). The following year, he was back at St. Andrews where he made up for his earlier indiscretion by defending his title, winning by six shots with a record total of 3-under 285. Jones had clearly done much in the six years since his regrettable debut at the Home of Golf to endear himself to the galleries. Not only was he the defending champion, he had also won two U.S. Opens and two U.S. Amateurs. He was vying with Walter Hagen to be the best player in the world, and had at last lost the temper that colored his early career. He had, in fact, become a dignified, gracious and very popular winner. As his name was announced at the prize-giving ceremony the Associated Press reported that "hats were thrown into the air, and stolid old Scots who hadn't danced a step for decades threw themselves into a Highland Fling with utmost abandon."

Jones earned the adulation of the Scots still further by saying he would not be taking the Claret Jug back to Atlanta, but that it would stay in the custody of the Royal and Ancient Golf Club.

DOUBLING UP
There are seven huge double-greens on the Old Course— the 11th hole shares a green with the 7th. Only the 1st, 9th, 17th and 18th have their own greens.

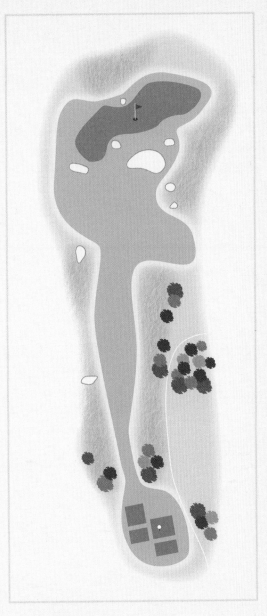

STEEPED IN HISTORY
St. Andrews is located on the east coast of the Kingdom of Fife, approximately 50 miles north of Edinburgh. The current town was established in the 12th century and is home to the oldest university in Scotland.

1822

8th Ratho Farm

Location: Bothwell, Tasmania, Australia

Distance: 165 yards, par 3

Original course designer: Alex Reid

Subsequent alterations: Paul Mogford, Neil Crafter (2010)

Australia is one of the world's great golfing nations, ranking fourth behind the U.S., U.K. and Japan in terms of adult participation—roughly 10 percent of the U.S. plays golf, 8 percent of Brits, 7 percent of Japanese and 6 percent of Aussies (according to the Australian Golf Industry Council). There are a little over 1,500 courses in the country and the major cities—Sydney, Brisbane, Adelaide, Perth and Melbourne—and each possesses a number of genuinely world-class courses. Melbourne, in particular, has more than its share of championship layouts dotted around the suburbs of Sandringham and Cheltenham, 10 miles southeast of the Central Business District. None of these great cities boasts the country's first course, however, a title that goes to the tiny village of Bothwell, 50 miles north of Hobart on the island of Tasmania, where, in the early 1820s, a Scottish immigrant built 12 holes around his backyard.

OVER THE WASHING LINE AND AROUND THE VEGETABLE PATCH

Ratho Farm is thought to have been laid out in 1822 and is generally considered Australia's oldest golf course, the oldest in the Southern Hemisphere, and one of the oldest courses in the world outside of Britain (the Royal Calcutta GC is regarded as the oldest golf club outside of Britain). It was created by Alex Reid, an Edinburgh merchant who emigrated with his wife and two children to Van Diemen's Land (now Tasmania), settling in the Clyde Valley, which several other Scottish families had begun to call home. Reid's original course consisted of six holes running north, away from the sheep-shearing shed, and six that first headed south toward the village, but which returned to the farmstead, finishing more or less outside the back door.

Following World War II, the course became a nine-holer when three of the original holes were abandoned. The other three were lost in the early 1980s when a bridge and road were redirected close to the old

BACK TO BASICS
If Ratho Links at Ratho Farm wasn't so significant a course, you probably wouldn't choose to play it very often. But what it lacks in architectural interest it makes up for in history and character.

1st hole. Government compensation allowed the current owner, John Ramsay, to hire Australian architects Paul Mogford and Neil Crafter to restore old holes and build new ones as close to the original style and retaining as much of the course's original character as possible. The bridge made replacing one original green impossible, and sourcing information showing the exact specifications of others wasn't easy. So there was some level of interpretation, but Crafter believes the 165-yard 8th hole is more or less identical to what it might have been. The hole plays back past the shearing shed, over a hedge and a ditch, and a vegetable garden sits to the right of the green. "Quite a hole," says Crafter.

The work was completed in two phases, starting in the summer of 2010 and concluding in 2012. Two of the new holes—the 450-yard 15th and 265-yard 16th—make wonderful use of the Clyde River, and although the holes are still routed through what is basically someone's back yard, it is a profound pleasure to play so historic a golf course.

Visitors pay a small fee to play the links at Ratho (which measure about 5,876 yards) and to become members of the Rural and Ancient Golf Society of Van Diemen's Land for the day (annual and life memberships are available). Stay overnight and you can sleep in one of the Convict Cottages which once housed the convicts Alex Reid was granted use of by the Government when establishing Ratho Farm.

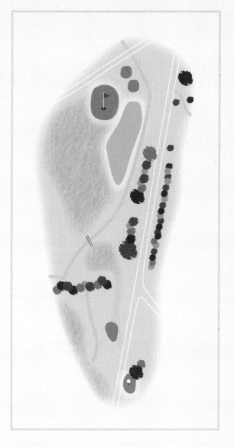

OLD SCHOOL
The aerial plan shows you tee off over a road, pass through a hedge and hit over a narrow stream. Sounds intriguing, though in reality it probably wasn't one of Alex Reid's best designs.

BACKYARD GOLF
Ratho Farm is located near the village of Bothwell, Tasmania. The course Alex Reid laid out around his farmhouse nearly 200 years ago was rudimentary to say the least.

"The visiting golfer is in for a special treat at Ratho, for here is golf as it once was. The course is laid out over the natural ground, and obstacles found on a farm such as sheep, hedges and ditches are all part of it. It is especially fun to play with hickory-shafted clubs."

Neil Crafter, Ratho Farm designer

1851

17th Prestwick

Location: Prestwick,
Ayrshire, Scotland

Distance: 394 yards, par 4

Original course designer:
Tom Morris Sr.

Subsequent alterations:
Charles Hunter (1882)

The 17th at Prestwick—the 2nd hole on Tom Morris' original 1851 12-hole layout—is a wonderfully old-fashioned challenge only a tiny number of present-day architects would even consider building, and which an even smaller number of course owners/developers would allow an architect to build. As a rule, modern golfers prefer not to have their path to the hole, green or fairway obscured by a natural landform like a huge sand dune, for instance.

BLIND SPOT

"Blind" holes were not uncommon in golf's early years. Without earth-moving machinery, the game's first course-builders had little choice at times but to route holes over or around ridges, dunes, mounds, etc. Unless they had an army of laborers at their disposal (like Charles Alison in Japan—see p.138), they didn't really have the option of removing what stood in their way.

Also, because water wasn't piped all around the course by hi-tech, multi-million-dollar irrigation systems, the first designers had to rely heavily on gravity to get water to a certain place, which is why a good many of their greens were built in punchbowls or hollows where rainwater would percolate and where good turf already grew.

ONE OF A KIND
You would never see a hole like the 17th at Prestwick built today. It's just too quirky, and contemporary architects, developers and golfers simply couldn't afford to wait for it to become iconic.

Golfers who appreciate the game's history revere these blind holes, saying they create intrigue, are only blind the first time you play them, and that there is nothing so thrilling as climbing the dune that sits between them and the hole to see the result of their shot. Others loathe what they regard as anachronisms, which have no place in the modern game.

With the huge sandhill dominating the hole 40–50 yards short of the green (preventing any sight of the putting surface or of the deep depression just in front of it known as the Slough of Despond), the forced carry off the tee over a corner of the Cardinal bunker (albeit a carry most should conquer), the 7-foot-deep Sahara bunker that sits between the Alps

and the green, and a shallow, half-pipe-shaped putting surface, the 17th is 394 yards of debate-inducing amusement. Visitors can hardly wait to finish the relatively benign 288-yard 18th so they can hash out the merits of the 17th over a pint of "dark" in the delightful stone clubhouse while perusing the club's magnificent collection of British Open and Morris-family-related memorabilia.

BOUNTIFUL
Prestwick is found in a stretch of glorious golfing terrain on the Ayrshire coast in southwest Scotland.

AMERICAN ALPS

As mentioned above, the idea of the Alps is just too quirky, too eccentric, too unpredictable for most developers and designers today. Modern golfers say the word "quirky" as if it's a bad thing. If a large mound sits in what will be a fairway, today's designer is apt to bulldoze it. Thankfully, though, a handful of architects over the last hundred years or so have recognized the charm of such features and sought to recreate them, most notably perhaps C.B. Macdonald, his associate Seth Raynor, and his disciple Charles Banks. Macdonald built a superb Alps at National Golf Links of America (NGLA) that he, not surprisingly, given his bravado and conviction, declared better than Prestwick's. More recently, the always-adventurous Mike Stranz, who sadly passed away in 2005, built a handful of great Alps-like holes. Tom Doak and Jim Urbina included a great Alps in their tribute to Macdonald at the Bandon Dunes Golf Resort in Oregon. Opened in 2010 and aptly named Old Macdonald, the course possesses a treasure trove of the template holes (Alps, Redan, Sahara, Punchbowl, Cape, Road, etc.) Macdonald used so effectively on his courses. All fit the land beautifully and don't seem at all forced. And none is better than the 16th which, unlike the Prestwick hole that inspired it, does allow the superior golfer who can drive it a long way down the right side of the fairway a look at the green.

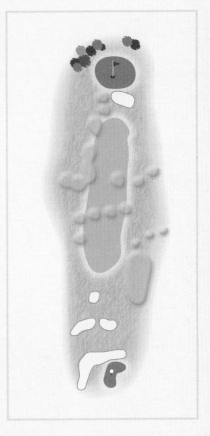

MOUNTAINOUS
The intimidating sandhill short of the green on the 17th is a strange obstacle. But, like all blind holes, it is only blind the first time you play it.

"I have never been an admirer of blind holes, and believe the old masters would not have tolerated them if they had modern machinery available to do an occasional nip and tuck."

Pat Ruddy, course designer

1852

17th St. Andrews (Old Course)

Location: St. Andrews, Fife, Scotland

Distance: 495 yards, par 4

Original course designer: The Good Lord

Subsequent alterations: Daw Anderson (1832), Allan Robertson (1848), Tom Morris Sr. (1869), Martin Hawtree (2012)

"No question it is the hardest hole in championship golf. But I think it's the finest par 4 in the world."

Seve Ballesteros, winner of the British Open at St. Andrews in 1984

Golf has been played on the links of St. Andrews since the 15th century (though it was banned in 1457 by King James II, as it interfered with soldiers practicing their archery. The ban was lifted by James IV in 1502). The ground was cropped by hungry sheep, forming fairways, and animals trying to avoid the bitter winds dug shelters that are now bunkers (do you think they knew they were playing a crucial role in the creation of the world's most famous golf course?) The Old Course has evolved a great deal over time, the latest modifications occurring under Martin Hawtree's watch in 2012/13. In 1754, when the Society of St. Andrews Golfers was formed (it became the Royal and Ancient Golf Club in 1834), there were 22 holes—11 out, 11 back. In 1764, however, the society combined the first four and last four holes into four total to form an 18-hole course. Scott Macpherson, author of *The Evolution of the Old Course: The Impact on Golf of Time, Tradition & Technology* says the western boundary of the Old Course was probably formed in 1852, when the Leuchars to St. Andrews train service opened. How close was the track to the hole? Well, the town's station was located where the Old Course Hotel now stands and railway outhouses had to be negotiated from the tee. And the famous Jigger Inn, where people now enjoy a pint of McEwan's ale or Irn Bru soda while watching their fellow golfers try to escape the Road bunker, was the stationmaster's house.

ROCKY ROAD
The second shot at the 17th approaches the green from the left of this image. The green is clearly very shallow and fronted by the notorious Road bunker.

WHERE THE RUBBER MEETS THE ROAD

Allan Robertson, the club- and ball-maker, and the best player of his day (first to break 80 on the Old Course—in 1857), had made several alterations to the course in 1848, including doubling the width of the fairways and building the shallow, angled green we now play at the 17th. There, he also dug the Road bunker—the menacing sand-filled hole that eats into the front of the putting surface. The green was the culmination of the 1st and 17th holes at the time, but Tom Morris Sr. separated them in 1863, giving the course four holes with their own green— 1st, 9th, 17th and 18th—and seven huge double greens, and changing the direction of the round from clockwise to counterclockwise.

An 1821 diagram of the course shows that the hole on which the 17th now sits was straighter than what became the 17th. When the railway sheds were built in the 1850s, however, the fairway became obscured and gave the hole a left-to-right kink. With Robertson's Road bunker and the railway sheds, the 17th was now one of the most demanding holes in Scotland. And the average score the world's best players have managed during recent British Opens (see box above) proves it is still one of the hardest par 4s in the world. The scores actually suggest it's a par 5, which it was until 1964.

The problem from the tee is obvious. You can't go through the sheds (at one time known as the Black Sheds because they were covered in soot from the steam trains' emissions, and which were taken down when the railway station moved into the town and replaced by the hotel, but subsequently rebuilt to restore the hole's former character) that stand at the corner of the dogleg, so you have to go over them, or around them to the left if you don't like the carry.

That carry was made a little more challenging for British Open competitors ahead of the 2010 Open, when a new back tee was built 40 yards behind its predecessor. The tee was now actually outside the boundary of the course, made the hole a monster par 4 of 495 yards, and was much maligned by Old Course disciples who maintain the 17th, or indeed any part of the course, should never be altered. Peter Dason, the Royal and Ancient Golf Club's secretary and Chief Executive of the R&A said the move would bring the road behind the green more in play than it had been in recent years, as players would need to hit lower-flying mid-to-long irons for their second shot, as opposed

SCORING AVERAGE

✦

The scoring average at the 17th hole during the British Open since 1984:

1984—4.79
1990—4.65
1995—4.62
2000—4.70
2005—4.63
2010—4.67

to the much shorter irons they had used in 2005. From the new back tee, the drive needed to travel roughly 260 yards to find a safe position in the fairway.

The approach shot from the fairway with a long-to-mid iron is surely one of the most challenging and exciting in the game. Because the surface is so shallow, it is more or less impossible to carry the ball on to the green and have it stop before it bounds off the back and on to the road behind. So a low, run-up shot works better.

But, of course, the insidious Road bunker lies in wait, gathering balls like a sink, and plunging golfers to the bottom of a 6-foot-deep pit.

Together with Martin Hawtree, the St. Andrews Links Trust, which manages the town's seven courses (the Old Course only became known as the Old Course after the town's second course—now the New Course—opened in 1895) has altered the bunker in recent years, expanding and re-contouring the surrounding area to make it easier for a ball to roll in, bringing it back from the green slightly, widening it by about 2 feet to give it a more oval shape, and making the base slightly more bowl-like rather than flat to make the recovery shot slightly easier. But it's still the Road bunker—the bunker golfers about to play the course for the first time have been thinking about since they scheduled their tee-time, and probably long before that.

The disciples write letters and form protest groups every time someone so much as goes near the bunker with a spade or digger, and that is perfectly understandable given its significance. But what alterations have happened have not changed the fact it is still the best-known hazard in the world, and assigns the golfer foolish or unlucky enough to find it an incredibly tough (but fun) dilemma— try blasting up, out and forward and risk hitting into the sod wall, or come out sideways, ensuring you get out perhaps but leaving another tricky shot.

Fifty yards short of the green and just to the left of the fairway is Scholar's bunker, which Alister MacKenzie regarded as superfluous, as it stopped balls headed for what he called the "danger zone." Cheape's bunker is a worry only for those completely mis-hitting their tee shot or not taking the risk of carrying the sheds. It should really only bother those going left off the 2nd tee.

The rough left of the fairway can be pretty unfriendly. Beyond the green there is the road, which was once covered in stone and gravel but is now covered in asphalt. Beyond the road is a stone wall.

It all adds up. Combine the shot over the sheds, Cheape's Bunker, Scholar's Bunker, heavy rough left, crumpled ground short of the Road bunker, the Road bunker itself, the very shallow green, the road beyond and the wall beyond the road, and the length of the hole (426/436/455 yards from the three forward tees) and you have a very distinctive, very scary, but thoroughly entertaining hole of which five-time British Open champion Peter Thomson, who won the 1955 British Open at St. Andrews, once said, "If one built such a hole today, he'd be sued for incompetence."

TROUBLE BOGEY

Stories of misadventure on the Old Course's 17th hole are legion. Seriously, where does one start? How about 1885, St. Andrews' fifth Championship, when local golfer David Ayton Sr. found trouble on the Road? After an opening 89, Ayton was six off Archie Simpson's lead heading into the second and final round, but played superbly over the first 16 holes to rise to the top of the leaderboard (they didn't have leaderboards in those days, but you get the idea). But it all went hideously wrong down the penultimate hole. Ayton actually hit a good drive, followed by a decent brassie up the fairway. But his chip-and-run to the green was weak and came up short of the Road bunker. The pitch over the sand is extremely delicate and Ayton misjudged it, going over

SPOILED FOR CHOICE
Fife is one of Scotland's most popular golf destinations. As well as the five full-length courses at St. Andrews, there's the Dukes Course, Kingsbarns, St. Andrews Bay, Crail, Elie, Lundin, Leven, etc.

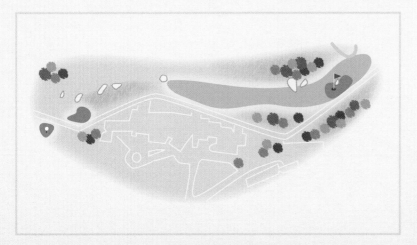

HAZARDS APLENTY
Tee off on the left, and somehow avoid the hotel, Out of Bounds, heavy rough, deep bunkers, and the road en route to a very well-earned par 4.

the back of the green and finding the road. His fifth shot failed to reach the putting surface and rolled back to where he was standing. He overcooked the next shot, the ball running back over the green and into the Road bunker. Three splashes later and he could use his putter at last. He missed his first effort then holed out for an 11. Ayton finished two strokes behind the winner Bob Martin. Had he made a straightforward par 5 at the 17th he would most likely have broken 80 (Allan Robertson had been the first man to do so 35 years earlier but it was still a rare feat) and won the British Open.

Fast-forward 93 years to the 1978 British Open. Japan's Tsuneyuki (Tommy) Nakajima, a 23-year-old two-time winner on the Japan Golf Tour (he would finish his career with 48 JGT victories), arrived at the 17th hole in the third round in contention for the title. On the right half of the green in two, he had a putt for a share of the lead. But instead of finding the hole at the bottom of the flagstick, Nakajima found the hole with sand at the bottom, having putted into the Road bunker. He then took not one, not two, not three but four shots to get out and two-putted for a 9. Asked after the round if he had lost concentration in the bunker, Nakajima replied, "No, I lost count." For years after, the Road Bunker was known as the "Sands of Nakajima."

Spain's Seve Ballesteros was also in the picture at the 1978 British Open but drove into the hotel grounds in the second round, eventually making a 6. He finished the week 6 over par for the hole and seven shots behind the winner, Jack Nicklaus. The following year, at the Colgate PGA Championship (the British PGA Championship now known as the BMW Championship), Ballesteros' relationship with the 17th hole grew worse still when he emulated Nakajima by putting into the bunker, having found the green in regulation. The Spaniard took two to get out then two-putted for a 7.

But, oh, how Ballesteros profited from another's mishap at the 17th during the final round of the 1984 British Open. Seve had made a bogey at the hole in each of the opening three rounds. In the fourth he went left off the tee and found thick rough. With just over 190 yards to go, he took a 6-iron and hit a superb short to the front edge of the green. After two putts he had his first par of the week at the 17th, putting pressure on the only other man in contention—Tom Watson—who was going for a sixth Claret Jug, which would have tied England's Harry Vardon for the record.

The American hit a bold tee shot down the right side, leaving himself the best angle into the green. But the ball rolled onto a small upslope about 195 yards from the hole and, given the extra loft the shot would have and that he felt a little wind in his face, Watson decided on a 2-iron instead of the 3-iron he says he would have taken had his lie been flatter.

It was too much club. Watson's ball went through the green, over the road, and ended up dangerously close to the wall. He was able to hit a jabby chip shot, but without any control. He made a 5 and ended up two shots behind Ballesteros, who made a birdie at the 18th hole and saluted the crowd with his famous fist-pumping routine. "If there was one shot in my career that I would like to have over again, it would be that 2-iron shot," Watson said years later.

MONUMENTAL
One of the most stirring views in the game—as you play the back nine the R&A clubhouse, Hamilton Grand (formerly a university hall of residence) and St. Rule's Tower are always in sight.

15th North Berwick

Location: North Berwick,
East Lothian, Scotland

Distance: 190 yards, par 3

Original course designer:
David Strath

FORTIFIED
Does it remind you of a
jagged notch protruding
from the walls of a
formidable fortress,
specifically one in
Sevastopol?

It seems a little far-fetched, not to say ridiculous, to liken golf holes to the design of military fortresses, but that is how the 15th at North Berwick came by its name—Redan. The hole, one of the most famous in the game, is thought to have begun as a 260-yarder but is now a tough par 3 of 190 yards. It was the sixth of nine holes when first played in 1869.

BIRTH OF THE REDAN

North Berwick GC had been formed in 1832 (13th oldest golf club in the world), the members playing over a six-hole course that extended from the clubhouse to a stone wall known as the March Dyke. When a wealthy member and landowner—the Right Hon. John Nisbet-Hamilton—donated a few acres beyond the wall in 1868, the club was able to add another three holes. The course grew further still in 1877 when Nisbet-Hamilton made more land available as far west as the Eil Burn, and the nine holes doubled. The club sought advice from Tom Morris in extending the course, and Davie Strath, appointed Keeper of the Green a year before, was also heavily involved. The 6th hole became the course's new 15th.

BATTLE SCENE
The Siege of Sevastopol took place between October 1854 and September 1855 and was part of the Crimean War fought between Britain, France and the Ottomans, against Russia. The Battle of the Great Redan brought the siege to an end.

North Berwick was an almost embarrassingly short 4,841 yards, however. The club continued its attempts to stretch even further west, but had to wait until 1895 when the course became a much healthier 6,095 yards, the work carried out by greenkeeper Tom Anderson adhering to a plan devised by the secretary of the Greens Committee Jack McCulloch.

Yet more land was found in 1932 and, under the supervision of Ben Sayers Jr., son of the famous club-maker who had worked in a small building adjacent to the 1st tee for 45 years, and Major Cecil Hutchison, the course took on the shape we are familiar with today.

When it first appeared, probably in 1869, the Redan is thought to have played to 266 yards, though this was possibly because there were no formal tees at the time and players simply teed up within a club's length of the hole they just finished. The 1886 and 1887 Amateur Championship winner Horace Hutchison most likely played the hole at this distance, as he said it required a "cleek or iron short over a wall, so far and no further, and then a full drive or brassy shot to carry over a bunker escarpment not inaptly called the 'Redan.'"

It is likely that when Hutchison played it first, the hole had been known by that name for 15 years—since Major John Whyte-Melville returned from the Crimean War and, on his first visit to the course, remarked that the 15th put him in mind of the formidable fortress, or redan, he had encountered during the Siege of Sevastopol, probably during the Battle of the Great Redan in September 1855.

The word "redan" is a form of the French *redent* (jagged notching) and means "salient" or "projection." It is used to describe protruding

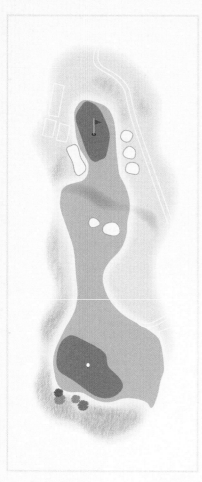

V-shaped kinks in fortress walls. Quite how the 15th at North Berwick, and the formation of the bunkers 30–40 yards short of the green in particular, reminded the major of a protruding V-shaped kink in a fortress wall is anyone's guess. But if it had something to do with it being difficult to penetrate then there is indeed some connection.

> **"Take a narrow tableland, tilt it a little from right to left, dig a deep bunker on the front side, and approach it diagonally."**
>
> *Famed course architect C.B. Macdonald*
> *on how to create a Redan*

PLAYING THE REDAN

In essence, the Redan is a par 3 (though the design of the green complex can be used on par 4s and par 5s) with a green angled at roughly 45 degrees to the line of play from front right to back left, with the front edge significantly higher than the back, creating a downward slope best negotiated with a low, running, right-to-left shot. The area around the front-right corner of the green is raised and thus kicks a ball hit with right-to-left spin to the left and toward the hole. This raised area is often referred to as a "kick plate." A deep bunker is positioned on the front-left side of the green.

The North Berwick hole, which has inspired numerous copies around the world, also has three man-deep bunkers to the right of the green and the two set in a mound 30–40 yards short of it, which actually obscures the golfer's view of the green from the tee.

The green on most of the world's Redans points front right to back left and accommodates the well-judged draw. There are a few, however, set on the opposite diagonal (called Reverse Redans)—short left to long right—and which therefore yield to a fade. The vast majority of post-North Berwick designers who build Redans usually dispense with the mound short of the green, preferring to make the putting surface at least partly visible from the tee.

HIDDEN DANGERS
Clearing the sandy ridge that cuts the hole in two, and which conceals your view of the green from the tee, is just the first of your problems at the 15th.

BONNIE BAY
North Berwick GC is found on the East Lothian coast overlooking the Firth of Forth, about 25 miles east of Edinburgh.

MACDONALD, RAYNOR AND BANKS
—THE REDAN'S BIGGEST FANS

When Charles Blair Macdonald moved from Chicago to Scotland in 1872 to study at St. Andrews University, he became devoted to the game, being tutored by the legendary Old Tom Morris and playing matches against his son, Young Tom, on the course which hosted the British Open for the first time the year after Macdonald arrived. He became intrigued by the great British links courses, growing especially fascinated with the design of certain holes—North Berwick's Redan included.

Having returned to the U.S. in 1874, Macdonald spent 17 years—a period he called "the Dark Ages"—as a stockbroker and playing very little golf. His interest stirred in the early 1890s, however, when he introduced the game to friends, together with whom he founded the Chicago Golf Club. In the spring of 1892 he built his first course—a short seven-holer on the lawns of Senator Charles Farwell ahead of the 1893 World's Columbian Exposition. He didn't much like it, but it attracted enough attention to inspire him to build something altogether more worthy. He rented some farmland in the western suburb of Belmont (now Downers Grove), and later in 1892 built nine holes, to which he added nine more a year later, creating the United States' first 18-hole golf course. The Chicago Golf Club was registered on July 18, 1893. (In December 1894, Macdonald was heavily involved as his Chicago GC joined Shinnecock Hills GC, Newport GC, The Country Club and Saint Andrew's GC in establishing the United States Golf Association—originally known as the American Golf Association. Macdonald became the first official U.S. Amateur champion at Newport the following year).

Belmont still didn't quite do it for him though so, in 1895, Macdonald moved the club to Wheaton, 30 miles from downtown Chicago, where he purchased 200 acres, financed development of the new course, recruited a new membership, built a house for himself, and designed every hole with the utmost precision, creating inner and outer circular nines much like those at Muirfield in Scotland, a course he admired greatly.

In 1900, wanting to play more top-flight amateur golf, Macdonald left for New York City where he became a partner in a Wall St. brokerage firm. He played a good deal but was largely unimpressed with most of the courses he visited, and he grew determined to build a world-class course himself. He visited Europe often to gain inspiration and knowledge and, after much searching, he finally chose a site

"I believe in reverencing anything in the life of man which has the testimony of the ages as being unexcelled, whether it be literature, paintings, poetry, tombs—even a golf hole."

C.B. Macdonald

for his wonder-course, to be christened the National Golf Links of America (NGLA), on Peconic Bay, near Southampton on Long Island. He offered founding memberships to 70 people at $1,000 each and began work in 1907, eager to build something that would compare favorably with the best he had played on the other side of the Atlantic, with holes modeled on his favorites.

The 2nd hole at NGLA would be a version of Royal St. George's Sahara hole, the 3rd a longer version of Prestwick's Alps (17th). The 7th was based on the Old Course at St. Andrews' Road Hole (17th), and the short 13th was a replica of St. Andrews' Eden Hole (11th).

The best of the lot, though, was undoubtedly the 4th, a Redan Macdonald sited on a perfectly tilted green with 5 feet of drop from front to back. The green—the front section at least—was visible from the tee—the reason many who have played both holes say NGLA's Redan is superior to North Berwick's. At NGLA, they say, a player can see the ball pitch and begin its roll toward the hole. Others say the original will never be bettered.

It was at NGLA that Macdonald first worked with Seth Raynor, a local civil engineer educated at Princeton. Raynor wasn't a golfer and had worked on drains, ditches and roads after leaving university. But Macdonald hired him to survey the land at Southampton and was so impressed with his "seriousness and dependability" he asked him to stay on as construction supervisor.

NGLA opened to great acclaim in 1911 and, 100-plus years later, it is still ranked inside the world's top 20 courses.

Raynor was heavily involved at every course Macdonald designed thereafter—Piping Rock, Sleepy Hollow, St. Louis CC, Old White at the Greenbrier, Blind Brook, The Lido, Mid Ocean, Deepdale, Gibson Island, the Creek Club, the Course at Yale—and learned a great deal about what made a golf hole great for both scratch players and the less competent.

He struck out on his own around 1914, becoming one of the best and most prolific architects in America's history. Among dozens of other noteworthy courses, Raynor designed a number of timeless classics such as Fisher's Island, Camargo, Shoreacres, Fox Chapel, the Country Club of Fairfield, the Country Club of Charleston, Lookout Mountain, Mountain Lake and Yeamans Hall, all of them with plenty of template holes including some exquisite Redans.

In 1923, Raynor was sent by his mentor to Chicago GC to perform some much-needed renovations. Course designer H.S. Colt had also visited—in 1913—and made some proposals of his own, but the club had just built a new clubhouse so wasn't able to implement them fully. Ten years later, Raynor arrived with Macdonald's instructions and transformed the course into what is regarded as one of the top 50 or so in the world—one that is jealously guarded by a small, exclusive, attention-eschewing membership.

Perhaps the best of the many template holes Raynor built at Chicago was the par 3 7th, a downhill Redan with two wide, horizontal bunkers short of the green.

Another of the great Redans can be found at The Course at Yale in Connecticut, which is often credited to Macdonald but was really the work of Raynor. It is also where he and Macdonald took on another pair of hands—those of Charles Banks, a Yale graduate who was working as a teacher at Hotchkiss Prep School just 60 miles away. Raynor was building a nine-hole course for the school and Banks was chosen to assist him. Banks recognized pretty quickly he had chosen the wrong line of work, and very soon joined Raynor at Yale. He too would learn the art and science of building template holes, helping Raynor find the superb 13th, a downhill 212-yard Redan that plays partially over water.

> **"When properly executed the play of this green is one of the most pleasing and interesting plays in golf."**
>
> *Charles Banks, Raynor's assistant,*
> *on the Redan at Yale*

1st Prestwick

Location: Prestwick,
Ayrshire, Scotland

Distance: 345 yards, par 4

Original course designer:
Tom Morris Sr.

Subsequent alterations:
Charles Hunter (1882)

RIDING THE RAILS
Today's 1st hole at
Prestwick is bordered
on its right side by the
Ayr–Glasgow railway line
(over the stone wall).
A scary prospect for
anyone with a tendency to
push or slice the ball.

Ask a golf historian something about Prestwick's 1st hole and they are liable to answer, "Which one?" No, it doesn't currently have two opening holes, rather there have been two remarkable and noteworthy 1st holes in the club's history. The first was an outrageously long hole for the time, the second a beguiling par 4 with a railway line just a slightly pushed shot from the tee.

MORRIS HEADS WEST

Most of the ancient clubs played their first shots on rudimentary courses with an arbitrary number of holes—basically wherever the topography and the property's boundaries allowed them to hit a feathery (a ball made of goose feathers stuffed into a leather pouch). After the Royal and Ancient Golf Club of St. Andrews first stated in the Rule Book that "One round of the Links, or 18 holes, is reckoned a match" (R&A members are actually thought to have begun playing 18 holes in 1764 when they turned four of their 12 holes into two and played eight of the remaining 10 twice), other clubs in Scotland—Montrose, Innerleven

(Dubbieside links, which no longer exists), Prestwick, the Honourable Company of Edinburgh Golfers, etc., followed suit, slowly adopting the 18-hole round themselves. Clubs with six holes played their links three times. Nine-hole courses were played twice. New courses, such as Muirfield (the location to which the Honourable Company of Edinburgh Golfers would move, from nine-hole Musselburgh, in 1891) were invariably built with the full complement of 18 holes.

As 18 became the standard, and longer, more durable, more affordable gutta-percha balls replaced the feathery, the old five-, six-, nine- and twelve-hole layouts were basically abandoned, the holes all but forgotten.

Prestwick GC was founded in 1851 by 57 gentlemen, led by the Earl of Eglinton who owned the land on which the course was to be built. Colonel James Fairlie, one of the club's founding members, a friend of the Earl's and a member of the R&A, persuaded Tom Morris (aka Old Tom Morris), who worked for club- and ball-maker Allan Robertson at St. Andrews, to head west and lay out the course at Prestwick then stay on to become Keeper of the Green.

MEMORABLE MORRIS
Tom Morris Sr. (Old Tom Morris) addresses his ball outside the clubhouse at Prestwick during the very first British Open in 1860.

Morris' first son had died the year before, so it's probable he and wife Nancy saw the move to the other side of the country as an opportunity to try and forget their sorrow. He got to work straight away, devoting himself to building his first course more or less by hand and with very little assistance. He had worked with Robertson in laying out 10 holes at Carnoustie in 1842, but this would be Morris' first solo effort.

The land was rough, utterly useless for arable farming but perfect for golf. The Glasgow–Ayr steam train whistled right by the property too, making it easily accessible for members who lived and worked in Glasgow.

Morris built 12 holes, a number of them crisscrossing because of limited space. But despite being somewhat hazardous, Morris' holes took full advantage of the crude but captivating land, collectively forming a course whose reputation spread far and wide with the help of the stream train.

No hole's reputation spread further or faster than that of the 1st. It certainly wasn't true of every course Morris would design but, if the difficult 1st hole at Muirfield and the 1st at Prestwick are anything to go by, he definitely wasn't opposed to making strong demands of the members from the very start.

His opening hole at Prestwick measured 578 yards—by far the longest hole in the game, and a colossal distance at a time when 200 yards was considered a good whack. Not only did the average member have to make four healthy swipes to reach the green, he had to hit the first of them well enough to clear an area of swampy marshland called the Goosedubs (now drained, re-turfed and site of the present 14th hole). A stone marker, a few yards to the west of the clubhouse, shows the position of Morris' 1st tee.

THE BRITISH OPEN AND TOMMY'S EAGLE

In 1859, Allan Robertson who, nobody refuted, was the best player in the game, died. Colonel Fairlie, who had held what amounted to a national club championship at Prestwick beginning in 1857, decided the club should hold a new tournament to identify Robertson's successor. Clubs were invited to send no more than three professionals but only eight entered, seven of them from Scotland (the eighth was England's George Brown). The first British Open was held on October 17, 1860, but, despite the name, was open only to professionals.

The winner was Musselburgh's Willie Park (his brother Mungo and son Willie Jr. would also win) who beat Tom Morris by two shots, playing three rounds of the 12-hole course in 174 strokes—55, 59, 60. Park won no money, but did take home a handsome red leather belt—the Challenge Belt—with silver clasps that had cost the Prestwick members £25 ($40).

WINNING STREAK
In 1872, after winning his fourth British Open title, Tom Morris Jr. was awarded this medal (actually called the Golf Champion Trophy).

The tournament became genuinely open the following year, when the field increased to 18 golfers of which eight were amateurs. Morris extracted full revenge on Park winning by four with rounds of 54, 56 and 53. Old Tom Morris would win three more titles, in 1862, 1864 and 1867.

Though he finished second in 1868, by which time he had returned to St. Andrews to become Keeper of the Green, Old Tom was far from unhappy with the result, as it was his son, Tom Morris Jr., who beat him. Young Tom shot 154 to beat Andrew Strath's record total of 1865 by eight shots. He was just 17 years old at the time, and he remains the youngest major championship winner in history. He repeated his victory in 1869, and in 1870 he won his third title in a row, becoming the permanent holder of the Challenge Belt.

Morris Jr. shot a record 149 over the 36 holes that year, helped to a large degree by the incredible start he made in the first round. With a sizable and excitable gallery following to see if he could capture the unprecedented three-peat, Morris Jr. played two shots safely down the fairway then holed his third for a scarcely believable 3. Par had not been conceived by this point, but a professional was generally expected to complete the lengthy 1st in 6 or better, making Morris' 3 an albatross or double-eagle.

Morris Jr. shot 47 in the opening round, beating his own course record by two and becoming the first player to average better than 4 per hole on the course his father had built. He would win the championship by 12 strokes over Davie Strath and Bob Kirk.

Morris was unable to go for victory in four consecutive years because the British Open was not held in 1871. The R&A and Honourable Company of Edinburgh Golfers had become interested in hosting the tournament and contributing to the purchase of a new belt, but no decision on what the winner's prize would be or which course would host the event were made in time.

Agreement was finally reached on September 11, 1872, when it was decided the three clubs would take it in turns to host the British Open and each contribute £10 ($15) for the purchase of a new trophy—a claret jug whose official name would be the Golf Champion Trophy.

There was no time to commission and make it in the two days before the start of the 1872 British Open at Prestwick, however, so the winner would collect a medal with the words "Golf Champion Trophy" inscribed on its face. Picking up where he had left off in 1870, the

LIKE FATHER,
LIKE SON
Old Tom stands behind
Young Tom in a portrait
taken some time between
1870 and 1875.

young Tom Morris won his fourth British Open title, coming back from five behind Davie Strath after two rounds with a final round of 53 to win by three. He was 21 years and 146 days old.

It's not very useful to compare Young Tom with modern day professionals, so much has the game evolved over the past 140-plus years. But it seems worth noting the next youngest player to win four majors is Tiger Woods, who was seven years and three months older than Morris when he clinched his fourth—the 2000 British Open.

In 1873, the British Open moved away from Prestwick for the first time, being held at St. Andrews, where Tom Kidd shot 91, 88 to beat Jamie Anderson by a shot. Young Tom Morris tied for third, his father, now 52 years of age, was seventh.

Tommy died tragically on Christmas Day 1875 at the age of 24. After returning home from a match with his father against the Park brothers at Musselburgh, he found his wife, Margaret Drinnen, and newborn baby both dead, following a difficult labor; three and a half months later Tom too had passed away. The official cause of Young Tom's death was a heart attack, but everyone that knew him would have told you profound grief was responsible.

THE "NEW" 1ST HOLE

By the early 1880s, St Andrews was considered the appropriate length for a layout worthy of holding the Championship, so Prestwick, having acquired additional land to the north of the existing course, extended the layout to the full 18 holes.

Club professional Charles Hunter did much of the work with assistance from his friend Old Tom Morris, who had been back in St. Andrews for 18 years but who still visited Prestwick frequently to play in the British Open and spend time with old

TOP-DRESSER TOM

✦

It's no fun putting on bumpy, inconsistent, thatch-covered greens that drain poorly and are prone to disease. Golfers prefer healthy turf and even surfaces on which they can be confident the ball will roll smoothly toward (and into) the hole.

To achieve top-quality putting surfaces, greenkeepers/superintendents aerate (punch holes) then "top-dress" the greens with a mixture of sand, soil, seed and fertilizer. Most do this twice a year, though some get better results applying less mixture more frequently. Old Tom Morris was very probably the first greenkeeper to ever adopt the practice, having discovered the more sand he applied to his greens at Prestwick the better they turned out.

friends. Hunter reconfigured Morris' original holes and built six of his own of which the new 1st might have been the best.

Named Railway because the Glasgow–Ayr line is just the other side of the boundary wall to the right of the fairway, the hole starts in front of the clubhouse and measures only 345 yards. The tracks are out of bounds of course, but the brilliance of the hole is that the nearer you get to them the easier the approach to the green will be. Take the safer line down the left and you must contend with bunkers, banks and ridges.

The course saw further changes in 1922 when James Braid and Harold Hilton modified the stretch between the 7th and the 11th.

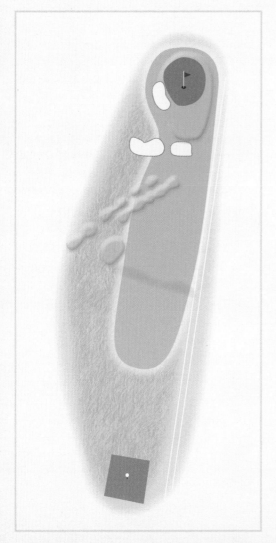

NARROW MARGINS
Can't go right, can't go left—gotta go straight. But it's better to be a little right of center, so you need to flirt with the wall to leave a better line for the approach.

TRAIN TOWN
A settlement at Prestwick, roughly 35 miles southwest of Glasgow, has existed for over 1,000 years, though the village rose to prominence in the 1840s when the steam train from Glasgow arrived.

8th Royal Troon

Location: Troon, Ayrshire, Scotland

Distance: 123 yards, par 3

Original course designer: George Strath

Subsequent alterations: Willie Fernie (1888), James Braid (1923), Martin Ebert (2013)

Royal Troon GC was founded in 1878. Members first played over six holes laid out by Charles Hunter, the professional at nearby Prestwick. George Strath, Troon's first professional, arrived in 1882 and extended the course to 12 holes, then 18, during his five-year stay. Strath's successor Willie Fernie made improvements, as did James Braid in 1923. The club's motto is *Tam arte quam marte*—Latin for "As much by skill as by strength." It is apt for the tiny, tantalizing, tormenting 8th.

LITTLE DEVIL

If you can direct a wedge, 9-iron, 8-iron or whatever you need to hit the ball 123 yards between the cavernous bunkers surrounding the green, then you'll probably make an easy par at Royal Troon's 8th hole and walk to the 9th tee wondering what on Earth all the fuss is about.

Mis-hit your tee ball into one of the bunkers, though, and there's a good chance you'll make a bogey or, God forbid, match the 15 German amateur Herman Tissies made here during the 1950 British Open.

> "The 12th at Augusta, the 7th at Pebble Beach and the 8th at Troon. They should be easy but you can run up a big score in a hurry at all of them if you're not careful."
>
> *Colin Montgomerie*

Or the 6 Tiger Woods carded in 1997. Woods, playing in his first British Open as a professional and coming off a 64 in round three, had begun the final round in a tie for eighth, eight shots behind leader Jesper Parnevik of Sweden. He still harbored faint hopes of winning as he boarded the 8th tee, but after finding the back right bunker, taking two to get out, then three-putting, those hopes quickly vanished.

The hole is the shortest in the British Open's history and became known as the Postage Stamp after 1887 and 1889 British Open champion Willie Park Jr. wrote in a 1909 edition of *Golf Illustrated* that the hole had a "pitching surface skimmed down to the size of a postage stamp."

Prior to the 2004 British Open, Scotland's Colin Montgomerie said the hole was his favorite in the world, dangerous too if you didn't give it the respect it deserved.

HOWDY NEIGHBOR
The 10th tee at the south end of Royal Troon is about a mile from the 10th green at the far north end of Prestwick.

TOUGH TARGET
The height of the dune
to the left of the putting
surface, the deep rough
covering it and the sharp
run-off to the right make
finding the green at the
8th paramount.

THREADING
THE NEEDLE
The hole is only 123 yards
long from the champion-
ship tee, but whether you
attack the pin with a sand
wedge or a 7-iron, your
tee shot had better
be accurate.

WELCOME BACK, GENE

In 1923, Royal Troon staged its first British Open and Gene Sarazen,
winner of the previous year's U.S. Open and PGA Championship,
attempted to qualify for his first British Open. The wind during the
qualifying round was so strong Aubrey Boomer hit a shot
from a bunker then watched as his ball curled back over
his head and into his jacket pocket. Unaccustomed to such
conditions, Sarazen failed to advance.

To commemorate the 50th anniversary of Royal
Troon's first British Open, and Sarazen's first try at qualifying, the seven-time major winner was given a special
invitation for the 1973 championship. This time, he was
able to take home much better memories.

The winner of the 1932 British Open at Prince's GC in
Kent, England, Sarazen was 71 years old and went out in
the first round with two fellow champions: Fred Daly who
won at Royal Liverpool in 1947, and Max Faulkner,
who had claimed his Claret Jug at Royal Portrush in 1951.
A stiff breeze was blowing into the golfers' faces as they
reached the 8th. Sarazen punched a 5-iron, curtailing his
follow-through to keep the shot below the wind. The ball
pitched 15 feet short of the hole, took a couple of hops
and rolled gently into the cup for an ace. The following
day, he found a deep greenside bunker, but holed his
explosion shot. One hole, two days, three shots: awesome.

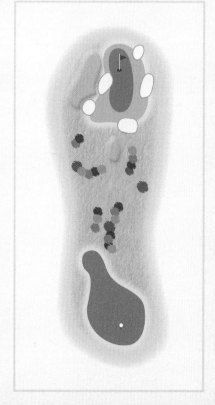

1887

5th Royal St. George's

Location: Sandwich, Kent, England

Distance: 416 yards, par 4

Original course designer: William Laidlaw Purves

Subsequent alterations: Frank Pennink (1975), Donald Steel (1980, 2002)

Royal St. George's polarizes opinion. For many, it's just too quirky and full of random, unexplained bounces; for others it is a charming and very special place. Jack Nicklaus apparently said British Open venues got worse the further south you traveled. He didn't much like Royal St. George's, but says he was misquoted and that he probably said the courses got better the further north you went. Walter Hagen, who won here in 1922 and 1928, said the front nine was tremendous fun, but the golf wasn't very good, while the back nine was tremendous golf but no fun at all. However, Bernard Darwin said, "This is as nearly my idea of heaven as is to be attained on earthly links." And two-time Masters Champion and golf course architect Ben Crenshaw thought RSG had the British Open's finest set of greens.

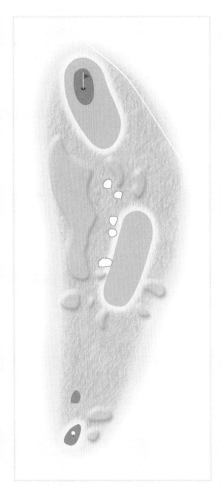

LINKS LOOKOUT

Royal St. George's is said to have been "found" by Dr. Laidlaw Purves—a Scottish native living in London, who was desperate to find golfing ground similar to that in his homeland—while scanning the coast from the top of St. Clement's Church in the nearby village of Sandwich. He had searched all through London and the Home Counties for land as suitable for the game as this, and once he had gathered sufficient funding and had his offer accepted, he, his friend Henry Lamb and their appointed greenkeeper/professional Ramsay Hunter laid out the course. It was immediately praised and, in 1894, became the first course outside of Scotland to host the British Open. It staged eight more Championships through 1949, at which point the players (and therefore the R&A) appeared to have finally had their fill of its eccentricities. It was another 32 years, following a Frank Pennink renovation, before Royal St. George's hosted the British Open again. The club a Scotsman named after the patron saint of England, and which was granted its Royal patronage in 1902, has now hosted 14 British Opens, the last of them in 2011, when 42-year-old Irishman Darren Clarke won his first major.

LONG RANGE

On the 5th, with the wind at their backs, the pros can blast a driver over the bunkers and the dunes, leaving them with an easy pitch to the green.

PICTURE PERFECT
After a long iron/hybrid
to a spot on the fairway
short of these two bunkers,
players get a gorgeous
view of the green between
the dunes.

BRADSHAW HITS THE BOTTLE

It was another Irishman that was involved in the course's best-known incident, however. In the second round of the 1949 British Open, County Wicklow's Harry Bradshaw, winner of five Irish PGA Championships (he would win five more) and an Irish Open (he would win his second three weeks

"If the ball had been in a Guinness bottle, I could not have brought myself to hit it."

Harry Bradshaw (reportedly)

later), hit his tee shot at the par 4 5th and was dismayed to discover the ball had rolled into the bottom of a broken beer bottle, probably discarded by a careless picnicker.

Unsure if he was entitled to relief or not (he could actually have dropped clear with no penalty), Bradshaw bit the bullet, closed his eyes and, swinging his blaster (equivalent to a 9-iron) as hard as he could, shattered the glass and sent the ball squirting forward about 30 yards. He wasn't wounded physically, thank goodness, but it clearly unsettled him and he wound up making a double-bogey 6. He was round in 77.

Composed again for the final day, Bradshaw shot 68 in the morning and 70 in the afternoon to complete 72 holes on 283. His closest competitor, South Africa's Bobby Locke, made a birdie at the 17th and par on the last to tie Bradshaw. The two met in a 36-hole playoff the following day when Locke was invincible, shooting 67, 68 to win by 12.

History has always sympathized with Bradshaw for the bottle incident. Had his ball rolled an inch either side, he could have thrown it away and surely saved a shot or two, thus winning the British Open. What isn't so well known is that, after topping his drive at the 14th hole in the final round, his ball hit a stone and hopped the stream—called the Suez Canal—that splits the hole in two. That surely saved him a shot or two.

SANDWICHED
Royal St. George's, Kent, sits between two other great links—Princes, which hosted the British Open Championship in 1932, and Royal Cinque Ports (Deal), venue for the 1909 and 1920 championships.

1888

3rd Biarritz Le Phare

Location: Biarritz, France

Distance: 220 yards, par 3; shortened to just 90 yards in the late 1890s; gone altogether by 1902

Original course designer: Tom and Willie Dunn

Subsequent alterations: H.S. Colt (1920)

In 1887, a group of British golfers who spent summers in the fashionable beach resort of Biarritz, in southwest France, began whacking balls on a stretch of high ground above the town called Le Plateau du Phare (*phare* meaning "lighthouse"). The following year, Tom Dunn, a club-maker and professional at North Berwick GC, joined his brother Willie in France after his doctor advised him to head south and rest up, following a bout of blood poisoning (Tom failed to notify North Berwick of his little trip, however, and subsequently lost his job). Together, the brothers laid out a nine-hole course at Biarritz on which the most notable hole was the 3rd—Chasm. It began on an 80-foot cliff, crossed 80 yards of beach and water, and fell to another cliff 30 feet below. Once over the Chasm, the golfer still had 120 yards or so to the green. Development of the area meant the Chasm hole had to be moved and shortened drastically in the 1890s, however (although the course was extended to 18 holes with nine separate holes for ladies). And it had disappeared entirely by 1902.

CHASM CONFUSION

In 1906, American golfer Charles Blair Macdonald (see p.25) visited Biarritz with two-time (1896, 1897) U.S. Amateur champion H.J. Whigham, who would become Macdonald's son-in-law in 1908. They were looking for holes Macdonald wished to imitate at the course he was planning to build (National Golf Links of America) on Long Island, New York.

Macdonald had most probably heard there was something at Biarritz worth seeing, as he is unlikely to have traveled to the southwest of France without good reason. And sure enough, he did find something to justify the trip—an architectural element he used at several courses

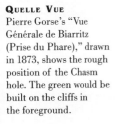

QUELLE VUE
Pierre Gorse's "Vue Générale de Biarritz (Prise du Phare)," drawn in 1873, shows the rough position of the Chasm hole. The green would be built on the cliffs in the foreground.

in the U.S. (though ironically not NGLA, probably because he just couldn't find the necessary topography) on long par 3s that he labelled Biarritz Holes, but which for a time were also called Macdonald's Folly by some contemporary architects and writers who thought its features a little eccentric.

"The best holes have not been found on the five British championship links alone," Macdonald wrote in a letter to the *New York Sun* in June 1906, explaining which features he found during his Europe trip he wished to use in America. "The idea for one hole comes from Biarritz in France. The hole in question is not a good one, but it revealed a fine and original principle that will be incorporated into my selection."

But which hole was it?

It's a question that causes a significant rift between respected golf course architecture aficionados, one group insisting it was the 3rd—Chasm—and another which says the short par 4 12th in the Chambre D'Amour—a sandy area below the cliffs that was first used for the course in 1897 and which apparently got its name after two lovers were drowned in a cave when trying to avoid the surging sea—is the more likely candidate (note, it is not today's 12th hole, as a hotel now sits on the Chambre D'Amour).

The distinguishing features of a modern Biarritz hole, or rather what the Biarritz hole has evolved into, are a longish carry over a

NOUVEAU TERRAIN
Today, Biarritz Le Phare is set back from the ocean. Most of the holes run through pleasant parkland half a mile or so inland.

Golfers on the 11th tee, heading down into the Chambre d'Amour at the turn of the 20th century. The hole, long gone, was an exciting 335-yard par 4.

hazard short of a very long green, which features a deep swale running from side to side with bunkers on both flanks. This is probably not how Macdonald envisioned the hole, however, as the dip was actually positioned in front of the green, with the turf maintained at fairway height. The front plateau before the swale became the front part of the green sometime later (greens with three distinct levels are technically Double-Plateau holes).

Whether that is true or not, the whole point of the Biarritz was to hit a shot high enough to carry the front hazard, but low enough so that it pitched short of the depression, disappeared into it, and emerged on the other side where the pin was invariably cut. Today's equipment allows good golfers to float a long or even mid-iron to the back tier carrying both the first plateau and the swale, which means if a modern Biarritz was to play the way Macdonald intended it would need to be about 260 yards long. Regardless of the quality of equipment though, the ground needs to be maintained fast and firm so a running shot is possible. If the ground is soft and the ball pitches and plugs or bounces softly, the hole's interest and drama are lost entirely.

The group convinced the Chasm Hole was Macdonald's inspiration was led by a gentleman named George Bahto who, after retiring from the dry-cleaning business, became probably the world's most credible voice on Macdonald's course design work. Sadly, Bahto passed away in March 2014, five years after consulting on the design of Old Macdonald—a tribute to the creator of some of America's very best courses—at the Bandon Dunes Golf Resort in Oregon (see p.211).

The problem with Bahto's assertion, say those that disagree with him, is that nowhere did Macdonald mention a chasm when writing about his concept for this long par 3 hole. And his description of the hole that interested him as "not a good one" would appear not to be a reference to the Chasm, which, by all accounts, was rather special. And, most significant of all, surely, is that according to the words of a 1902 *Country Life* article which said, "the Chasm has gone altogether—even the modified form of Chasm that replaced the more tremendous one of the original course," it would appear the hole wasn't even there when Macdonald and Whigham showed up.

The Chambre D'Amour holes, including the 12th, first appeared in 1897 and definitely were there when Macdonald inspected the course. The 12th featured a ridge, or hog's back, running straight down the fairway and stopping about 30 yards short of the green. The ground then dropped before running up to the putting surface.

Again, it's not an ideal explanation for Macdonald's Biarritz concept because his first Biarritz hole—at Piping Rock GC in Locust Valley, New York, which opened in 1912—did not possess a significant hog's back. And nor did any of his subsequent Biarritz holes.

It's important to note however that, though Macdonald certainly was inspired by what he thought were the best holes in Britain and Europe, he didn't seek to build exact copies.

BONNES VACANCES
Biarritz is a handsome resort town in southwest France, located on the Bay of Biscay just 22 miles north of the Spanish border.

CLIFFHANGER
The original Chasm hole, built in 1888, was something of a brute—220 yards across a gap in the cliffs to a raised green.

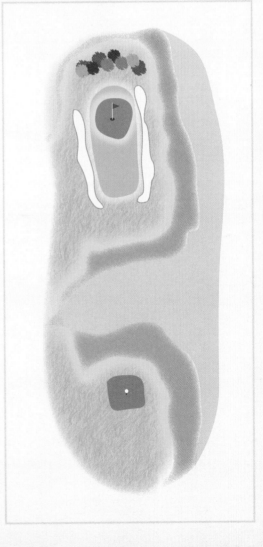

It's also possible the green at the 16th at North Berwick in Scotland—a hole called Gate, which features two plateaus with a 5-foot gully in between—and the Valley of Sin, a similarly deep swale short of the 18th green on the Old Course at St. Andrews (Macdonald would have been familiar with both)—may have influenced Macdonald's Biarritz greens.

Whatever you believe, there is no doubt these greens, if built correctly and maintained properly (and, ideally, if the pin is located on the back plateau, never in the swale) provide great entertainment, and there are several fine examples from which to choose the best. The 9th at Yale University's course in New Haven, Connecticut, which opened in 1926, often gets the nod, though it isn't actually credited to Macdonald, but rather his protégé and course-building associate Seth Raynor, who stepped out from Macdonald's far-reaching shadow in 1915 or thereabouts and built an impressive design career of his own. Macdonald did consult with Raynor at Yale, but it is the younger man who gets the credit.

Raynor built a number of excellent Biarritz greens besides Yale as did Charles Banks, the prep school teacher who aided Raynor with the construction of a nine-hole course at the school he worked at, and who would likewise go on to build a solid course design portfolio.

"Yale's 9th is a shot from an elevated tee over a lake to a monstrous 70-yard-deep green that is divided in two by a swale so deep you could hide a parked SUV."

Gary Van Sickle, Sports Illustrated

Other notable Biarritz holes include the 219-yard 3rd at Chicago GC, which Raynor built in 1923 after getting his mentor's blessing to redesign the original course and where the swale is in front of the green; the 5th at the Raynor-designed Fisher's Island in New York, where the swale likewise appears before the putting surface; the 3rd on the Old White Course at the Greenbrier in West Virginia, where there is no front hazard but a slim green and two bunkers on each side; and the 17th at Forsgate CC in New Jersey, where Banks built a 75-yard-long green with similarly long bunkers left and right on this difficult 235-yard hole.

BIARRITZ—AN AMERICAN THING

The Biarritz green was conceived by Charles Blair Macdonald and sustained by Seth Raynor and Charles Banks, all of whom worked exclusively in the U.S. (the furthest Raynor got was Hawaii—Waialae CC in Honolulu). And because Macdonald wound down his design career in the mid-1920s, Raynor passed away in 1926, and Banks died in 1931, construction of Biarritz greens more or less stopped not long after it had begun. A few have been built by Macdonald/Raynor/Biarritz enthusiasts in recent years, however. Here are five of the best:

• 4th Dunes Course at Monterey Peninsula CC, California—Seth Raynor (1925)/Rees Jones (1998)

• 17th Black Creek, Tennessee—Brian Silva (2000)

• 8th Old Macdonald, Oregon—Tom Doak (2010)

• 16th Streamsong (Red), Florida—Bill Coore and Ben Crenshaw (2013)

• 15th Guacalito de la Isla, Nicaragua—David McLay Kidd (2013)

INCONSPICUOUS COLT
✦

An interesting footnote to all this is that when H.S. Colt was called upon to update/redesign any course, as he was at Biarritz in 1920, his work would normally result in a much-improved layout and heightened exposure. In short, the course invariably became great. Biarritz's best-known period, however, and the one which interests most people who find the evolution of classic golf courses a fascinating subject, happened several years before Colt was hired.

16th Askernish

Location: South Uist, Scotland

Distance: 363 yards, par 4

Original course designer: Tom Morris Sr.

Subsequent alterations: Gordon Irvine, Martin Ebert (2006), Tom Doak (2011)

For a number of die-hard old-schoolers, the most enjoyable golf is played on an ancient and untainted golf course like Askernish on the Outer Hebridean island of South Uist. Yes, the present course is a slightly modified version of Old Tom Morris' original layout, but it's still pretty raw. The journey to Askernish takes you to Glasgow, where you hop on a propeller plane bound for Benbecula, one island to the north. You then hire the island's rental car (there may be more than one now) and head south on the A865, crossing the channel between the islands and squeezing through some very constricted sections of road. You pass a million small ponds and cruise through terrain so bleak and seemingly unpopulated you occasionally wonder if you'll ever see civilization again. It's not long though before you spy the course on your right-hand side, and what a welcome sight it is.

MEMORABLE MORRIS

Askernish GC was originally laid out by Tom Morris Sr. in 1891, the same year his design at Muirfield opened on the mainland. The course is set on wild, dramatic, crude sand dunes that toss and turn and dip and dive as randomly as any stretch of dunes in the country.

In 1922, however, local crofters (small-scale farmers) took over much of the course, and that combined with a general lack of maintenance and organization saw interest in what was left of it decline significantly. Over the next 70 years, either local enthusiasts or visiting golfers intrigued by the possibility that a Morris original was concealed under the dunes were able to get it up and running to some degree or other, but by the 1990s Morris' course was all but lost.

PREACH
The green on "Old Tom's pulpit" is raised well above the fairway and possesses some of the wackiest contours you're ever likely to see on a golf course.

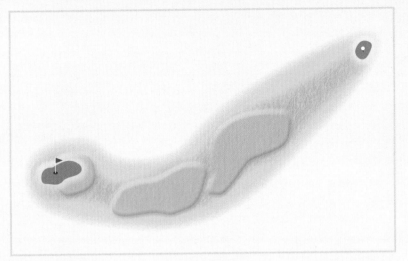

UPHILL STRUGGLE
The amazing 16th is one
of the most anticipated
and talked-about holes at
Askernish. Hit a hybrid/
3-wood into the fairway
and a short iron up the
hill to the pulpit.

In September 2005, master greenkeeper and
course consultant Gordon Irvine telephoned
the island's factor (estate manager) Tim
Atkinson to discuss plans for a fishing trip,
whereupon Atkinson told Irvine about an old
golf course that some famous golfer or other
had built on the island a hundred years ago …
Old Tom Morris or something like that. Irvine
didn't believe it.

FAR-FLUNG
Askernish is found on
the remote island of South
Uist in the Outer Hebrides,
about an hour's flight
from Glasgow.

He did, though, after Atkinson persuaded him to come and see it for
himself. Irvine's visit in December 2005 was instrumental in generating
another attempt at restoring the course. He returned the following
March with acclaimed architect Martin Ebert (who had worked under
course architect and former *Sunday Telegraph* columnist Donald Steel
for many years renovating several British Open courses) to find and
restore Morris' original holes. With a great deal of work by greenkeeper
Colin MacGregor and club members, the course slowly took shape over
the next year or so and was ready for play by May of 2008. It officially
reopened on August 22.

The 16th hole, named Old Tom's Pulpit, is 363 yards long and bends
slightly from left to right before finishing on a green you have to see to
believe. For starters, it's perched on a dune that rises 15 feet about the
fairway (hence "Pulpit"); second, it's tiny; and third, the surface doesn't
so much undulate as palpitate. Actually Ebert, along with American
designer Tom Doak, altered the green in 2011, extending the putting
surface at the back and turning the wrinkles at the front of the old green
into part of the approach. Losing the wild contours was controversial

certainly, as they were a unique feature that made the hole utterly unforgettable. But while quirky and fun, the contours were perhaps a little "crazy golf," and not really suitable for a course that wanted to retain its character but also be considered a worthy test of golf. And anyway, Doak isn't convinced the mad undulations on the old green were part of Morris' original design. And the hole is still unforgettable.

GATSBY GOLF

Playing a wild, unadorned golf course that looks now much as it did when it first opened is tremendous fun and a refreshing change from modern courses that often place too much emphasis on length. A lot of enthusiasts take it one step further by playing these antique courses with equally aged equipment—hickory-shafted clubs and replica gutta-percha golf balls (see box)—while wearing period dress: plus fours, a shirt and tie, and a flat cap.

DAPPER
The flat cap, plus fours, the hickory club, the guttie ball—it could be Scotland c.1920. Actually, it's Florida, 2014.

Most of the early courses that started out with six, nine or 12 holes on rough, unimproved ground were either developed, cultivated and manicured, turning them into something barely recognizable, or abandoned altogether. A small number of what are really "museum courses" still exist around the world, however, and remain largely unaltered, every bit as charming now as they were 100 or even 150 years ago. Oakhurst Links in White Sulphur Springs, West Virginia, is a nine-hole course on 30 acres now owned by the nearby Greenbrier Hotel. It looks much the same now as it did when Russell Montague and his friends laid it out in 1884, making it one of the first golf courses in the U.S. (some say the oldest, but a University of St. Andrews historian recently discovered documents showing golf was played in the Charleston, South Carolina area as early as 1739—although there is no evidence that an actual course was laid out there). Visitors use hickory clubs and gutta-percha balls and can purchase knickers, tall socks, caps, shirts and ties in the golf shop.

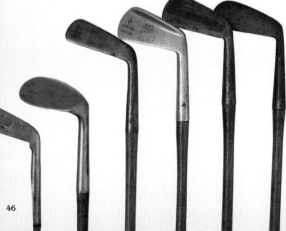

STICK SHAFT
Strong, durable Hickory replaced ash and hazel in shafts and remained the standard material until steel took over in the 1930s.

HICKORY AT HOME

Original equipment is used at Kingarrock GC in Cupar, Fife—about 9 miles from St. Andrews and where jute manufacturer Frederick Sharp built an imposing family home in 1904 so he could be closer to the Old Course, and in which he could house his impressive antiques collection. The course Sharp built in front of the house was abandoned at the start of World War II and remained unused until the Anderson family, the current owners of the property, reopened it in June 2008. The green fee includes use of five hickory clubs, golf balls, "reddy" tees and an old golf bag. A glass of Da Anderson ginger beer and some Fisher & Donaldson shortbread is also handed out at the end of the round.

Hickory clubs can also be rented at Musselburgh Old Links, a few miles east of Edinburgh and which claims to be the oldest course in the world with documentary evidence the links existed in 1672.

The nine holes which staged six British Opens and on which more than 60 clubs and societies—including the Honourable Company of Edinburgh Golfers—played various competitions, are now maintained by the East Lothian Council and measure a total of 2,968 yards.

The course, designed by H.S. Colt, at Fort Augustus GC at the southern end of Loch Ness stretches to only 5,100 yards but is extremely entertaining. Opened in 1924, the course possesses tiny greens and is about as natural as a course gets, with livestock responsible for keeping the grass at a reasonable height.

Askernish now measures 6,259 yards and might be a very tough proposition for anyone using hickory, especially in a cold wind. But whatever you use here, you cannot fail to come away charmed and exhilarated by a course as raw and natural and historic as this.

GUTTIE

✦

Gutta percha is a natural polymer with a rubbery quality made from the milky sap of a Malaysian Sapodilla tree. In 1848—five years after it had been introduced to the West as an ideal electrical cable insulator—a Dundee missionary named Rev. Robert Paterson discovered it could be used to make a golf ball cheaply and could be re-conditioned when misshapen.

The "guttie" had a profound impact on golf as it opened up the game to a new section of society, previously unable to play due to the excessive cost of "featheries." A dozen gutties could be produced in the same time it took to make a single feathery.

1891

18th Muirfield

Location: East Lothian, Scotland

Distance: 473 yards, par 4

Original course designer: Tom Morris Sr.

Subsequent alterations: H.S. Colt (1923), Tom Simpson (1933), Martin Hawtree (2010)

HONORABLE MENTION
The clubhouse of the Honourable Company of Edinburgh Golfers stands behind the 18th green at Muirfield and was designed by a former captain of the club, Hall Blyth.

The Honourable Company of Edinburgh Golfers is not a club to seek much limelight and tends not to make grandiose statements when a simple description will do. So when it says the 18th hole at its Muirfield home is one of the great finishing holes in golf, you can be confident the line is watertight. In order to remain a fitting challenge for the closing hole at the British Open (which the course has now hosted 16 times, along with 26 other national and international competitions), the 18th has evolved a good deal over the last 120-plus years, now measuring close to 100 yards more than it did in 1891.

BLEAK AND BEAUTIFUL

Muirfield is the Honourable Company's third home and was laid out on a stretch of barren links land 20 miles east of Edinburgh. The club was first mentioned in 1744, when Edinburgh's Town Council presented a silver club for an annual competition contested over the five holes at Leith Links by a group referred to as the Gentlemen Golfers. On March 26, 1800, the City Council and Lord Provost granted the club a charter and it became the Honourable Company of Edinburgh Golfers.

By 1830, Leith had become seriously overcrowded so club members began playing on a new nine-hole layout within the racecourse at Musselburgh, 5 miles to the east. Mary Queen of Scots is said to have hacked at some sort of ball on this ground in 1567, although the first documentary evidence of golf being played at Musselburgh appears in 1672.

The Honourable Company eventually severed ties with Leith and officially moved to Musselburgh in July 1836. Musselburgh and the Honourable Company hosted the British Open six times between 1874 and 1889. (Incidentally, the reason why holes are 4¹/4 inches in diameter is because the implement used to cut the holes at Musselburgh happenedto be this size. The Royal and Ancient Golf Club of St. Andrews—R&A—which assumed the responsibility of writing the game's rules in the late 19th century, adopted the dimensions in 1893.)

HONORABLE CAPTAIN
The regal-looking William Inglis (1712–1792), Edinburgh surgeon and gentlemen golfer, was captain of the Honourable Company.

But as St. Andrews' influence on the game continued to grow and the 18-hole course was accepted as standard, and because Musselburgh was now being used by four clubs and becoming "disagreeably crowded," the Honourable Company felt the need to move again. Ironically it landed at another racecourse—the Howes—on the Archerfield Estate at Dirleton where King Edward I's bowmen had established a settlement during the prelude to the Battle of Falkirk in 1298.

Tom Morris Sr. laid out the first course at Muirfield with the help of head groundsman David Plenderleith, who was clearly impressed with the nature of the turf. "Without a doubt, it's the finest turf that ever was seen," he said.

At the time, courses were built on narrow strips of sandy dunes land between the sea and flatter, arable land and they tended to move away from the starting point for nine holes before turning around and heading back for nine. Muirfield's shape was more circular, however, so Morris abandoned convention, avoiding holes that ran parallel to each other. But while it may have been shaped differently, the property wasn't overly large—just 117 acres, bordered by stone walls—so Morris and Plenderleith originally built only 16 holes.

Two more holes were added ahead of the 1892 British Open, won by English amateur Howard Hilton with a score of 305 (it was the first time the Championship was played over 72 holes), but the course drew a good deal of criticism. Contrary to Plenderleith's assessment, many of the players complained that conditions were actually very poor. The large sandy areas on the western half of the property proved difficult to maintain, while other parts of the course were waterlogged. One competitor, Andrew Kirkaldy, was somewhat scathing, calling the course "naething but an auld water meadie."

Over a period of many years, the land was drained and cultivated and the course enhanced by a number of the club's top amateur players—most notably Robert Maxwell, who twice won the Amateur Championship at Muirfield (1903 and 1909).

An additional 13 acres were found in 1907, but it wasn't until 1923 when Maxwell, a former club captain and highly respected businessman and administrator, persuaded the club to purchase 50 more acres to the north, closer to the Firth of Forth, and hire H.S. Colt to redesign the course that Muirfield finally began to realize its potential. With the new acreage, Colt was able to build 14 new holes, alter the routing and thus create the course that's still challenging the best players in the world today.

> **"In golf course design, the obvious thing is almost invariably the wrong thing."**
>
> *Tom Simpson in his 1933 report on Muirfield*

Though Colt is invariably credited with establishing Muirfield's innovative routing comprised of an outer loop of nine holes running clockwise and an inner nine moving counterclockwise, the direction his front nine took was similar to that of the previous front nine. It was on the back where he made his most significant changes, creating a sequence of holes that bears little resemblance to what was there before.

Before Colt came to Muirfield, the 18th hole did run in roughly the same direction—from the middle of the course back toward the clubhouse, but it measured only 382 yards and was flanked by the 13th to the left and 17th to the right. A string of three linear bunkers separated the 18th and 13th, and the tee shot had to carry a large sandy area, while the approach needed to clear three smaller bunkers traversing the fairway about 40 yards short of the green.

Colt added 43 yards and a left-to-right kink, increasing the hole's challenge ahead of the 1929 British Open—won by Walter Hagen who claimed the last of his four Claret Jugs with a six-shot victory over fellow American Johnny Farrell.

Tom Simpson, a great rival of Colt's and a confirmed eccentric who traveled by chauffeur-driven Rolls-Royce and wore a beret and sunglasses, visited the course in 1933 and wrote an extensive report recommending numerous changes. In the report, Simpson said many holes lacked subtlety and were "featureless, by reason of their obvious and straightforward character."

Only a handful of Simpson's proposals were implemented, however, the most significant of them at the short 13th. Simpson shifted the hole to the left and took out several of Colt's bunkers (Simpson thought 55 bunkers ample for 18 holes and was perhaps the profession's first conscientious minimalist). He also built a flatter, more accommodating putting surface than the virtual ski slope Colt had left behind.

As for the 18th, it became straighter and continued growing throughout the 20th century. By 2013, when Muirfield hosted its 16th British Open following a 2010/11 renovation by England's Martin Hawtree, the hole had become a 473-yard beast—24 yards longer than it was for the 2002 British Open—with three fairway bunkers (two left, one right), two large bunkers short of the green, and one either side of the putting surface.

WHAT TOOK YOU SO LONG, LEFTY?

What drama the crowds surrounding the 18th hole at Muirfield have witnessed over the years, never more so than in 2013 when Phil Mickelson made a birdie on the last to win his first Claret Jug and cement his place among the game's all-time greats with five major championships.

Mickelson, a flamboyant player incapable of resisting the urge to hit the heroic, all-or-nothing shot, had had a rough time at the British Open. In 19 starts prior to 2013, he had recorded just two top-10 finishes after taking 12 tries to record his first. He'd also missed four cuts.

After rounds of 69, 74 and 72, Mickelson began the final round at Muirfield in a tie for ninth, five shots behind leader Lee Westwood. But as the Englishman and the other contenders—Adam Scott, Henrik Stenson, Tiger Woods, Hunter Mahan—began to falter Mickelson took control with birdies at the 13th, 14th and another at the 575-yard 17th, where he hit two towering 3-woods onto the front of the green.

At the last, the 43-year-old put the icing on the cake when he hit a superb 6-iron against the left-to-right wind that flirted with the left bunker but bounced right and curled to within 12 feet of the hole. He made the putt to notch his fourth birdie in the last six holes and cap a round of 66, which he described as probably the best of his life.

BETTER LATE THAN NEVER
After 19 attempts, Phil Mickelson at last won the Claret Jug—at Muirfield in 2013.

WHERE CHAMPIONS ARE CROWNED

MINEFIELD
At the 18th, finding either
of the two bunkers to the
left of the fairway, or one
on the right, brings the
two bunkers short of the
green into play.

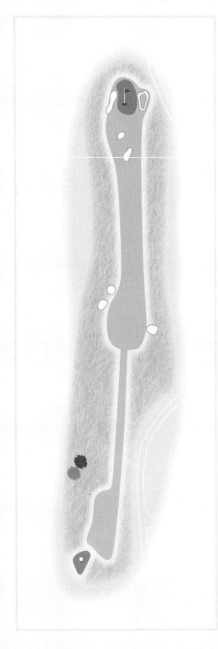

No major venue, apart from Augusta National, which has a big advantage as the permanent host of the Masters Tournament, can boast as formidable a roll call of champions as Muirfield. In 16 championships the East Lothian course has produced only one winner whose victory might be considered surprising—in 1935, a club pro from Surrey, England, named Alf Perry beat fellow Englishman Alf Padgham by four strokes to win his first professional tournament (he only won three more).

Besides Perry, the list of players that have won at Muirfield includes a number of World Golf Hall of Fame members and some of history's greatest players—Phil Mickelson, Ernie Els, Nick Faldo (twice), Tom Watson, Lee Trevino, Jack Nicklaus, Gary Player, Henry Cotton, Walter Hagen, Ted Ray, James Braid (twice), Harry Vardon and English amateur Harold Hilton who won two British Opens, four Amateur Championships and one U.S. Amateur.

"The design is highly intelligent. It has got more variety of shots than any course I know. The rough is good and the bunkering is absolutely exquisite."

Gary Player on Muirfield

BEMBRIDGE AND NICKLAUS x2

Before the 2014 event at Gleneagles, the Ryder Cup had been played in Scotland just once—in 1973 at Muirfield. The American team, captained by Jackie Burke, included Jack Nicklaus, Arnold Palmer, Lee Trevino, Billy Casper and Tom Weiskopf and was considered the strong favorite.

But it was Great Britain & Ireland that made the better start, finishing day one with a $5^{1}/_{2}$–$2^{1}/_{2}$ lead. The home side's heroes in the morning foursomes had been Bernard Gallacher and Brian Barnes who beat Casper and Trevino on the 18th hole. Maurice Bembridge and Brian Huggett were similarly successful in the afternoon fourballs, beating America's Blue Ribbon pairing of Nicklaus and Palmer.

UNDERACHIEVER
England's Maurice
Bembridge was probably
a better golfer than his
record suggests. At the
1973 Ryder Cup at
Muirfield, he took the
great Jack Nicklaus to the
wire twice in one day.

After a U.S. comeback on day two, however, the sides were level on eight points heading into the final day and two sessions of eight singles matches.

Bembridge, from Worksop in England, and Nicklaus were drawn together in the morning session and competed ferociously all the way to the 18th. Both were on the green in two when the afternoon pairings were announced over the public address system. The two would be squaring off again after lunch.

The 18th was halved in four, each player winning half a point. The afternoon match was similarly hard-fought, with no more than one hole separating the two. At the long 17th, Nicklaus was on the green after two big hits—ball-striking that Bembridge just couldn't match. Nicklaus went 1-up and when Bembridge made a bogey at the 18th Nicklaus capitalized, taking the hole with a par and the match by two holes. Nicklaus though was impressed with Bembridge's performance. "Hey you son of a b-----, you really can play this game," he told him. The U.S. team took 11 of the 16 points available that day and won the match 19–13.

GOLF COUNTRY
Muirfield is located on the
East Lothian coast, 23 miles
east of Edinburgh and
about two and a half miles
west of North Berwick.

10th Atlantic City

Location: Northfield, New Jersey

Distance: 488 yards, par 4

Original course designer: John Reid

Subsequent alterations: Willie Park Jr. (1915), William Flynn (1925), Tom Doak (1999)

Atlantic City Country Club was founded in 1897 in Northfield, New Jersey—9 miles west of the coastal city that resembles a mini Las Vegas, with its mega casino hotels visible across Lakes Bay. The first nine holes were laid out by Scotsman John Reid who, nine years before, had founded the Saint Andrew's Golf Club (the United States' oldest) in Yonkers, New York. Willie Park Jr., another Scot, built a second nine in 1915, and William Flynn added his touches in 1925. The course then remained largely untouched until 1999, when Tom Doak gave it a much-needed revamp. Besides the evolution of the course, there is much to interest the golf historian here. The bell outside the clubhouse was used in the early 1900s to warn golfers the last trolley would soon be leaving for Atlantic City. John McDermott, the first American-born winner of the U.S. Open (in 1911, aged 19) was the club professional from 1911 to 1914. A young Coast Guard trainee called Arnold Palmer played the course frequently in 1951 and 1952 when stationed at Cape May, 40 miles south. And six USGA championships have been played here. None of that, though, is why Atlantic City CC will forever hold a special place in the game's archives.

AB'S BIRD

OFF TO A FLYER
The details surrounding how the term "birdie" originated are hazy to say the least. However, we can be sure it happened here at Atlantic City Country Club.

Of much greater significance perhaps, is that the term "birdie" was coined at Atlantic City CC—then called the Northfield Links—in 1899. Or was it 1903?

Actually, there's not a lot anyone can be sure of. We do know that somewhere on Atlantic City CC sometime around the turn of the 20th century, one of the Philadelphia golfers who spent winter weekends on the coast to escape the snow, hit an excellent iron shot which his partner (or partners), immediately (or later) called a "bird of a shot"—at the time, "bird" was used to describe anything good. Actually, one report also said the term stemmed from someone's ball hitting a bird en route to the green, but that has been discounted.

The facts surrounding how, when and why "birdie" became universal are elusive. We know the year is in doubt.

But we can be confident it happened on the 12th hole ... until we read it was actually the 2nd ... or 4th. And is that today's 12th or the 12th in 1899 ... or 1903 (when, um, the course didn't have 12 holes)? The current 2nd or 4th, or the old holes? Muddying the water further is the fact that the 10th, which moves away from the clubhouse, is now called Birdie, but the club insists the green on which the incident took place is currently a chipping green near the clubhouse.

Likewise, details on the personnel involved are hazy. Virtually every account involves one Abner Smith, but nobody seems sure with whom he was playing. George Crump, the force behind Pine Valley (see p.98), is mentioned often, as is Smith's brother, William. But were they a threesome or was A.W. Tillinghast their fourth?

In his book *Fifty Years of American Golf*, H.B. Martin quotes Abner Smith as saying it was a threesome, he hit the shot that finished within a few inches of the cup and he labeled it "a bird of a shot." *The Press of Atlantic City*, however, said four were in the group and that William Smith had issued the bird call. Another commentary says Crump hit the shot.

At least everyone does agree that once Smith (or Crump) had made the putt, the group decided that beating par by one stroke would henceforth be called a birdie, and that the prize for making one would be two balls instead of the usual one Philadelphia Ballsome members received when winning a hole.

The term soon became popular among members, and vacationing golfers took it home. Before long, America and then the world were calling it a birdie.

CITY LIMITS
Atlantic City Country Club is actually located in the suburb of Northfield, about 10 miles west of downtown Atlantic City, and 60 miles southeast of Philadelphia.

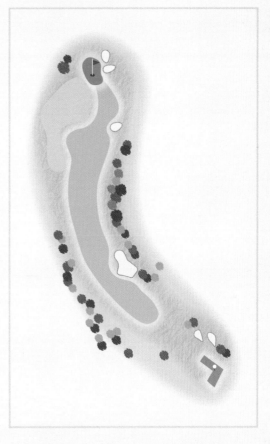

BIRDIE HOLE
Though the 10th hole at ACCC is named Birdie, it's unlikely Ab Smith's eureka moment took place here.

16th Royal Lytham & St. Annes

Location: Lytham St. Annes, Lancashire, England

Distance: 358 yards, par 4

Original course designer: George Lowe

Subsequent alterations: H.S. Colt (1919–1922)

Lytham is something of an anomaly—a genuine links course with no views of the sea. The ground here is firm, the lies sandy, the bunkers deep and revetted, the fescue rough fierce in places, and the flags often lean one way or the other in stiff winds—everything you'd expect of an British Open venue. And yet nowhere over the course's near-200 acres do you ever catch a glimpse of the Irish Sea. The course is less than a mile from the coast, but suburban Fairhaven gets in the way. The club, founded in 1886, admits on its own website it is "not a conventionally beautiful golf course," but convention be damned when the ground is this good and the holes this challenging. The original course hosted the inaugural British Ladies Amateur in 1893, but the club's first professional George Lowe gave us today's routing in 1897. From 1919 to 1922, H.S. Colt added tees and length, and he also put in a few bunkers—206 of the things are now scattered throughout the course. The bones of Lowe's course remain, however.

UP AND DOWN FROM EVERYWHERE

A teenage Seve Ballesteros had announced his arrival during the British Open at Royal Birkdale in 1976 (see p.122). That year, he had slashed his way around the links, playing absurdly adventurous recovery shots and demonstrating almost supernatural short-game skills. He generated the same excitement Arnold Palmer had when he won at Birkdale in 1961.

DREAM GREEN
The 16th green at Royal Lytham, where Ballesteros made critical birdies in the final round of both the 1979 and 1988 British Open.

When he arrived at Royal Lytham & St. Annes for the 1979 championship, Ballesteros was a nine-time winner on the developing European Tour, and had played his first three Masters Tournaments and two U.S. Opens. He had finished tied for 15th in the British Open at Turnberry in 1977, and tied for 17th at St. Andrews the following year. He was only 22, but already established as one of Europe's best players. But when would he show his true class and win a major?

In his two tournaments leading up to the British Open, Ballesteros won the English Classic at the Belfry, then came second in Sweden.

He arrived in Lancashire brimming with confidence, so an opening 73 that put him in a tie for 16th, eight shots behind the surprise leader Bill Longmuir, was a little disappointing. He was a different player in the second round, though. An electric closing stretch, in which he made four birdies over the final five holes, resulted in a 65 that put him two back of U.S. Open champion Hale Irwin.

Despite shooting a less-than-memorable 75 on the Saturday, he didn't lose any ground to Irwin, who stumbled to the same number. But it did allow the ever-dangerous Jack Nicklaus to make up a little ground.

Ballesteros entered the final round two behind Irwin and a shot clear of Nicklaus and England's Mark James.

It is extraordinary to note that in the entire 72 holes of the 1979 British Open, Ballesteros found the fairway off the tee just nine times. He was especially wayward on that final afternoon, for some reason persisting with his driver with which he found the short grass once in nine tries. At the short par 4 16th, he sliced his tee shot well right, the ball coming to rest beneath one of a handful of cars parked 25 yards to the right of the fairway. The situation

UP NORTH
Royal Lytham and St. Annes is located on the Lancashire coast, 55 miles north of Liverpool and 6 miles south of Blackpool.

SEA OF SAND
There are more than 200 bunkers at Royal Lytham— 10 or more a hole. The 16th certainly has its share with 15.

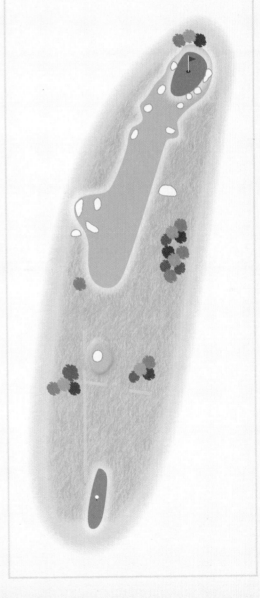

"I don't aim for the rough. It just goes there. My caddie tells me to close my eyes and hit it and maybe it goes in the fairway."

Seve Ballesteros, 1979 British Open

begged two questions: one, who on Earth had allowed these cars to park so close to the course, and two, with such a poor record with the club, was there any need for Ballesteros to take the driver, especially on a short par 4 where the need to be accurate trumped the need for distance?

Of course he didn't need to take a driver. But the young, headstrong Ballesteros wasn't born to hit the percentage shot. With Irwin struggling again and none of the other contenders posting any birdies, Ballesteros was riding a fiery chariot all the way to the Claret Jug and no amount of prudence or caution was going to stand in his way.

After dropping clear of the car without penalty, Ballesteros caught a good lie and actually had a straightforward short iron to the green. He pitched to about 20 feet and knocked in the putt for a 3.

Super Seve
Seve Ballesteros burst onto the scene at Royal Birkdale in 1976, tieing for second six shots behind Johnny Miller. But no one could catch him three years later at Royal Lytham.

A final-round 70 saw Ballesteros ease home with a three-shot cushion over Nicklaus and Ben Crenshaw. Afterwards, Ballesteros was somewhat disapprovingly labeled the Car Park Champion. It was a cheap shot, and though Ballesteros always believed Irwin had coined the phrase, the American denied it.

On his return to Lytham for the 1988 British Open, Ballesteros once again made a birdie on the 16th in the final round, this time taking the long iron off the tee, then hitting a 9-iron to just a few inches from the hole. That day (a Monday, following awful weather on the Saturday) he was round in 65—one of the finest rounds of an illustrious career and good enough for a two-shot victory over Nick Price and his third Open title.

I Don't Care Who You Are

It might not have much to do with the 16th hole, but we can't leave Royal Lytham, and the first of Bobby Jones' three British Open victories in particular, without mentioning the difficulty the American amateur had getting back into the course following lunch in his hotel between the third and fourth rounds in 1926. Jones forgot his player's badge and an overzealous security guard didn't buy his story, so he had to pay his admission fee just like everyone else.

One other footnote to this British Open— Walter Hagen, finishing after Jones, came to the 18th needing a 2 to tie. A shameless grandstander, Hagen had his caddie tend the flag as he took his second shot from the fairway. He missed … but not by much, the ball almost pitching in the hole. Unfortunately, it bounded into a back bunker and he took six to finish fourth.

MORE LYTHAM CHAMPIONS

✦

Lytham has hosted the British Open 11 times, most recently in 2012 when Ernie Els took advantage of Adam Scott's disastrous back nine to win his second Claret Jug. Lytham's first winner, in 1926, was Bobby Jones who in the final round hit a famous shot from 175 yards out of sandy scrub to the left of the 17th fairway and on to the green. A plaque now indicates the spot from which Jones hit the shot that ripped the heart out of his closest opponent, and playing partner, Al Watrous.

The female version of the British Open, the Women's British Open, has been contested at Lytham four times. America's Sherri Steinhauer won two of her three titles here and, in 2009, Scotland's Catriona Matthew won less than three months after giving birth to her second child.

Two Ryder Cups have also been held at Lytham—in 1961 and 1977. In 1961, the U.S. won $14^1/_2$–$9^1/_2$, and in 1977 the U.S. won again, $12^1/_2$–$7^1/_2$, despite a young Nick Faldo winning his three matches.

1899 17th The Country Club

Location: Brookline, Massachusetts

Distance: 370 yards, par 4

Original course designer: Willie Campbell

Subsequent alterations: Two club members (1908), William Flynn (1927), Rees Jones (1987)

QUIET RIOT
The green at the 17th seems an unexceptional place for a couple of the most significant incidents in the sport's history to have taken place.

The Country Club dates back to 1882, when it focused solely on equestrianism and social activities. John Reid and his Apple Tree Gang (see p.54) hadn't become active yet so golf wasn't even in the picture at Brookline. In 1893, however, five years after the Gang had formed the Saint Andrew's Golf Club, the Country Club created a golf committee and had three members—Messrs. Hunnewell, Curtis and Bacon—lay out six holes. They were basic and didn't last long, but it was a start. The club needed a professional, and in 1894 it took on Willie Campbell, a Musselburgh man not long off the boat from Scotland. Campbell soon expanded the course to nine holes. Later in 1894, the club became one of the five charter members of the United States Golf Association. Campbell added a second nine holes in 1899. Soon, however, the Haskell Ball rendered the course short and insubstantial, so more land was needed for further expansion. In 1908, with 30 more acres, two club members—Messrs. Windeler and Jacques—added three new holes. It was this configuration that would stage the club's first U.S. Open in 1913. Philadelphia's William Flynn was hired to add a separate nine-hole course in 1927. Three holes from Flynn's Primrose nine have been added to 15 from the Main Course to create the Composite Course that has been used for every major event since the 1934 U.S. Amateur.

Well Met, Ouimet

The first official U.S. Open was played at the Newport CC in Rhode Island in 1895. English-born Horace Rawlins won, and it was native British golfers that claimed the title every year until 1911, when Philadelphia's John McDermott became the first U.S.-born champion. McDermott would win again the following year, and was highly fancied to make it three in a row at the Country Club on September 18 and 19, 1913, especially after beating a strong field, including Britain's Harry Vardon, at the Shawnee Open in August.

To win in Boston, though, McDermott would not only need to overcome Vardon, a five-time British Open winner (he won a sixth in 1914) and the 1900 U.S. Open champion, but also his fellow Jersey native, Ted Ray. Vardon was a superstar, Ray too, though to a lesser degree, and they were in the U.S. to play a series of exhibition matches. In 1900, Vardon had spent 11 months in the country playing 88 exhibitions, of which he is said to have lost 15, but only two singles.

> **"He is a credit to American golf."**
>
> *Harry Vardon after being defeated by*
> *Francis Ouimet at the 1913 U.S. Open*

The two Jersey golfers' exhibition schedule in 1913 was so full the U.S. Open had to be pushed back a little, causing some resentment among the American players. Indeed, McDermott, a feisty young man, got into trouble after making some impolite remarks during his victory speech at Shawnee.

Also in the field at the Country Club were Vardon's younger brother Tom, Walter Hagen, J.H. Taylor, Jock Hutchison, Jim Barnes and the Smith brothers—Alex and MacDonald who led after a first-round 71 on the 6,245-yard course. By the end of Thursday's two rounds, the elder Vardon was out in front by two, following an afternoon 72. At lunchtime on Friday, three were tied for the lead—Vardon, Ray and a 20-year-old amateur who had grown up across the street from the Country Club. Francis Ouimet was from working-class stock and had worked as a caddie at the club. Carrying his bag was a 10-year-old boy named Eddie Lowery.

The three were tied on 6-over 225, and all three shot 79 in the final round to set up an 18-hole playoff the next day. Boston newspapers estimated 20,000 spectators turned out on Saturday, a gallery unheard of for a golf tournament.

PIONEER
Francis Ouimet may not have been the first American-born winner of the U.S. Open, but his victory in 1913 triggered a rapid surge of interest in the tournament.

After nine holes the trio were tied on level-par. Ouimet then opened up a two-shot cushion over both opponents after 12 holes, but Vardon got one back with a birdie at the 13th. Ray shot himself out of it with a double-bogey at the 15th, but Vardon was still only one behind as they arrived at the 17th.

A bunker sits on the corner of the right-to-left dogleg hole and Vardon, with the honor, found the sand. He would make a bogey and fall to 2 over. Ouimet, however, made a birdie 3 and, at 1 under par, went into the 410-yard final hole with a three-shot lead.

Ray made a consolation birdie at the last to be round in 5-over 78. Pushing for a birdie of his own, Vardon found trouble and took six. He shot 77. Ouimet, though, was down in four to complete a 1-under-par 72.

The crowd went wild, lifting their new hero onto their shoulders and carrying him to the clubhouse.

MUDDY RIVER
The Country Club is located in Brookline (once known as Muddy River), 5 miles west of downtown Boston.

INNOCUOUS
The 17th at the Country Club is a gentle par 4 of 370 yards that bends left around a collection of bunkers and moves slightly uphill to a green surrounded by more sand.

The vanquished Brits were magnanimous in their praise of the young champion. "He certainly played a great game, and stood under the strain like the man he is," said Vardon.

"He deserves all the cheers he got," added Ray. "One of the best young golfers I ever saw."

It was a seminal moment in American golf. Interest in the game surged and, combined with the good health of the U.S. economy, it led to a dramatic increase in the number of

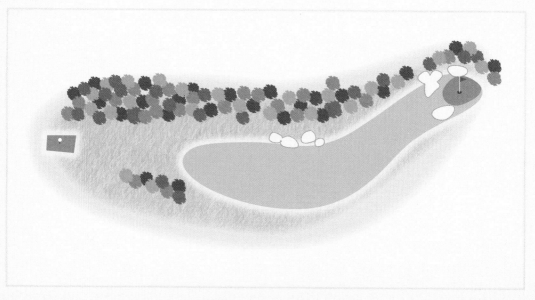

courses. Before Ouimet's incredible victory, there were roughly 700 in the U.S. Within 20 years there were 6,000.

Ouimet never turned professional, choosing instead to go into business. He won the U.S. Amateur the following year, and again in 1931. He played on eight Walker Cup teams (best U.S. amateurs against best GB and Ireland amateurs) and captained four. He entered the World Golf Hall of Fame in 1974.

RUB IT IN

Eight years after the acrimonious "War by the Shore" Ryder Cup (first played for officially in 1927 between a U.S. team and team from Great Britain at Worcester Country Club in Massachusetts. Players from Northern Ireland joined GB in 1947, players from the Republic of Ireland became eligible from 1953 onwards, and Continental players were added in 1979) at Kiawah Island in 1991, the bitter taste left in Europeans, mouths hadn't faded entirely, and relations between the two sides were still rather strained. Not surprisingly perhaps, the 1999 match became known as the "Battle at Brookline."

The U.S. started as favorite, fielding seven major champions and only one rookie—the world No. 2 David Duval—to Europe's two major winners and seven rookies.

> **"I'm a big believer in fate. I have a good feeling about this, that's all I'm going to tell you."**
>
> *U.S. Captain Ben Crenshaw to the press the evening before his team's amazing comeback*

It was Europe that performed better over the first two days though, establishing a seemingly unassailable 10–6 lead with just the singles to go. But the U.S. came out strong on Sunday winning the first six singles matches to move two points ahead. Europe fought back, and it seemed the match between Spain's José Maria Olazabal and the United States' Justin Leonard would ultimately decide the outcome. Olazabal was 4-up with seven to play but lost the next three holes. Leonard then holed from 40 feet at the 15th to draw level. They halved the 16th then, at the 17th, Leonard holed an uphill 45-footer for a 3. American players, wives, officials and cameramen ran onto the green to celebrate—an unfortunate reaction given that Olazabal still had a 25-foot putt for a 3 of his own. Had he holed it, the two would have gone to the last all square. But he missed, and the U.S. had the guaranteed half-point it needed to reach the all-important 14^1/2 points. Colin Montgomerie beat Payne Stewart in the final match on the course, but by then it didn't matter.

<table>
<tr><td>1901</td><td># 16th Glen Echo</td></tr>
</table>

Location: St. Louis, Missouri

Distance: 434 yards, par 4

Original course designer: James Foulis

Subsequent alterations: Robert Foulis (1914, 1927), Geoffrey Cornish (1985), Spencer Holt (2011)

St. Louis, Missouri, was the host city for the 1904 Olympic Games and the second Olympic golf competition, the first having been played four years before in Paris and staged concurrently with the Exposition Universelle (World's Fair). In 1904, St. Louis was the venue for the Louisiana Purchase Exposition, while Chicago had been chosen to host the Olympics. St. Louis didn't much like the idea of the Olympics stealing publicity away from its event, however, so informed the International Olympic Committee (IOC) that unless the Games were moved to St. Louis, it would organize its own international sporting competition. Baron Pierre de Coubertin, founder of the Olympic movement, gave in and awarded the Games to St. Louis.

WINNER OF THE GOLD MEDAL

Just as they had in Paris, however, the sport became something of a sideshow to the exposition with very little attention paid to the outcome of each event. In Paris, the golf tournament had been an afterthought, scheduled quickly by the Mayor of the City of Compiègne, an hour north of the French capital, and played in October—six months after the Games had begun. Charles Sands of New York won the Men's Gold Medal, but Peggy Abbott, an art student and member at Chicago GC who was visiting Paris with her mother and had decided to check out the golf tournament and then won it with a score of 47, had no

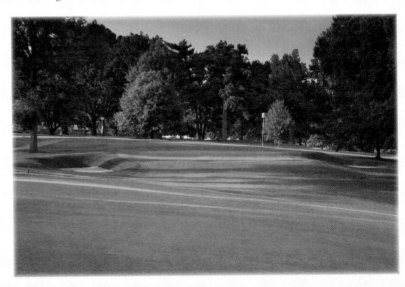

OLYMPIC GLORY
Though roughly the same length as today's 16th, the hole on which George Lyons won the 1904 Olympic Gold Medal was slightly straighter and the green much closer to a creek on the right.

idea she had become America's first female Olympic champion. As far as Abbot was concerned, she had won the Paris Ladies' Amateur. Or was it the International Women's Medal, or the Paris Ladies' Golf Championship?

At least the golf tournament in 1904 was a little better planned. Played at the Glen Echo Country Club, 10 miles northwest of downtown St. Louis and founded in 1901, the tournament was organized by two of the city's most prominent individuals—Colonel George McGrew and his son-in-law Albert Lambert.

Lambert had competed four years earlier in Paris, winning the handicap event (a competition not really based

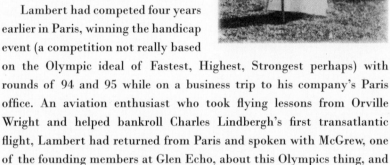

on the Olympic ideal of Fastest, Highest, Strongest perhaps) with rounds of 94 and 95 while on a business trip to his company's Paris office. An aviation enthusiast who took flying lessons from Orville Wright and helped bankroll Charles Lindbergh's first transatlantic flight, Lambert had returned from Paris and spoken with McGrew, one of the founding members at Glen Echo, about this Olympics thing, and together they hatched a plan to bring it to their club.

Twenty-two golfers representing four nations (Great Britain, United States, France and Greece) had played in 1900. In 1904, 77 men showed up, but they came from only two countries—74 were from the U.S., the other three from Canada. They entered into a number of competitions—long drive, putting, handicap events, team Nassaus, flights for matchplay losers, a two-round strokeplay team competition on Saturday, September 17, and a week-long (19–24) matchplay tournament to decide the individual Olympic champion.

Six teams were entered for the team competition but only two showed up—the Western Golf Association (WGA) and Trans-Mississippi Golf Association (TMGA). Ten other golfers hanging around the clubhouse were gathered together to form a third team, which, it was decided, would represent the United States Golf Association (USGA). The WGA, led by Chicagoan and Harvard University sophomore Chandler Egan, won easily.

Seventy-five golfers were present on Monday morning for the start of matchplay tournament. To qualify for the knockout stage, they first needed to play 36 holes of strokeplay and two St. Louis CC members—

Stuart Stickney and Ralph McKittrick—were co-medalists with a score of 163. One hundred and eighty-three was sufficient to advance, but only one of the three Canadians managed it—Toronto's George Lyon, an all-around athlete who had taken the game up just eight years before after several years as a renowned cricket player.

Lyon made it through to the semifinals along with Egan, Frank Newton of Seattle and Burt McKinnie of St. Louis. Egan trounced McKinnie, while Lyon beat Newton.

Egan would start the final a very hot favorite. Not only had he won the U.S. Amateur at Baltusrol two weeks previously, he was also a sprightly 20 years old. After a week of 36-hole days, Egan's youth would surely count against Lyon who, though a fine player (he would win the Canadian Amateur eight times), was now 46.

But Egan just didn't have it. Frustrated by the constant rain and his own scrappy play, he struggled in the morning round, coming off the 18th green 1-down. The rain cleared for the start of the second round, but still Egan couldn't click into gear. At one point he was four holes back to the long-hitting Lyon, who was said to own a "coal-heaver's swing." Around the turn, Egan at last found some form, whittling the lead down to one by the 15th hole.

He hit a bad drive left into a lake at the 15th, however, and suddenly found himself 2-down with three holes to play. At the 16th, a fairly straight downhill hole of 433 yards with more water to the right of the green, Egan hit another bad drive and ended up taking five. Lyon, meanwhile, made four, winning the match 3&2.

Still brimming with energy, Lyon accepted his gold medal after walking the length of the clubhouse dining room on his hands.

Golf was planned for the 1908 Olympics in London, but a bitter controversy arose among the press, golfers and Olympic officials over the format and choice of Royal St. George's GC in Kent as host club, instead of the R&A in St. Andrews. Royal St. George's was fully prepared for the event, but the British Olympic Association decided to

FAST LEARNER
Canada's George Lyon was an impressive athlete who excelled at cricket before turning his hand to golf at the age of 38.

"I am not foolish enough to think I am the best golfer in the world, but I am satisfied I am not the worst."

George Lyon to a reporter following his Olympic victory, aware that many of America's top players had not competed

cancel it two days before it began. Lyon, who had traveled to Britain to defend his title, was offered the gold medal by default but refused it.

Golf, then, has not been played at the Olympics since that 1904 final, meaning the 16th hole at Glen Echo is the last hole ever played in an Olympic golf competition.

RIO RETURN

In October 2009, International Olympic Committee (IOC) members voted 63–27 in favor of golf returning to the Olympics at Rio de Janeiro in 2016. Brazil's existing courses weren't up to the task of hosting so important an event, so a new course would need to be built. Seven design firms, including those belonging to Jack Nicklaus, Greg Norman and Gary Player applied but, in March 2012, it was announced Gil Hanse, a little-known but highly respected architect from Pennsylvania, had won the contract to build the course in the Barra da Tijuca neighborhood.

In May of 2014, however, a public prosecutor raised concerns that environmental laws weren't being followed, halting construction. By the middle of October, little had been resolved and it became apparent the non-native grass that had already begun growing on the site—Zeon Zoysia—might need to be removed.

The construction timeframe had been so severely compromised that it wasn't clear what might happen, even if the judge in the case ruled in favor of construction continuing. The planned test-run tournament in the summer of 2015 was surely in jeopardy, meaning the first tournament ever played on the course could possibly be the Olympic tournament itself.

MOUND CITY
Glen Echo Country Club is located in the American Midwest, just a few minutes' drive from downtown St. Louis.

BENDABLE
Today's 16th at Glen Echo bends to the left, though not enough for the hole to be considered a genuine dogleg. A lone bunker guards the slightly raised green.

18th Oakmont

Location: Oakmont,
Pennsylvania

Distance: 484 yards, par 4

Original course designer:
Henry C. Fownes

Subsequent alterations:
William C. Fownes (Henry's
son), Ferdinand Garbin
(1962), Robert Trent Jones
(1960s), Arnold Palmer,
Ed Seay (1978), Arthur Hills
(1991, 1995), Tom Fazio
(2001, 2006)

Like Pine Valley in New Jersey, Oakmont Country Club, outside Pittsburgh in Pennsylvania, wasn't the work of a full-time architect but a man with a profound appreciation for the game, an innate understanding of what made a golf course interesting and consistently challenging, plus the means to devote a good part of his life to creating his one and only course—his masterpiece. Henry C. Fownes left school at 15 to work in the family iron business, following the death of his father. Before long he was running the company with his brother William, though it was on Henry's desk that the buck invariably stopped. In 1896, the Fownes brothers sold their company to the Carnegie Steel Corporation, making Henry sufficiently wealthy to retire. He maintained a presence in the business community by serving on several boards, but mostly he played golf. The only problem was he didn't much like the majority of courses in the Pittsburgh area. They were short and a little dainty as a rule, and Henry C. wanted something altogether more testing. The 18th was one of the most taxing holes of all on the course he built—a long, uphill par 4 of 400 yards with a huge, undulating green. It was a fitting end for so difficult a round and just the sort of hole on which to crown a champion.

FOWNES' BRUTE

Henry C. put an investment group together, purchased 200 acres of largely treeless farmland bordering the Allegheny River 14 miles northeast of Pittsburgh, and got to work with 150 men gathered from the city's steel mills and over 20 mule teams. He had staked the course out in

September 1903 and it was playable the following spring. It's not altogether clear where Fownes got his inspiration for the design of the course as he never kept a record of its development and didn't contribute to *The Golfer* or *American Golfer* magazines.

LINK TO HIS PAST
H.C. Fownes had Scottish blood in his veins, so it's no surpise that Oakmont bears a strong resemblance to the ancinet links.

HARSH BUT FAIR
Oakmont never lets up and
finishes with this almost
inhumane par 4 which,
perhaps fittingly, was the
scene of the greatest ever
golfer's first major
championship victory.

After taking up golf when a misdiagnosis of arteriosclerosis gave him
two or three years to live (turned out his vision problems were the result
of failing to put a mask over his eyes when welding a bicycle wheel at
home) Fownes had quickly become proficient at the game—he would go
on to qualify for five U.S. Amateur Championships—and a keen
student. He knew the recently invented Haskell ball, that featured a
wound rubber core, would soon make the old gutta-percha and bramble
balls obsolete, and that if his course was going to be genuinely demanding for him and the game's best players, it would need to be long. It
measured 6,406 yards, making it 500–1,000 yards longer than most
courses, and possessed roughly a hundred bunkers, though that number
would more than double by the 1940s (some say it even tripled). The
bogey was 80 (what the imaginary Colonel Bogey—your matchplay
opponent if you were playing alone—would be expected to shoot),
another indication of how tough the course was.

Henry C. owned 51 percent of the club and kept control until his
death in 1935, when his son William C. (named after his uncle) took
over. Henry and William were only 21 years apart in age and William's
influence over the course had been significant before his father's death.
But it grew substantially after it and, determined to continue his
father's aspiration of creating a course to test the very best, William
began digging bunkers wherever he suspected players were missing the
fairway. It is said that a few years after H.C.'s death, the bunker count
at Oakmont almost reached 350, though no one can be sure of the
exact number.

Because of the heavy clay soils, however, William and the course's Superintendent, Emil "Dutch" Loeffler, couldn't build terribly deep bunkers. But they would often take the fill and build up the faces, meaning that though the bunkers were quite small, they were genuine hazards and best avoided.

There was just no breather at Oakmont. Getting to the green was tough but, once there, getting into the hole was even tougher as the greens possessed some major pitch and were considerably quicker than any other course's thanks to Loeffler's expertise and devotion.

Fownes (William C.), himself an excellent golfer who won the 1910 U.S. Amateur, was playing Captain for the U.S. Walker Cup team in 1922 and, four years later, became the President of the United States Golf Association, conspired with Loeffler to design bunker rakes that left deep, parallel ridges of sand, making the bunkers even more hazardous (the members got rid of them in the mid-1950s, a few years after Fownes' death). Fownes obviously had no qualms about building so penal a course, saying that "a poor shot should be a shot irrevocably lost." The Golden Age of Architecture, a period that ran from roughly 1910 to roughly 1937 championed strategic design, which aimed to give players multiple options on how to play the hole. Oakmont, by contrast, basically gave you one option, and if you failed to execute the shot properly you would be roundly punished.

It is the reason why Gene Sarazen said Oakmont had all the charm of a sock to the head, even though he won the PGA Championship there in 1922 beating Emmet French 4&3 in the final (the PGA Championship was a match-play tournament until 1958). It is why Tommy Armour, winner of the first of Oakmont's eight U.S. Opens (it will stage its ninth in 2016) in 1927, said

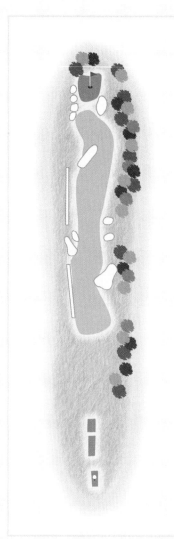

TO THE BITTER END
On the ground, to the side, up close, far away or, like here, from up above—it doesn't matter where you view it from; the 18th at Oakmont is simply terrifying.

THE BURGH
Oakmont Country Club is situated 14 miles east of downtown Pittsburgh in Pennsylvania— about 360 miles east of New York City.

every hole bordered on being a nightmare and caused "muscle-tightening terror." And it is why, in 1962, Herbert Warren Wind, writing in *The New Yorker*, called the course an "ugly brute."

The members and club president weren't terribly pleased with Wind's remark and decided to beautify their course by planting thousands of trees. From the mid 1960s to the mid 1990s, Oakmont morphed into a parkland course having lost the wide-open, exposed aspect H.C. Fownes had found so appealing.

Following the 1994 U.S. Open, the trees started coming out. In all, more than 5,000 were removed over a period of many years and only two remained in the course's interior. Naturally some of the members were very unhappy about it, which meant the superintendent, John Zimmers, had to do much of the work during the cover of night. But as the views opened up and the turf became healthier and firmer, most of the members began to concede Oakmont was better with fewer trees. It had always been tough, even with the trees, which shielded players from the wind and caused

SILVER SCOT
Tommy Armour was born in Edinburgh but moved to the US in his mid twenties. He won the 1927 U.S. Open at Oakmont, beating displaced Englishman Harry Cooper in an 18-hole playoff.

the turf to be a little softer than it should have been. But it was back to its unforgiving, exacting, remorseless best for the 2007 U.S. Open when Argentina's Angel Cabrera won with a 72-hole total of 5-over 285, saying, "I beat everybody here, not only Tiger Woods. But I wasn't able to beat the golf course. The golf course beat me." The average score for the last round was 75.72, the cut had fallen at 10 over par, and not one of the 18 holes played to an average below its par. The Fownes were looking down from the clubhouse in the sky grinning from ear to ear.

DETHRONING THE KING

"Let the clumsy, the spineless, and the alibi artist stand aside!"
William C. Fownes, who clearly thought bad shots should be penalized

Oakmont had been the stage for much drama during the U.S. Open down the years. Scottish expat Tommy Armour beat English expat Harry Cooper in a 36-hole playoff in 1927, eight years before local boy Sam Parks Jr. surprised a strong field including Walter Hagen, Gene Sarazen and winner of the inaugural Masters Tournament Horton Smith. In 1953, Ben Hogan went wire-to-wire to beat rival Sam Snead by six and win his fourth and final U.S. Open. Twenty years later, Johnny Miller shot a brilliant final-round 63, aided by overnight rains that softened the greens, to come from six strokes back and beat John Schlee by one.

In 1983, Larry Nelson shot an amazing 10-under 132 over the weekend to storm back after a miserable first two days and beat Tom Watson by a shot, and in 1994 Ernie Els won his first major beating Colin Montgomerie and Loren Roberts in a playoff (when Montgomerie was eliminated after 18 holes, Els beat Roberts at the second sudden-death hole). In 2007, Angel Cabrera was the last man standing after Oakmont extracted its usual pound of flesh.

Galleries at Oakmont have enjoyed some of the more compelling U.S. Open action (plus three PGAs, two U.S. Women's Opens, and five U.S. Amateurs), but never have they been treated to anything quite as momentous as the final round and 18-hole playoff in 1962, when a 22-year-old Jack Nicklaus took on 32-year-old Arnold Palmer in his own backyard. Nicklaus was from Columbus, Ohio, only 200 miles away, but Palmer came from Latrobe, Pennsylvania, just 35 miles from Oakmont.

After 54 holes, Palmer was tied for the lead with Bobby Nichols, with Nicklaus two strokes back and tied for fifth. In Saturday's final round, the two emerged as the leading contenders, Nicklaus finally drawing level after Palmer made a bogey on the 13th. Both players missed make-able birdie chances on the 18th that would have won them the Championship, and finished tied on 1-under 283—two clear of Nichols and Phil Rodgers in third.

"Now that the big guy is out of the cage, everybody better run for cover."
Arnold Palmer after losing the playoff

Ten thousand people turned out for Sunday's playoff, the group support-ing Nicklaus probably numbering no more than the number of holes he and Palmer were scheduled to play. Though he had turned pro only seven months before and was yet to win a pro tournament, Nicklaus was well known to the galleries. He had won the U.S. Amateur in 1959 and 1961 and, in 1960, finished second behind Palmer at the U.S. Open in Denver (see p.116). He was also low amateur at the Masters that year and then won the individual title at the World Amateur Team Championship at Merion by 13 shots, shooting an incredible 11-under 269. He finished tied for fourth at the 1961 U.S. Open.

He was Palmer's heir apparent. But the five-time major champion who had won his third Masters just two months before wasn't close to being ready to give up his crown.

Elements in the pro-Palmer crowd continued to taunt Nicklaus, calling him "Ohio Fats" and "Fat Jack," but after half a dozen holes most of Arnie's Army had fallen silent. When Nicklaus made a birdie 2 at the short 6th and Palmer a bogey 4, the seemingly unshakable young pretender had moved four clear.

It was time for a Palmer charge. Birdies at the 9th, 11th and 12th took him back to even par for the round and pulled him to within one of Nicklaus. The reignited crowd hoped the birdies would keep coming, but Palmer made a bogey on the 13th to fall two back and then the pair matched pars all the way to the 18th.

Then 462 yards, the home hole was full of danger, so Nicklaus certainly couldn't cruise. But he made a solid 4 while Palmer capitulated. At the back of the green in three, he hit his par putt past the hole then carelessly missed the bogey putt to finish on 74, three shots behind.

It was the first of Nicklaus' 115 professional victories and 18 professional majors.

CREAMER RISES

✦

As well as hosting the game's best male players at eight U.S. Opens, three PGA Championships and five U.S. Amateur Champion-ships, Oakmont has twice welcomed the world's top female golfers. In 1992, Patty Sheehan won the U.S. Women's Open after defeating Juli Inkster 72–74 in an 18-hole playoff. The championship returned in 2010 when the course measured 6,613 yards—301 yards longer than it had 18 years previously. Thanks to a brilliant birdie 3 at the 445-yard 18th on the Saturday, California native Paula Creamer took a three-shot lead into the final round. Playing with a bandaged left thumb following surgery in March of that year, Creamer actually pulled further away in the final round, shooting a 2-under 69 and winning by 4 over Norway's Suzann Pettersen and Korea's Na Yeon Choi.

17th Pinehurst (No. 2)

Location: Pinehurst Village, North Carolina

Distance: 205 yards, par 3

Original course designer: Donald Ross

Subsequent alterations: Richard S. Tufts (1950), Peter Tufts (1976), George and Tom Fazio (1978), Ed Connor (1987), Rees Jones (1996), Ben Crenshaw and Bill Coore (2010)

James W. Tufts, born in 1835, was an ambitious young man. A pharmacy apprentice at 16, he built his own pharmacy at age 21, and within a few years had a thriving chain of drugstores. He sold them all though when the invention he had been perfecting became so popular, its production and distribution required his full attention. Tufts' Arctic Soda Apparatus made him a wealthy man. In 1891, he merged with three of his competitors to form the American Soda Fountain Company, for which he served as president the rest of his life. In addition to his phenomenal business acumen and determination, Tufts was an altruistic man, interested in the well-being of his employees and other working-class folk from the industrial northeast. His own health, impaired by the demands of his position, was also a concern. He often journeyed south in the winter and on one trip to North Carolina in 1895 he was made aware of a 5,000-acre property in Moore County, 100 miles due east of Charlotte, that could be bought for roughly $1.25 an acre.

SHARP SHOOTER
Born Phoebe Ann Mosey
in rural Ohio in 1860,
famed hunter and trapper
Annie Oakley was hired in
1916 to run the resort's
gun club.

VILLAGE PEOPLE

Before Tufts bought it in July of 1895, the land had been covered in pine trees—the resin of which was used in the manufacture of turpentine—making it moderately useful. Once the trees had gone, though, all that was left was a sandy wilderness that everyone who knew of it assumed would be good for nothing. Tufts felt very differently and immediately began planning a village and resort that invalids and low-income workers from New England could visit to restore their health and vitality. Though most certainly a business venture, Tufts described the project as "semi-philanthropic."

He hired Frederick Olmstead, the creative brains behind Central Park in New York City, to design the village. Streets were built, public buildings went up and 222,000 decorative trees and shrubs were planted. Water pipes and sewer lines were installed, telephones and electricity were made available, and the first hotel—the Holly Inn—opened on New Year's Eve. Various names for the new village were tested, but the locals usually went with Tuftstown in deference to its founder.

Tufts, though, eventually chose Pinehurst, which he got from a list of names that had been suggested for Martha's Vineyard.

The resort offered its guests a number of recreational opportunities—horse-riding, hunting, archery, bicycling, lawn-bowls, polo and tennis. Sharp-shooting Annie Oakley opened the Pinehurst Gun Club and gave exhibitions and lessons. And when Tufts received complaints from a local farmer that his cows were distressed because of

UNFORGETTABLE
Bill Coore and Ben Crenshaw added sandy scrub and wire grass areas to the course during their redesign in 2011, yet the beauty of the 17th remains.

stray golf balls hit by enthusiastic golfers, he decided to add a nine-hole golf course. To build Pinehurst's first holes, Tuft's engaged Dr. Leroy Culver, a former New York City public health official and one-time resident physician at the Piney Woods Inn in nearby Southern Pines. Culver had visited St. Andrews to play this curious stick-and-ball game and was thus regarded as some sort of expert. The course possessed square, sand greens and opened early in 1898. And, though rudimentary, it proved extremely popular. Nine more holes soon became necessary.

In 1899, John Tucker—cousin of Willie Dunn (see p.38) and the resort's first golf professional—laid out the second nine, which, together with Culver's original holes, became Pinehurst No. 1.

Ross' Arrival

Seven hundred and fifty miles to the north, a 27-year-old Scottish professional, risking everything he had in coming to the New World, was settling into his job at the newly formed Oakley CC in Watertown, Massachusetts. Donald Ross, a native of Dornoch on the northeast coast of Scotland, had served an apprenticeship during his mid teens under Tom Morris Sr. in St. Andrews where he learned to build golf clubs. Following that he worked in Carnoustie for a year, before making it home to Dornoch in 1893, aged 21. A good player, with club-making skills and a knowledge of greenkeeping, Ross was installed as Royal Dornoch's first professional.

FOUNDING FATHERS
The Donald Ross (left) and Richard Tufts statues at Pinehurst honor two of the most influential men in the resort's history.

A Harvard astronomy professor named Robert Willson, who visited Scotland to play golf, met Ross in Dornoch and encouraged him to cross the Atlantic where he could work at his golf club giving lessons and redesigning the somewhat inadequate course.

It was his first attempt at design, but Ross did a sound job transforming Oakley in relatively short order. James Tufts, who owned land locally, saw what Ross had achieved and offered him a job at Pinehurst where he would direct all golf operations.

Ross arrived in North Carolina in 1900 and set to work upgrading the No. 1 course. Again, he did a fine job, paving the way for his next big project—No. 2.

**PALACE IN
THE PINES**
The 230-room Carolina
Hotel at the Pinehurst
Resort opened in 1901
and is known as "the
Queen of the South."

Pinehurst No. 2, undoubtedly the course for which Ross is best known, opened ahead of the fall season in 1907—a few months after Donald's brother Alex had won the U.S. Open. The greens were 60 square feet and built using clay and sand as no turf had been identified that could be reasonably maintained during the hot Carolina summers.

The course was an instant success and soon became the permanent home of the prestigious North and South Amateur and British Opens.

The North and South Open was played from 1902 to 1951 and winners included brothers Donald and Alec Ross who shared the title for the first seven years, Walter Hagen, Jim Barnes, Horton Smith, Byron Nelson, Ben Hogan, Cary Middlecoff and Sam Snead. It was cancelled when Pinehurst President Richard Tufts, a champion of amateur golf, became angry following the players' demands for a bigger tournament purse.

The amateur version was first played in 1901 and continues to this day. Winners include Walter Travis, Chick Evans, Ed Furgol, Frank Stanahan, Jack Nicklaus, Curtis Strange, Hal Sutton, Corey Pavin, Davis Love III and Jack Nicklaus II.

Ross would design or redesign four courses at Pinehurst (the resort now owns nine following the June 2014 acquisition of the Jack Nicklaus-designed course at National GC, just 3 miles from Pinehurst) and roughly 400 elsewhere in the U.S. But he would always return, each winter, to

Pinehurst and his favorite course, of which he said, "No. 2 has always been a pet of mine."

He tinkered with it until his death in 1948, overseeing the transition to Bermuda-grass putting surfaces in the mid 1930s, alongside his construction foreman and the Director of Grounds, Frank Maples. He also added greenside mounds and built intimidating, flash-faced bunkers. The greens complexes were his lasting masterpiece though. Large and tantalizingly contoured, they were pushed up slightly, putting emphasis on the approach shot and resulting in all manner of thought-provoking pitches and chip shots.

STEWART'S ENDURING IMAGE

No Pleasure Without Payne
By the time he won his second U.S. Open (and third major) at Pinehurst in 1999, Payne Stewart had become one of the most popular players in the game.

By the time Pinehurst No. 2 hosted its first U.S. Open in June 1999, 42-year-old Payne Stewart had become one of the most popular players in the game. But it had taken a while for him to get there. Often thought of early in his career as a little arrogant, caustic with the press and not terribly gracious towards the fans, Stewart had mellowed considerably. Winning two major championships (1989 PGA Championship, 1991 U.S. Open) was a big part of that, and fatherhood, faith and watching his good friend Paul Azinger survive cancer were also factors. And he'd been wearing his now familiar plus fours and flat cap for 17 years, overcoming the inevitable gibes to become something of a style icon.

The 1999 season had gone well thus far. Yes, he'd missed the cut in two of his three previous tournaments, but Stewart had notched his 10th PGA Tour win at Pebble Beach in February, and had recorded two runner-up finishes.

A first-round 2-under 68 put Stewart in a tie for fifth, one shot behind the four players tied for the lead. His 69 in the second round saw him climb to the top of the leaderboard alongside David Duval and Phil Mickelson. And though a 2-over 72 on Saturday wasn't his best effort, it was good enough to give him sole possession of first as Mickelson shot 73 and Duval 75. On 1-under 209, Stewart was one shot clear of Mickelson and two in front of Tim Herron and Tiger Woods, the 24-year-old who had won the Masters by 12 shots two years before.

By the 10th hole on Sunday, Stewart and Mickelson were tied, with Fijian Vijay Singh just one behind and Woods two back. It was a tense and gripping back nine. Mickelson was one clear by the time they reached the 16th green. There, Stewart holed a nasty right-to-left breaking putt from 35 feet to save par, while Mickelson missed from 6.

Tied on the tee of the 191-yard 17th, Stewart hit a fantastic 6-iron 5 feet right of the hole. Mickelson answered by putting his tee shot a foot outside Stewart's. Mickelson missed again, however, over-reading the break just as he had on the 16th. Moments later, Stewart poured in another putt and was now one clear heading to the last.

He drove into the right rough and, from a thick, wet lie, chopped out 75 yards short of the flag. From there he hit a lob wedge to about 15 feet while Mickelson was 20 feet right in two. Mickelson gave his birdie try a good run, but it slid by on the right, leaving Stewart his putt for a 4, a four-round total of 279, and the Championship.

A year earlier, he had gone into the final round at the Olympic Club in San Francisco with a four-shot lead, but a closing 74 allowed Lee Janzen in. Before the 1999 tournament began, Stewart said he just wanted the chance to win it again.

Well here he was, 15 feet from victory. The putt was very slightly uphill and mostly straight, and he gave it a beautiful rap, the ball hugging the green and falling into the cup with perfect speed. Stewart thrust his right arm out in front of him, his right leg out to the side. It was a memorable reaction, forever immortalized by a bronze statue unveiled in November 2001 near the green on which he won his third major, his wife Tracy and children Aaron and Chelsea in attendance.

That moment came just a little more than two years after Stewart was tragically killed in a plane crash when the Learjet he was flying in from Orlando to Dallas lost cabin pressure, causing Stewart and the five other people on board to suffer fatal hypoxia. The plane eventually ran out of fuel and crashed into a field just outside Mina, South Dakota.

ANOTHER TRAGIC LOSS

◆

Payne Stewart's tragic death rekindled sad memories of another great American golfer that died prematurely in a plane crash. In July 1966, Californian Tony Lema was killed alongside his wife Betty and two others when the Beechcraft Bonanza taking them from Akron, Ohio, to Lansing, Michigan, ran out of fuel and crashed into a lake less than a mile from the runway. Lema was just 32 and had beaten Jack Nicklaus by five strokes to win the British Open at St. Andrews in 1964. Peter Thomson, Arnold Palmer and numerous other professionals said they believed Lema was as talented a player as they had ever seen.

RESTORING ROSS

After 75 years of ownership, the Tufts family sold Pinehurst to the Diamondhead Corporation in 1973. Intent on maximizing profits rather than preserving one of the country's historic golf resorts, the new owners built condos that lined the fairways on No. 3 and No. 5, and reserved 2,700 acres for single-family houses. Worst of all perhaps, they turned No. 2 into a clone of Augusta National, rejecting the firm and fast conditions in favor of soft and green, abandoning completely Donald Ross' vision.

Diamondhead sold to Robert Dedman's ClubCorp in 1984, but it too was keen on the green. It wasn't until 2010, in fact, by which time Dedman had sold all of ClubCorp's assets except Pinehurst, that a decision was made to restore the course that Ross built. Dedman, together with then-Pinehurst-president Don Padgett, hired the team of Bill Coore and Ben Crenshaw to rediscover the strategy and shots Ross had intended. It was a major risk because, as Padgett admitted, the business model was working. Only a golf architecture obsessive could really know how great No. 2 had been back in the day. Modern golfers, who probably didn't know any better, still loved it. But Pinehurst No. 2 was half the course it had once been and Dedman and Padgett were willing to take the gamble to restore it.

Coore and Crenshaw had built a fine reputation in the industry for designing strategic, lay-of-the-land courses and with Crenshaw's love of golf's history they were the perfect choice. They took out 35 acres of Bermuda rough, replacing it with sandy waste areas dotted with clumps of wiregrass. They widened the fairways and removed 650 irrigation heads, saving the resort roughly 40 million gallons of water a year.

YOUNG AT HEART
The bronze Putter Boy statue, sculpted by Lucy Richards in 1912, is one of Pinehurst's most beloved features.

"Coore and Crenshaw are the best at what they do. Pinehurst No. 2 is now so much fun to play."
Phil Mickelson on seeing the restoration of Pinehurst No. 2 for the first time

And because it was the greens for which No. 2 was best known, Coore and Crenshaw wisely left them alone, enlarging a couple to find extra pin positions but mostly concentrating on the fairways and approaches. Large, fast and with severe banks or slopes at their edges that shrink the area on which it is safe to land an approach shot, the greens are incredibly demanding and are thought to have become more crowned, and thus even more challenging, over time. The theory is that decades of top-dressing had raised the centers of the putting surfaces by as much as a foot, making the drop-offs increasingly steep. Kyle Franz, one of Coore and Crenshaw's crew members, refutes this though, saying that because the edges of the greens were mown lower than they used to be and that the greenside bunkers had become grass-faced as opposed to sand-faced, it just appeared the greens were higher. Franz added that if Ross were to see the course's greens today, he would definitely recognize them.

Because of the reduced irrigation, the edges of the fairways during the 2014 U.S. and U.S. Women's British Opens looked dry, if not burnt—a result of the remaining irrigation heads all being positioned down the middle of the fairways. Some said No. 2 looked brown and ugly, but everyone that knew how much water Coore and Crenshaw had saved, and how much more fun firm and fast is compared to soft and green, just smiled and ignored them.

IN THE PINES
Pinehurst Resort is found in the North Carolina Sandhills, in the central part of the Tar Heel State, 100 miles east of Charlotte.

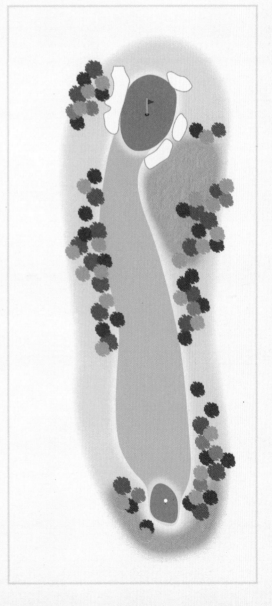

SANDS OF TIME
Like every other hole at Pinehurst No. 2, the 17th was transformed during Coore and Crenshaw's major renovation. With a relatively large green, however, the sand here doesn't really come into play for the pros.

11th Merion (East)

Location: Ardmore, Pennsylvania

Distance: 367 yards, par 4

Original course designer: Hugh Wilson

RIGHT PLACE, RIGHT TIME
Though only 367 yards long, and positioned in the middle of the round, the 11th at Merion (East) had greatness thrust upon it when Bobby Jones won the 1930 U.S. Amateur here.

English course architect Tom Simpson said the vital thing about a golf hole was that it should either be more difficult than it looks or look more difficult than it is. "It must never be what it looks," he added. Though Simpson had nothing to do with Merion's design, the short, teasing par 4 11th fits the theory well. You would expect the world's best players to post more 3s than 4s on any two-shot hole measuring less than 400 yards. In the final round of the 1934 U.S. Open, however, Gene Sarazen found the creek off the tee and wound up with a 7, eventually finishing one stroke behind the winner, Olin Dutra. At the 2013 U.S. Open, the hole played to an average of 4.21 with the 70 birdies overwhelmed by 102 bogeys, 21 double-bogeys, and six ugly "others."

INSTANT SUCCESS

On December 22, 1894, four East Coast clubs—Newport, Saint Andrew's, Shinnecock Hills, and the Country Club—together with the Chicago GC formed the Amateur Golf Association which soon became the United States Golf Association (USGA). Golf was

beginning to take root in America, and a sporting club with a growing reputation like Merion needed to offer this intriguing stick-and-ball game from across the Atlantic to its curious members.

Merion Cricket Club had been founded in 1865 when 15 young enthusiasts met for twice-weekly games on a few acres in Wynne Wood, about 8 miles northwest of downtown Philadelphia. It wasn't long before the group had outgrown its original site, however, so it moved a mile west to Ardmore in 1875. In 1892, it moved again, this time to 12 acres near Haverford College, where it continued to prosper and offer the membership additional sports—squash, field hockey, soccer and lawn tennis. There clearly wasn't sufficient space for those interested in golf to swing their hickories, so 100 acres were leased from the railroad company in Bryn Mawr, a mile or two northwest of Haverford. Nine rather crude holes were "built" and opened for play in May 1896. Nine more were added four years later on land belonging to a member, and for 10 years the club's golfers made do with their rather mundane layout.

It was a situation that couldn't last very much longer. The golfers wanted their own land, a much better course, and a place they could call their own. A site committee, given the task of finding the golfers suitable land, was established.

A couple of shrewd and astute local businessmen who became aware of what the club was looking for began buying up parcels of land near Haverford College. By 1910, they had put a consortium together, which included a handful of members, and began operating as the Haverford Development Company. In total, they acquired roughly 300 acres, of which they were willing to sell 100, or however many were needed to build a course, to the club for the discount price of $726.50 an acre. The hope was that by building a first-class golf course on a chunk of their land the value of the rest of it would skyrocket.

An English-born golf professional and course architect by the name of H.H. Baker who was based at the Garden City GC on Long Island, New York, was hired to make a plan for the course. The site committee chose not to follow Baker's plan, however, but involve C.B. Macdonald and H.J. Whigham instead. Macdonald and Whigham were both very fine amateur golfers who had worked together to find land for the National Golf Links of America on Long Island. Their expertise was much in demand, and they journeyed to Merion to advise the committee on where their holes should go.

They envisioned a course requiring 120 acres, but not all of the land they needed was controlled by the Haverford Development Company, which moved fast to purchase more acreage for the course. Even after the acquisition of the 21-acre Dallas Estate, however, they were still 3 acres short—acres owned by the Philadelphia and Western Railway. It is not entirely clear how the club eventually came by this land but it is now home to the short 13th and much of the par 4 12th.

With the course planned in its entirety and the land now purchased, the club set up a course construction committee headed by an insurance broker who had captained the Princeton golf team—the sole reason, it seemed, for his appointment.

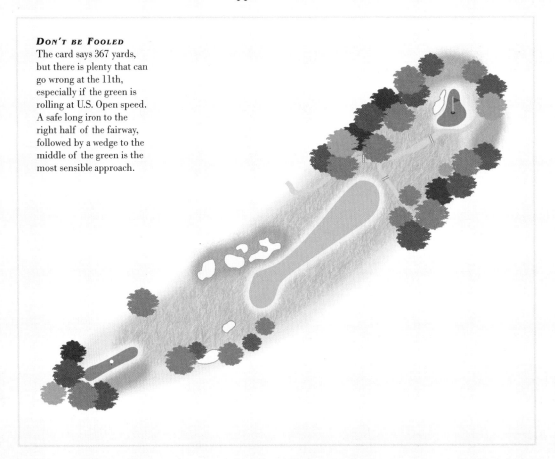

DON'T BE FOOLED
The card says 367 yards, but there is plenty that can go wrong at the 11th, especially if the green is rolling at U.S. Open speed. A safe long iron to the right half of the fairway, followed by a wedge to the middle of the green is the most sensible approach.

Much like Philadelphia hotelier George Crump, who played a crucial part in the creation of Pine Valley GC, Pittsburgh iron manufacturer Henry Fownes who financed, founded and designed Oakmont CC, and accomplished California amateur golfers Jack Neville and Douglas Grant who designed Pebble Beach, Hugh Wilson was no expert in matters of golf course architecture.

MAIN LINE
Ardmore is a suburb of Philadelphia, Pennsylvania located just over 9 miles northwest of the Liberty Bell.

One of Wilson and the committee's first moves was to travel to Southampton on Long Island to consult with Macdonald and Whigham who had devised the initial routing and who now taught Wilson the rudiments of laying out a golf course. Construction got underway sometime in spring of 1911 before Macdonald and Whigham made one final visit.

In September of 1911, the course was seeded and then, in the spring of 1912, Wilson left for Britain where he would spend seven months studying the country's finest links courses in great detail.

The question as to why Wilson went to Britain after Merion had already been built baffled historians for a long time, but there now seems little question he went with the intention of discovering interesting design elements he would be able to incorporate into the bare bones of the course at Merion on his return to the U.S.

> "The members of the committee had played golf for many years, but the experience of each in construction and greenkeeping was only that of the average club member. Looking back on the work, I feel certain that we would never have attempted to carry it out, if we had realized one-half the things we did not know."
>
> *Hugh Wilson, Merion's designer (1916)*

Indeed, Macdonald himself always encouraged golf clubs not to build everything straight away, but add hazards and other finishing touches after it had become clear where poorly directed shots would finish.

Wilson would follow this advice while forsaking Macdonald's tendency for building template holes. Though certainly influenced by what he saw in Britain, Wilson never wanted to build exact replicas of any hole, no matter how much he liked it.

The East Course at Merion (Wilson also created the West Course) opened to the club's members on September 14, 1912, but Wilson would continue to tweak it right up until his untimely death in 1924, aged 45.

Merion has now hosted 18 USGA events including five U.S. Opens —won by Olin Dutra in 1934; Ben Hogan, who hit a 1-iron up the hill to the 18th green in 1950, enabling him to earn a spot in a 36-hole playoff with Lloyd Mangrum and George Fazio which Hogan won (see p.91); Lee

Trevino, who beat Jack Nicklaus in an 18-hole playoff by three strokes in 1971; David Graham, who shot a brilliant final round 67 in 1981; and Justin Rose, whose excellent approach shot to the 72nd green in 2013 rivalled that of Hogan and set up a two-shot victory over Phil Mickelson.

Though C.B. Macdonald and H.J. Whigham contributed a great deal to Merion's initial routing and layout, credit for the course that evolved into the treasure it is today must go to Hugh Wilson, whose great achievement is perhaps summed up best by architect Tom Doak who said Merion has an aura of perfection and that it should be one of the first courses any young architect studies.

Impregnable Quadrilateral

Put yourself in Eugene Homans' shoes. It's September 27, 1930, and today is the biggest day of your golfing career so far, as you've reached the final of the U.S. Amateur championship at Merion GC. The day before you battled back from 5-down in a 36-hole match against a player named George Seaver and won on the final green, the first time you had the lead all day. You've won the New Jersey Amateur five times already, and earlier in the year you took the prestigious North and South Amateur at Pinehurst. You're young, confident and clearly very talented. And who knows how far a victory today could take you.

Your opponent, however, is Bobby Jones—winner of the U.S. Open and the Open and Amateur Championships of Great Britain this year, and just a victory at the U.S. Amateur away from achieving the

NEVER AGAIN
Because the best amateur and U.S. college players invariably turn professional some time in their early twenties (if not before) these days, we can safely assume Bobby Jones' amateur Grand Slam will never be repeated.

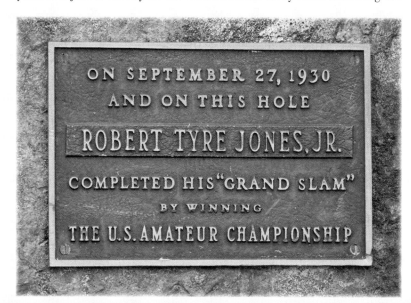

ON SEPTEMBER 27, 1930 AND ON THIS HOLE ROBERT TYRE JONES, JR. COMPLETED HIS "GRAND SLAM" BY WINNING THE U.S. AMATEUR CHAMPIONSHIP

LINE 'EM UP
The British Open's Claret
Jug, the U.S. Amateur's
Havemeyer Trophy, the
Amateur Championship
Trophy, the U.S. Open
Championship Trophy—in
1930 Jones won them all.

impossible—what *Atlanta Journal* writer O.B. Keeler termed the "Grand Slam," and what George Trevor of the New York *Sun* called the "Impregnable Quadrilateral."

Since the U.S. Open at Interlachen in Minneapolis in July, the golf world and much of society outside the game has been abuzz with talk of the Grand Slam. And today, 18,000 excited spectators feverishly anticipating, indeed hoping, for a Jones victory have come to Merion to see history made.

What's more, Jones has very happy memories of Merion, having made his national debut here in 1916 when, aged just 14, he competed in his first U.S. Amateur, making it all the way to the quarterfinals. And then, eight years later, he won his first U.S. Amateur title here, beating George Von Elm 9&8 in the final.

How could Homans, a bespectacled 22-year-old Princeton graduate whose uncle sat on the same USGA committee as Jones, possibly perform under such circumstances? Though no doubt a fine, upstanding young gentleman, few people outside his immediate family would have wanted Homans to win.

It was really no surprise, therefore, when he failed to make a par in the first five holes and found himself 3-down after six.

As the match went on, Homans did begin to hit the ball cleanly, but whatever he threw at Jones it wasn't enough to keep pace with the 28-year-old Georgia Tech and Harvard law student, who found another gear altogether playing the back nine in three under-4s and walking off the 18th green with a seven-hole lead.

> **"Acre for acre, Merion may be the best test of golf in the world."**
>
> *Jack Nicklaus, who shot 269 in the 1960 World Amateur Team Championship at Merion to win individual honors and lead the U.S. to a 42-stroke victory*

When the match resumed after lunch, Jones quickly went nine up, but the pressure of the situation and the nervous exhaustion he frequently suffered began to take their toll. His play around the turn was erratic but, thanks to mistakes by his opponent, he lost only one hole.

Thus he arrived on the 11th tee, the 29th hole of the match with an eight-hole lead that Homans would need extra holes to overcome. Jones split the fairway then hit an easy pitch that settled about 20 feet from the cup. Homans also found the putting surface in regulation, leaving himself at the back of the green slightly inside Jones.

Jones putted first, running his ball down the hill to the side of the hole, meaning Homans had to sink his putt for the match to stay alive. Halfway there, it was obvious his ball had taken too much break and would miss on the low side. Jones won the match 8&7, claiming his fifth U.S. Amateur and 13 major title (four U.S. Opens, three British Opens, five U.S. Amateurs, one British Amateur).

A group of Marines surrounded him in an effort to keep the jubilant hordes at bay and escorted him back to the clubhouse where he chatted with his father and had a little time to reflect on the enormity of his achievement. Writing in *Sports Illustrated*, Herbert Warren Wind noted that Jones looked younger during the prize ceremony than he had in recent weeks, as the strain of the last few months seemed to disappear from his face. Two months later, Jones announced his retirement from competitive golf, leaving a legacy that few, if any, amateur sportsmen have ever equalled.

Fortunately for golf, he remained active in the game, establishing the Augusta National Golf Club in Augusta, Georgia in 1933, alongside his friend, investment banker Clifford Roberts, and in 1934,

TIMELY
On September 22, 1930, the week before he would win the Grand Slam, Bobby Jones appeared on the front cover of *Time* magazine—a rare honor for any golfer.

TIME
The Weekly Newsmagazine

ROBERT TYRE JONES JR.
It's only just not. Percy.
(See Sport)

Volume XVI   Number 12

WARM WELCOME
On July 14, 1930, Bobby
Jones (seen arriving with his
wife) was given a hero's
welcome outside City Hall
in Atlanta, Georgia. Jones
had just won the U.S. Open
to go with the Open
Championship and (British)
Amateur Championship he
had already won that year.

inaugurating the tournament that soon came to
be known as The Masters (see pp.154 and 155).

During the Bobby Jones era, the Amateur
Championships of the United States and Great
Britain were considered the game's two most
important tournaments. With the passage of
time and the rise of professional sport, however,
these amateur events have been replaced by
the PGA Championship and The Masters—the
tournament Jones conceived. After winning
the 2001 Masters, Tiger Woods held all four professional major championship trophies, having
won the U.S. Open, Open Championship and
PGA Championship the previous year, but no
one has ever won all four in the same calendar
year. Jones is therefore the only player to have
won a Grand Slam. Chances are it's a record that
will remain intact as long as golf is played.

JUST IN CASE

✦

Situated in the southeastern
corner of the course, at the property's
lowest point and close to where Cobb's
Creek (also known as the Baffling Brook)
intersects with another stream, the green
at the 11th is rather prone to flooding,
something that happens at least once a
year. To avert disaster during the 2013
U.S. Open, USGA Executive Director Mike
Davis had Matt Schaffer, Merion's Director
of Course Operations, maintain two holes
on the club's West Course to U.S. Open
conditions, just in case the 11th green and
12th fairway remained under water for two
days. Davis said the possibility of that
happening was "very, very remote," and
called it the "doomsday of all doomsday
scenarios" and fortunately, despite heavy
rainfall at the beginning of the week, the
holes survived and the tournament
concluded in good time.

1912 18th Merion (East)

Location: Ardmore, Pennsylvania

Distance: 521 yards, par 4

Original course designer: Hugh Wilson

WOLF IN SHEEP'S CLOTHING
It may look tranquil, but the 18th at Merion is extremely challenging, a stringent test for players who have their sights set on winning the U.S. Open.

If not for the memorable shots that have been played there to win major championships, it's unlikely the 18th on the East Course at Merion would be particularly well known. Just the sort of hole to conclude a U.S. Open, it is a long par 4 that has little of the charm found elsewhere on Hugh Wilson's magnificent course, but all the demands that separate champions from also-rans. Usually 463 yards from the members' back tee, the hole gained an extra 58 yards in time for the 2013 U.S. Open. The drive crosses the quarry that affects the course's closing three holes before falling downhill slightly to a fairway cantered from right to left. Players hanging back off the tee find the flat part of the fairway but are left with a long iron or hybrid to the dome-shaped green, while those that power a driver further down the hill leave a much shorter approach, but must deal with an awkward downhill lie. Any way you slice it (actually, best if you don't), it's a brute.

HERO HOGAN

The year 1949 began in typical fashion for 36-year-old Ben Hogan. With 51 PGA Tour wins, including three major championship victories, he had established himself as one of the best players in the world alongside Sam Snead and fellow Texan Byron Nelson, and he added to his victory haul that winter by winning the Bing Crosby Pro-Am at Pebble Beach in January and the Long Beach Open at Lakewood CC 10 days later when he beat Jimmy Demaret in an 18-hole playoff. A week after that, he finished runner-up to Demaret in Phoenix following another 18-hole playoff.

GOLDEN SHOT
On the left side of the fairway at the 18th, about 220 yards short of the green you'll find this plaque commemorating one of the finest shots ever played.

After what had been a successful road trip, Hogan and his wife Valerie were ready to go home to Fort Worth, Texas. From Phoenix, they drove 550 miles east to the small Texas town of Van Horn where they spent the night at the El Capitan Motel. The next day, Wednesday February 2, the couple made an early start on the remaining 480 miles.

Shortly after setting out on what is now Interstate 20, the Hogans' Cadillac hit a thick patch of fog, reducing visibility significantly. Hogan slowed to 25 mph but was alarmed to see four headlights in the road ahead, two belonging to a slow-moving truck, the other two to a Greyhound bus overtaking it.

The head-on collision was inevitable. At the last second Hogan hurled himself across his wife in the passenger seat, saving her life and, as it turned out, his own as the steering column was shunted back as far as his seat cushion and would have crushed him. Valerie was dazed but Ben blacked out.

An ambulance, which took an hour and a half to reach the scene, took Hogan to the Hotel Dieu Hospital in El Paso, 120 miles back in the direction he had come from.

Hogan had survived the crash but his injuries were extensive—a fractured left collarbone, a double fracture of his pelvis, a broken ankle and a broken rib.

Still, his doctors were so impressed by his determination they said he could make a complete recovery within about two months. But while the bones were healing nicely, Hogan's lungs began giving the doctors concern. Clots had formed in Hogan's legs and it wasn't long before his lungs were affected too. Abdominal surgery was performed to tie off the inferior vena cava and prevent the clot from reaching his heart. It meant another painful month's stay in the hospital.

Hogan, only 137 pounds before the accident, lost 20 pounds while in El Paso before finally making it home to Fort Worth on March 29. He was still in a lot of pain and very weak, and his doctors were now unsure as to just how complete a recovery Hogan was going to make. His legs had atrophied significantly. There was a possibility he might not play golf again.

Hogan spent the rest of the year recuperating, though he was able to travel to Ganton GC in Yorkshire, England, to serve as non-playing captain for the U.S. Ryder Cup side which won the match 7–5.

In January 1950, with his legs bandaged to stop the swelling, Hogan made his highly anticipated return to the PGA Tour at Riviera CC where he had won the Los Angeles Open in 1947 and 1948, and his first U.S. Open also in 1948, after which the course came to be known as Hogan's Alley.

Surely, it would be just a token effort though, a ceremonial outing to show the fans he was doing OK. He couldn't possibly contend, could he?

Well, this was Ben Hogan, as gutsy a golfer as ever played the game, so perhaps no one should have been too surprised when he struggled through the pain and tied Sam Snead after 72 holes (he would lose the 18-hole playoff 72–76 after a week delay due to bad weather).

Hogan now set his sights firmly on Merion and the U.S. Open, always a physically and mentally demanding event, for which his calm, efficient, almost robotic game seemed perfectly adapted. To preserve energy before the first round, he played only 23 practice holes—none on Monday, 18 on Tuesday, five on Wednesday.

HAWKING IT
Hogan fought a damaging hook early in his career and spent countless hours on the range in an attempt to eradicate the shot. It prompted his famous saying that the secret was "in the dirt."

An opening 2-over 72 put Hogan in a tie for 18th, eight back of surprise
leader Lee Mackey. A 69 in round two pushed Hogan up into a tie for
fifth, two behind leader E.J. "Dutch" Harrison. So far so good for Hogan,
but would 36 holes on the final day prove too much?

At one point during the third round, Hogan did take the lead. But he
faltered over the closing stretch to finish the round two behind Lloyd
Mangrum, the 1946 champion. In the final round, Mangrum shot 41 on
the front nine, making a bogey on six of the first seven holes, thus opening the door for several other players, one of whom was Hogan. As he
reached the 15th green, the Hawk stood two clear and had a 25-foot putt
for a birdie.

But he missed, and then he missed again from less than 2 feet. He
made par on the 16th, but after another bogey at the 17th he came to the
458-yard home hole needing a par 4 to force a playoff with Mangrum,
who had shot 76, and George Fazio, who had finished with a level-par 70
to complete the four rounds on 7-over-par 287.

After a good drive to the left center of the fairway, Hogan faced a
slightly uphill shot of about 220 yards from a slightly downhill lie. A
gallery five or six deep ringed the entire length of the hole, craning to see
what promised to be one of the greatest comeback stories in all of sport.
Hogan's legs still gave him tremendous pain—he would later say he
had considered walking in from the 13th hole—so catching the ball

cleanly and powerfully enough to send it all the way to the green was a little too much to ask.

With one final, enormous effort, Hogan summoned perhaps the best swing of his career, catching the ball flush and sending it safely onto the green, about 40 feet from the hole. He two-putted for par, to tie with Mangrum and Fazio on 287.

Given the circumstances—final hole of a U.S. Open needing a par to have any chance, uphill 1-iron, sore, aching legs—Hogan's approach to the 18th ranks among the very greatest shots ever hit. But it would have been largely forgotten had it not resulted in victory.

The following day's 18-hole playoff was a tight, tense affair all the way to the 14th tee. At that point, Fazio began dropping strokes and would eventually finish with a 75. On the 16th green, Mangrum, just one stroke behind Hogan, was assessed a two-stroke penalty when he marked, lifted and cleaned his ball after noticing a bug on it. In the preceding years, players had been allowed to lift and clean on the greens at PGA-run events, but at the time the USGA

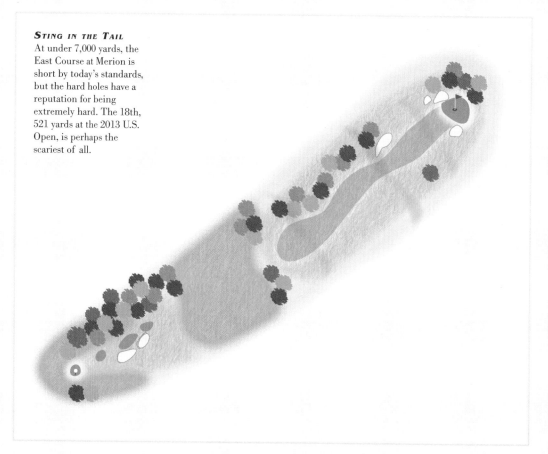

STING IN THE TAIL
At under 7,000 yards, the East Course at Merion is short by today's standards, but the hard holes have a reputation for being extremely hard. The 18th, 521 yards at the 2013 U.S. Open, is perhaps the scariest of all.

said a ball could only be lifted if it interfered with another player's line. Mangrum apparently forgot the rule momentarily and was given the penalty by USGA official Isaac Grainger as he left the green. Mangrum fell to 3 over par, giving Hogan a three-stroke cushion for the final two holes.

Mangrum's reaction was characteristically stoic for a man who understood the triviality of golf. The Texas native had earned four Battle Stars and two Purple Hearts fighting in the 9th Division of General Patton's Third Army during World War II. He landed on Omaha Beach on D-Day, fought in the Battle of the Bulge, and was one of only two people from his platoon to survive the war. The story goes that after Grainger had spoken to him, Mangrum calmly put his putter back in his bag, shrugged his shoulders and said, "Well, at least my kids will eat tomorrow," or words to that effect.

Hogan then made a birdie at the short 17th and the lead was four. He made a 4 at the last for a round of 69 and a four-stroke victory. The fairytale comeback was complete, ensuring Hogan's shot from the day before could now receive the recognition it most assuredly deserved.

Hollywood made a movie depicting Hogan's life and comeback called *Follow the Sun* which premiered in March 1951 and starred the hopelessly miscast Glenn Ford, who was far too soft and smiley to play a man with the cagey reticence and frosty detachment of Hogan.

CAREER SHOT

Ben Hogan wasn't the only person doing something extraordinary at the precise moment he hit the 1-iron to the 18th green. Hy Peskin, a photographer for *Sports Illustrated* and *Life* magazine, was also busy, ensuring the moment would never be lost.

Peskin, the son of a Russian immigrant, was an intense, volatile man, a law unto him himself and described as something of a renegade. He took his first pictures at a low-key boxing match

"It was the purest stroke I've ever seen."

Cary Middlecoff, Hogan's playing partner, on the 1-iron Hogan hit to the 18th green in the final round of the 1950 U.S. Open

shortly after World War II and was so nervous about running out of film he pressed the shutter release button only three times. All three pictures turned out perfectly, however, and he was able to sell them to the editor of *Look* magazine—a general interest biweekly for which a young Stanley Kubrik was a staff photographer.

1934—Olin Dutra—Eight
back after 36 holes, Dutra
overcomes stomach pains to shoot
13-over 293 and beat Gene
Sarazen by a shot.

1971—Lee Trevino—Defeats
Jack Nicklaus in a playoff 68–71
after the pair ties on even-par 280.
1981—David Graham—Hits 17
fairways and 18 greens in an
immaculate final round 67 to
finish on 7-under 273 and
win by three.

2013—Championship returns to
Merion after 32 years. Course 452
yards longer than in 1981 but still
under 7,000 yards. But a typical
U.S. Open set-up with narrow
fairways and heavy rough keep
scores high. England's Justin Rose
wins on 1-over 281, hitting a
superb 4-iron approach from 10
yards behind the Hogan Plaque
(commemorating Hogan's 1-iron in
1950) to set up a winning par. Phil
Mickelson finishes runner-up for the
sixth time at the U.S. Open.

Peskin shot hundreds of covers for sport publications, but he also took a very famous picture of John Kennedy and his then fiancée Jaqueline Bouvier on a sailboat near Cape Cod that appeared on the cover of *Life* magazine in July 1953.

In the final round of the 1950 U.S. Open, Peskin followed Hogan for all 18 holes, mindful that history—significant, momentous, immortal history— was very much in the making. But he didn't take a single photograph until the 18th hole, apparently unconvinced anything he saw was worth shooting. As Hogan prepared to hit his approach to the final green, most of Peskin's colleagues, competitors and contemporaries rushed ahead to photograph Hogan's face post-impact. But Peskin held back, wanting to catch the entire scene.

The picture he took (with what he supposed was a Graflex Speed Graphic camera—standard issue among press photographers at the time) became one of the best-known golf photographs ever taken. Hogan has hit the shot and the ball is on an unerring path to the green. He stands perfectly balanced at the end of what was clearly another well-executed swing—weight on his left foot, right foot on tiptoe, hips fully cleared, a small divot on line with the green, the Stars and Stripes floating in the background, the gallery not yet aware how great a shot they are watching.

BASKET CASE

The 1950 U.S. Open was the only time the wicker baskets that Merion GC attaches to the end of its standards were absent, the USGA insisting flags be used instead. Though numerous weird and wonderful stories have been offered to account for why Merion chose baskets over flags 100 years ago, the club admits their origin "is a mystery to this day." What is known is that the superintendent William Flynn, who would go on to become a fine course architect (see p.114), received patent approval for his basket design in the summer of 1915 and that the club has used them ever since (apart from the 1950 U.S. Open).

The USGA was applauded for agreeing the baskets be used at the 2013 U.S. Open, but one player wishing they hadn't was Lee Westwood, who hit the basket on the 12th green during the opening round. Westwood, tied for the lead at 3 under par, found the rough to the right of the 403-yard par 4 and, after hacking out, was left with a 60-yard uphill pitch shot for his third. Today's top players are pretty accurate with their wedges, so it was no great surprise when the Englishman hit the basket and had to watch helplessly as his ball rebounded 30 yards back down the fairway. His next pitch wasn't much good and he missed his first putt, eventually winding up with a double-bogey 6.

Another striking feature of the course is its distinctive bunkering. Known as the "white faces of Merion," the bunkers here, like those on all good championship venues, are genuine hazards and really best avoided.

"I think Justin Rose hit a better 4-iron than Ben Hogan hit a 1-iron and under the same pressure as well."

Bernard Gallacher, three-time European Ryder Cup team captain

SEEING RED
Merion's wicker baskets are a piece of curious club history that has gladly not been lost to the past—even if the story of their origin is somewhat undecided.

1913

13th Pine Valley

Location: Camden County, New Jersey

Distance: 450 yards, par 4

Original course designer: George Crump

Subsequent alterations: Tom Fazio (member and long-time consulting architect)

Ranking golf courses is always a subjective process—one man's fantasy layout might be another man's dog track. Given that undeniable truth, it could be argued rankings have no value and are really just a waste of time and perfectly good paper or cyberspace. Really, how accurate can you be when separating courses that are often profoundly different from each other? How, for instance, can you evaluate a bleak and windswept links course like Muirfield, near Edinburgh, against an extravagantly beautiful inland layout in suburbia that's surrounded by trees, like Pine Valley Golf Club, near Philadelphia?

APPLES AND ORANGES?

Don't be so cynical. Ranking courses is great fun, and allows for amusing debate among players eager to reason with their fellow golfers why their choices are better, but ultimately aware everyone is right … and wrong. And you can compare Ballybunion—an Irish links course with fantastic views, a barren landscape and springy, sand-based soil, with Augusta National—the suburban parkland course with considerable flora and heavy clay soil—using an established set of criteria that makes an awful lot of sense and by which it is reasonable to judge a golf course.

The first consideration is location, location, location—is the course set in an attractive place, somewhere you're happy to spend a few hours? Given the choice between playing something designed by a master architect in an area with a gray, chilly climate and with views of a smoke-belching industrial estate, and a tame, ordinary design hugging the turquoise waters of the Caribbean, most people would go for the second option. There would be a number of golf course architecture geeks who chose the first, but they are a dogged, unshakable, sensitive bunch of fanatics (guilty) whose logic isn't always to be trusted.

Next, is there sufficient variety among the holes and the shots required to play them to keep your brain alert and your senses keen—is it an engaging challenge? Say you like holes that sweep beautifully to the left, and have a pretty lake to the left of the green and an interesting putting surface. You'll enjoy playing that hole, certainly, but what if it looked and played much the same as the course's 17 other holes?

Early photographs of
Pine Valley show the wild and
rugged nature of the terrain.

Top: George Crump stands on what
will become the 3rd tee.

Middle: Can't you just see a long,
uphill par 3 going in here—the 5th?

Bottom: The rough, sandy scrub in
front of the 2nd green.

You'd soon get bored. Is it
designed so well a beginner
can have as much fun as a
scratch handicapper? Is it in
good condition? Are your
good shots given the reward
they deserve?

In a nutshell, you can
assess the quality of a golf
course by asking yourself
how much fun you had (also
influenced by how well you
played, of course) and how
much you want to go back
and play it again.

Given the sheer number of golf courses spread across the globe
(approximately 35,000), the mix of types—links, parkland, heathland,
moorland, downland, forest, desert, mountain, etc.—the assortment of
design styles—heroic (by taking on and clearing a significant obstacle
or carry, the golfer gains a favorable position), penal (no options: only
one way to play the hole with often a severe punishment for missing it)
and strategic (multiple options, with players taking on the more difficult route and executing a good shot gaining an advantage over players
taking the easy option), plus the judges' fickleness and shifts in taste,
you'd think it highly unlikely one course in particular would frequently
top the lists of the game's most respected publications.

THE UNDISPUTED BEST?

But such a course does exist. Pine Valley, a half-hour drive southeast of Philadelphia, currently sits atop virtually every meaningful ranking and, despite some pretty powerful competition from the likes of Augusta National, Cypress Point, the Old Course at St. Andrews and Royal County Down in Northern Ireland, has done for some time.

Those that don't think it the greatest course in the world point to the fact it has hosted only two major international events—the 1936 and 1985 Walker Cups—and no doubt regard it as too uncompromising for the average golfer. They may have a point. Pine Valley is extremely tough to score well on, as there are no breather holes. No hole is ridiculously difficult and par can be made with sound decision-making and equally good execution, but the cumulative effect of having to concentrate 100 percent on every single shot, lest you run up a quick and unexpected triple-bogey, can wear a player down.

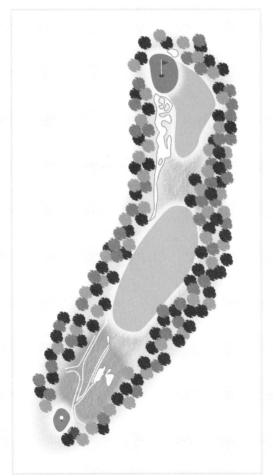

IRRESISTIBLE
Don't you just want to play the shots this fabulous hole demands—especially the low, drawing approach starting right of the long bunker and curling left?

IN THE VALLEY
Pine Valley is located on the other side of Philadelphia and the Delaware River from Merion, just over 20 miles southeast of downtown.

But how can a course with so many superb holes be thought of as anything other than, well, superb? Robert Trent Jones, the most prolific golf course architect in history, once said 10 of its 18 holes were classics and that, of the remaining eight, five were outstanding, two were good, and one, the 12th, was ordinary. Most people fortunate to have played Pine Valley think Trent Jones was actually mistaken—the 12th isn't ordinary at all.

The 13th, meanwhile, was surely among those holes Trent Jones considered the very best. Numerous renowned designers visited and even contributed to some degree or other during the construction of Pine Valley—H.S. Colt, A.W. Tillinghast, George Thomas, Walter Travis, C.B. Macdonald, William Flynn, Hugh Wilson, C.H. Alison, Perry Maxwell—but the 13th is really all George Crump's. A brilliant 450-yard par 4, it heads over a sandy ridge from the tee to a hog's back fairway then moves slightly downhill and to the left. From the fairway you have a choice of taking on the carry over a huge sandy area to the left of the fairway and green or hitting a lower, running-type shot down the right and hoping the ball catches the slope pushing it toward the flag—kind of like a Redan. The 13th satisfies every benchmark of greatness—it is strikingly beautiful, it fits into the landscape perfectly, it provides options for the good golfer and his not-so-capable opponent, it is well groomed. Most of all, once you hole out you want to rush straight back to the tee and try it again.

> **"My God, he's still in there."**
>
> *A Pine Valley member who witnessed a guest having trouble getting out of the bunker left of the 18th green one day, then happened to see the same man in the same bunker the following day*

ONE MAN'S DREAM, AND DOWNFALL?

Without the vision, wealth and determination of Henry Fownes, eight-time U.S. Open venue (nine in 2016) Oakmont Country Club would never have been built (see p.68). Likewise, C.B. Macdonald's considerable zeal was required to make National Golf Links of America on Long Island, New York, a reality—so too Chicago Golf Club. But though Fownes and Macdonald were crucial to the birth of their respective clubs, neither went to quite the same lengths as George A. Crump in creating Pine Valley.

Crump was a hotelier and part of a group of eight or so fine Philadelphia golfers who would abandon their home city on winter weekends and head south and east on the train to Atlantic City, where it was a little warmer and free from snow. They alighted at Pleasantville, the penultimate stop on the line, and headed to Atlantic City Country Club where they would indulge in a game that became known as a Philadelphia Ballsome, a sort of skins game in which they all played together.

Crump was married to Isabelle Henry, daughter of a wealthy businessman. For the first few years of their marriage, the couple lived in the Colonnade Hotel that Crump owned, but in 1906 Crump began work on a large house in Merchantville, 3 miles the other side of the Delaware River from the Liberty Bell. It was their dream home, but sadly Isabelle would never see it, as she died unexpectedly on a trip to New York City in September 1907.

Crump was devastated and, it seems, played significantly less golf over the next couple of years. But as he slowly became more active, he and his friends began discussing the possibility of building a top-quality course in the Philadelphia area to rival the fine venues they played elsewhere in the country, specifically New York, Boston and Chicago.

Crump was the driving force behind the dialogue and invited the group to the Colonnade to firm up plans. They imagined a course near the sea that could be played year-round.

In 1910, the hotel was sold and later that year Crump put some of the proceeds to good use by heading to Europe on a three-month golf junket. He and his friend Joseph Baker played St. Andrews, Prestwick, Turnberry, Hoylake, Sandwich, Deal, Princes, Sunningdale, Walton Heath plus a handful of courses on the Continent in France, Switzerland, Austria and Italy. Crump was particularly impressed with Sunningdale, a Willie Park Jr. design on sandy ground 30 miles west of London that had opened in 1901.

On his return, Crump flung himself into the search for a site, but ultimately gave up on the coast partly, it is believed, because of the mosquitoes and partly because it was just too far from Philadelphia. He began looking nearer to the City, in particular around the Camden area where he had spent much of his childhood.

Although it isn't known when exactly he found it, we do know that in September 1912, Crump wrote to his friends telling them of a marvelous site he had found 14 miles below Camden "at a stop called Sumner on the Reading Railroad to Atlantic City."

"There are ridges and rolls in every direction—big ones and little ones; long ones and short ones; hills and knolls, with every variety of shape and size. You could not fancy any contour of ground more admirably suited for golf purposes."

Crump's associate, Simon Carr, on the landscape that was to become Pine Valley

SANDPIT
A lone golfer makes his
way up the hill to the
fairway at the 6th hole in
April 1946. Just look at all
that glorious sand.

It is puzzling why Crump felt it necessary to be so specific about the stop, when his friends would surely have been familiar with it after so many weekend trips to Atlantic City on that same line. Though it's possible he was writing to acquaintances that weren't part of the regular weekend trips, and because the stop was merely a flag stop serving the estate of Virginia Sumner Ireland, trains would not have stopped there regularly.

Whatever, Crump was excited to show it off to his friends, who all agreed it was a stellar property. One of his closest comrades, a Catholic priest named Simon Carr, said it looked like the "upheaval of the bed of the sea in bygone ages."

There are two theories as to how Crump came across the land. First, he is thought to have been familiar with it already from hunting trips, and second he is likely to have seen it out of the train window on the way back from Atlantic City.

Later A.W. Tillinghast would write, "On several occasions I observed him [Crump] looking intently from the train window as we passed through a section about 20 miles out [of Philadelphia]. As a matter of fact, his attention had been attracted by a freakish bit of country in South Jersey, freakish because it was so totally different from the monotonous flat lands of those parts. At first he said nothing to anyone, but quietly, as was his wont in everything he did, he visited the tract and took option on 180 acres of gently hilled, pine-covered, sandy land—the tract which he had so intently studied from the passing trains."

However he found it, the parcel fitted his needs perfectly, so Crump purchased the 184 acres for approximately $9,000 using his own money and set to work, pitching a tent near to where the clubhouse is now and spending days surveying the land in great detail.

Clearing began in early 1913, with 22,000 trees being uprooted, but Crump stopped counting (the final figure was probably double that). A letter was sent to two hundred or so prospective members outlining the cost of founding membership—each share cost $100 and there was no cap on the number a person could buy. One hundred and forty-one people responded.

The original idea was for each of the 18 holes to be designed by a different person, though this idea was abandoned, thankfully, in 1913 following a visit to the site by H.S. Colt, the great English architect whom Crump may have met during his trip to Europe in 1910 (Colt had been the club secretary at Sunningdale, outside London, at the time) and who also represented the seed company—Carter's—that Crump was considering for Pine Valley. Crump had possibly recognized just how good the site was by now and felt he shouldn't proceed without expert counsel. Two of his friends—Walter Travis and A.W. Tillinghast—would become renowned course designers in their time, Tillinghast especially, but right now they were probably a little too inexperienced.

Like Crump, Colt pitched a tent and spent a week walking the land with the owner discussing possible holes and, eventually, comingup with a routing plan that differed slightly from an existing plan Crump had devised with his friends. There were to be no parallel holes, no more than two successive holes running in the same direction and each hole was to be more or less cut off from the rest.

Crump was thrilled with Colt's very positive impression of the land's potential but, rather than build the user-friendly course Colt envisioned, Crump wanted his course to test the very best with no quarter given the less than competent player.

Eleven holes were seeded in September/October 1913, and the course took on its first greenkeeper—Jim Govan, originally from St. Andrews in Scotland. Crump and Govan would become firm friends, frequently

SPORTS ILLUSTRATED

AUGUST 25, 1958 ★

America's National Sports Weekly

25 CENTS
$7.50 A YEAR

PINE VALLEY
WORLD'S MOST DEMANDING
GOLF COURSE

heading out onto the primitive course to identify the position for Crump's uncompromising hazards.

By January 1914, Crump had completed his bungalow near what became the 5th hole and moved in, walking the course by day and pouring over his plans by lamplight at night. Later that year, 11 holes were opened to members, and Crump discovered what would become the fabulous 13th hole.

Quite how Crump, Colt and everyone else who walked the site had missed this particular ground isn't clear, but as soon as he saw it, Crump felt it was too good to pass up, even if it did mean altering the routing. Plans for the existing 13th, 14th and 15th holes had to change to some degree but, as has become abundantly clear, the changes were worth it.

Everything seemed to be proceeding as planned but, in the autumn of 1915, the turf took on an odd color and all but died. The fescue Crump had planted was not taking as he had hoped and, in an effort to revive the turf and achieve better coverage, he threw manure, fertilizer and seed on it in vast quantities. It came back slowly, but progress suffered another setback when the U.S. joined the World War I in April 1917 and work on the course more or less stopped.

By now, reports were circulating Crump had spent upwards of $200,000 of his own money on the course, which many were calling "Crump's Folly." And there were still four holes—the 12th, 13th, 14th and 15th—to build.

Tragically, Crump would never see them completed. On the morning of January 24, 1918, he shot himself in the head at his house in Merchantville. Who knows if financial issues were to blame, or if society's reaction to his over-spending was somehow responsible? This seems unlikely, though, as Tillinghast wrote years after Crump's death that he had received $172,000 in bonds from the club and that "without a doubt, he intended putting these bonds aside, that they might not hinder the club in the work of maintaining and further developing the great course which he had hewn from the rough." Theories abounded. It was even reported Crump's poor mental state might have been caused by toothache. Or maybe six or seven years of persistent grind working on his dream course and the frustration of dealing with so many setbacks finally took its toll.

Crump was greatly mourned by his friends and associates. Eulogies and tributes appeared in *American Golfer* and the *Philadelphia Record*, Tillinghast writing, "Without shame, I confess that the writing on the paper before me is blurred by tears and there is a choke in the throat. George Crump was not only a golf comrade through many years, but also one the staunchest of friends, a man that I admired and loved."

The club fell silent following Crump's death, the air taken from its sails and no one sure what the appropriate response might be. Eventually, a year or so later, Crump's brother-in-law Howard Street took up the reins, becoming the club secretary and Chairman of the Greens Committee. Alan Wilson, agronomy expert and the brother of Merion designer Hugh Wilson, resolved the turf issues. Grinnell Willis, a local retired textile merchant and Crump's neighbor in Merchantville, donated $20,000 to fund construction of the final four holes, and Hugh Wilson built them. H.S. Colt's design partner, Charles Alison, visited the course at Colt's request, making several recommendations to an advisory committee the club had established.

By 1921, three years after his death and 10 years after the project began, all 18 holes of Crump's masterpiece were finally in play.

BALLER
A.W. Tillinghast was a great friend of George Crump and member of the Philadelphia Ballsome. He chronicled the construction of Pine Valley in his regular *American Golfer* column.

18th The Lido

Don't go looking for the Lido. It's not there anymore; hasn't been for over 70 years. It's a great shame, because every significant figure that played it during the 28 years it existed described the Lido as possibly the greatest course in the world and certainly the equal of America's other great courses—National Golf Links of America, Merion and Pine Valley. The Depression certainly didn't help, but the final nail in the Lido's coffin was driven home by World War II and the U.S. Navy, which took over the entire site in 1942.

AND THE WINNER IS ...

The Lido GC, located on Long Beach Barrier Island, the westernmost of the outer barrier islands off Long Island's south shore, opened in 1914 and was created by C.B. Macdonald and his protégé Seth Raynor, whose exceptional National Golf Links of America had opened 75 miles to the east three years earlier. It cost a fortune to build as 2 million cubic yards of sand were pumped from nearby Reynolds Channel in order to stabilize the barren marshland. Macdonald, as was his style, modeled many of the holes on his favorites in Britain (he had studied at St. Andrews University in Scotland) plus a few at NGLA and Piping Rock, which had opened in 1912.

The course thrived for a decade, but when the Depression hit the membership dwindled dramatically and, according to Peter Lees—the superintendent whom Macdonald had bought over from England for his expertise at growing fine fescue—there were days when "not half a dozen would venture over the course." (A new Lido GC, designed by Robert

YOU CHOOSE
One word that might sum up Alister MacKenzie's design philosophy is "options"—he loved to have players choose their route to the hole according to their ability. The 18th at Lido captured this thinking beautifully.

BEACHING
The Lido was situated on the southern coastline of Long Island, 25 miles southeast of Manhattan.

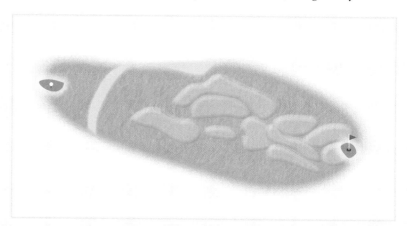

Trent Jones, opened half a mile to the west of the original in 1956. Though Jones recreated a couple of Macdonald's holes, the newer course has nothing of its predecessor's cachet.)

Of all its holes, the 18th was perhaps the most significant, as it was adapted from a plan drawn up by Dr. Alister MacKenzie, a former surgeon, who had entered and won a design competition sponsored by England's *Country Life* magazine (a couple of the 69 other entries were also used). It isn't clear why Macdonald chose a British publication for the competition, but his love of the old country and poor relationship with American titles, specifically the *American Golfer*, probably had a lot to do with it. Two of the judges—Horace Hutchinson and Bernard Darwin—were also good friends of Macdonald's.

Winning did wonders for MacKenzie's design career. Following World War I, during which he was called upon for the knowledge of camouflage he had developed during the Boer War in South Africa (1899–1902), MacKenzie abandoned his medical practice in favor of golf course architecture, basing his philosophy on his stated belief that "the chief object of every golf course architect worth his salt is to imitate the beauties of nature so closely as to make his work indistinguishable from nature itself."

Prior to the war, MacKenzie had already built a solid reputation as a designer, having created the excellent Alwoodley GC in Leeds, England, among others. H.S. Colt, who had been hired as a consultant at Alwoodley, had been immediately impressed with MacKenzie's work. So MacKenzie was no armchair amateur when he entered the Lido competition, but the publicity he earned from winning it gave his reputation a massive boost in America.

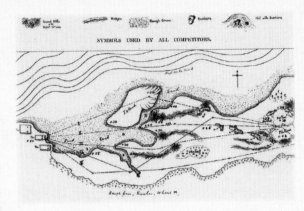

MASTER PLAN
One wonders how long the judges considered the other entries after seeing MacKenzie's brilliant plan for the 18th. One look and you just can't wait to play the hole.

"A first-class hole must have the subtleties and strategic problems which are difficult to understand, and are therefore extremely likely to be condemned at first sight even by the best of players."
Alister MacKenzie in The Spirit of St. Andrews

PRIZE ENTRY

MacKenzie's hole was never actually built as he had envisioned it, as Macdonald didn't have sufficient space. But on paper it showed all the characteristics MacKenzie considered important. It would look entirely natural, despite the course having to be constructed with all that pumped sand. It would be playable for scratch golfers and high handicappers, providing options for both. And it would look a good deal harder and more complicated than it actually was.

1922

4th Baltusrol (Lower)

Location: Springfield Township, New Jersey

Distance: 199 yards, par 3

Original course designer: A.W. Tillinghast

Subsequent alterations: Robert Trent Jones (1953), Rees Jones (1990s, early 2000s)

Baltusrol GC was named after a farmer who owned land between Springfield and Summit, New Jersey, and was brutally murdered on the night of February 22, 1831, by two men who came to his house demanding money. Baltus Roll, son of a Dutch immigrant, was a thrifty man by all accounts and rumored to keep a large sum of cash somewhere in his house. Sixty years after his death, Louis Keller, who now owned the farm but derived little income from it, decided to build a golf course. The publisher of a magazine that listed members of high society and reported gossip, Keller invited his socialite friends to become members of the club he founded in 1895. The original course was designed by Englishman George Hunter and improved by the club's first pro, George Lowe. But it became too cramped for the members so, in 1918, Keller hired A.W. Tillinghast to build him two new courses on 500 acres of additional land he had purchased to the west of the existing property.

PUT THAT IN YOUR PIPE AND SMOKE IT

The Lower Course at Baltusrol GC, 20 miles west of Manhattan, has been ranked among America's top 100 courses since golf course rankings began. It is set in beautiful parkland and is a classic Tillinghast design with tightly guarded greens, diagonal hazards, big, deep bunkers and an absence of parallel fairways thanks to a typically clever routing. It has been the site of seven U.S. Open championships, the last in 1993 won by Lee Janzen. Jack Nicklaus won here in 1967 and 1980. It has also hosted four U.S. Amateur championships, a U.S. Women's Open and, in 2005, the 87th PGA Championship which Phil Mickelson won with a birdie 4 at the last after tapping the Nicklaus Plaque (which commemorates Nicklaus' superb 1-iron to the 18th green from 237 yards in 1967) for good luck.

"I shall always count Baltusrol among my favorite courses—it is certainly one of the finest in the world."

Jack Nicklaus who won the 1967 and 1980 U.S. Opens at Baltusrol

The course for the 1954 U.S. Open—won by a journeyman pro named Ed Furgol whose crooked left arm, caused by a gymnastics injury at the age of 12, was responsible for his very awkward-looking swing—had been fortified by Robert Trent Jones after the club feared it was becoming too accommodating for the game's top players. Indeed, Tillinghast had warned it wouldn't take long for the rapidly improving professional golfer using rapidly evolving equipment to overwhelm both the Upper and Lower Courses.

Jones, together with Francis Ouimet who served as a consultant, made several alterations to the Lower Course while attempting to keep the character of Tillinghast's design intact. Four hundred yards were added to the total length, new fairway bunkers were built, and greenside bunkers enlarged. The biggest change, though, came at the short 4th, where Jones pushed back the championship tee 70 yards (to 186 yards), put a terrace in the green, reshaped the bunkers behind it, and replaced the logs and compacted soil that shored up the pond between tee and green with a stone wall.

The members didn't care for Jones' changes, however, complaining bitterly the hole was now too difficult. But Jones was so sure his changes were appropriate, he apparently offered to bear the expense himself. And he invited the most audible of the members, along with club professional Johnny Farrell, the 1928 U.S. Open champion, and C.P. Burgess, chairman of the 1954 U.S. Open Championship, to test the hole with him.

After his three "partners" had all found the green, Jones reportedly took out his "mashie" (though steel-shafted clubs had been in use for about 20 years by now, so it's more likely he actually elected a 4-iron or 5-iron). Jones, now 46, hit a beautiful, high shot that pitched 6 feet short of the hole, took one hop and fell into the cup for an ace.

STATELY
The Lower Course's beautiful par 3 4th hole (in the foreground) has challenged the best players in the world.

With considerable satisfaction, Jones turned to the onlookers and said, "Gentlemen, I think the hole is eminently fair."

Well, that's one version. The punch line inevitably changed a few times over the years. Whatever he did say though, Jones certainly made his point. No mention was ever made of how the chief critic responded, but one can picture him looking on in utter disbelief, squirming a little, and eventually conceding that, OK, the hole was fine.

Jones proved it perfectly playable that day, but during the 1954 U.S. Open, the 4th was among the toughest holes on the course, the field recording as many bogeys (or worse) as pars.

Three years previously, Jones had done much the same at Rockrimmon GC in Stamford, Connecticut. There, members of the Greens Committee believed a 170-yard par 3 looked a lot longer than the stated yardage, and would require a full wood shot. Jones, playing the course with a committee man, sent his associate Frank Duane back to his car to fetch a 4-iron and a couple of balls. He needed only one, hitting his first shot to 3 feet.

OPEN DOCTOR

In 1947, Donald Ross was asked to return to Oakland Hills CC in Bloomfield Township, Michigan, 20 miles north of Detroit, to make revisions ahead of the 1951 U.S. Open. Ross passed away in 1948, however, meaning the club had to find another architect to implement his suggestions. Robert Trent Jones had been hired to co-design Peachtree GC in Atlanta with the great Bobby Jones (RTJ told Bobby there could be only one Bobby Jones in Atlanta, so insisted he would go by Trent Jones) and was fast becoming the architect *du jour*, so Oakland Hills was confident it had the right man.

Jones went a good deal further than Ross had intended to, however, removing 80 bunkers and adding 60 of his own. He narrowed the fairways and advised the club to grow the rough long and thick.

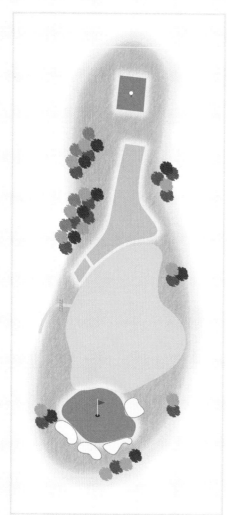

Ben Hogan's winning score of 7 over par was a fair reflection of just how tough it had become. After shooting an impeccable final-round 67, Hogan said he was "glad to have bought this course, this monster, to its knees." The South Course has been called the Monster ever since.

Despite the course's difficulty, Jones' work received many compliments and Joe Dey, Executive Director of the USGA, began recommending him to other clubs scheduled to host the U.S. Open. He altered the Olympic Club in San Francisco for the 1955 U.S. Open, Oak Hill CC in Rochester, New York for the 1956 championship, and Southern Hills in Tulsa, Oklahoma ahead of the 1958 event. He was next called upon by Oakland Hills for the 1961 U.S. Open and, three years later, the changes he had made to the Devereaux Emmet-designed Blue Course at Congressional CC outside of Washington DC, were in play. The 1965 tournament was played on a course of his own design at Bellerive CC, and he was brought back to Baltusrol in time for the 1967 U.S. Open, then Oak Hill for the following year. In 1970, the U.S. Open was held at his own Hazeltine CC, which received some fairly unkind feedback, prompting some drastic alterations.

That was the last U.S. Open venue remodeled by Trent Jones, who also worked on venues for the PGA Championship, U.S. Women's Open and U.S. Amateur Championship.

He was known as the Open Doctor but, as Ron Whitten, *Golf Digest* magazine's architecture editor, points out, he was really a Major Doctor. In the 1990s and early 2000s Trent Jones' second son, Rees, took on the title, updating the venue for seven U.S. Opens, six PGA Championships, four Ryder Cups, two Walker Cups and a Presidents Cup.

"The sun never sets on a Robert Trent Jones golf course."

Jones was fond of saying this and, with over 500 course projects in 35 countries, he probably wasn't wrong

THE DOCTOR IS IN
Robert Trent Jones "doctored" Oak Hill CC ahead of both the 1956 and 1968 U.S. Open Championships. Shown here with a model of the par 5 13th hole.

1st Cherry Hills

Location: Denver,
Colorado

Distance: 389 yards, par 4

Original course designer:
William Flynn

Subsequent alterations:
Press Maxwell (1958), Arnold
Palmer, Ed Seay (1974)

It must have been a big deal for a Philadelphia man to make the journey across the United States in the early 1920s. But Philadelphia and the East Coast were where the majority of the country's best golf course architects were based, so that's where the wealthy businessmen that founded Cherry Hills Country Club had to look to find their man. William Flynn was well established in his home city and well known for his course construction and agronomic expertise, and, says biographer Wayne Morrison, would have relished the opportunity to design and build a course on the other side of the U.S.

THE USGA REACHES THE ROCKIES AT LAST

It became a little more adventurous in the second half of the 20th century, thanks to better transport and communication links, but for a long time the USGA seemed somewhat reluctant to take the U.S. Open away from the Mid-Atlantic and the Northeast, where the organization is based and where a good percentage of the country's population lives.

Because of its size and, no doubt, the influence of the rather immodest C. B. Macdonald, Chicago did host the event a few times in the tournament's early years, but the furthest west the U.S. Open went in its first 21 editions was Minnesota—Minneapolis' Minikahda Club in 1916. Suburban Minneapolis hosted the event again in 1930, when the

CHERRY PICKED
Had Arnold Palmer not
triggered his amazing
comeback at the 1960 U.S.
Open by driving the green
at the 1st, it's highly
unlikely anyone but the
club's members would
know anything about this
straightforward par 4.

Interlachen Club was the scene of Bobby Jones' fourth and final U.S. Open victory and the third "major" of his Grand Slam year (see p.86), but the tournament didn't go beyond the Rocky Mountains and reach California until 1948. Actually, there were zero U.S. Opens in the western half of the U.S. (assuming Minnesota sits on the east side of the divide) before 1938—the year the USGA went out on a limb and took its premier event to Colorado and the Cherry Hills Country Club.

Cherry Hills had been founded by a group of wealthy businessmen 16 years before in a beautiful area of parkland 10 miles south of downtown Denver. The course was designed by William Flynn who, like the USGA, hadn't ventured very far outside his native Northeast and the Mid-Atlantic.

NATURE FAKER
Unlike Robert Trent Jones, C.B. Macdonald, A.W. Tillinghast and other architects who weren't scared to tout their work, Flynn never enjoyed the limelight.

Flynn had hoped to set up a design company with Hugh Wilson, the architect at Merion (see p.82), but Wilson did not enjoy the best of health so, instead, Flynn teamed with Howard Toomey, a civil engineer specializing in railroad construction. Flynn owned the design company and prepared all the routings, while he partnered with Toomey in the construction company—Toomey & Flynn.

World War I obviously impacted golf course construction, and though Flynn had worked at Merion on the construction crew and then as superintendent for many years, his design career had yet to take off.

Wayne Morrison, co-author of the absurdly thorough 2,280-page Flynn biography, *The Nature Faker*, suspects Flynn was chosen for the job because he was well known for his turfgrass expertise. Morrison adds Dr. C.V. Piper and Dr. R.A. Oakley, two U.S. Department of Agriculture scientists, who were instrumental in the development of the USGA Green Section (an authority on turfgrass management for golf), believed Flynn was the foremost golf architect of the day for his all-round knowledge on course development and maintenance.

Flynn is thought to have spent a month in Colorado, not only designing Cherry Hills CC but also working on a revision of Denver CC, originally designed by James Foulis. At Cherry Hills, Flynn produced a typically thoughtful, if complex, routing full of strategy and interest, the inspiration for many of the holes coming from Pine Valley where he had been involved during the course's design phase.

The 1st, like so many of Flynn's other opening holes (Shinnecock Hills, Manufacturers CC, Indian Creek CC, Huntingdon Valley CC, Philadelphia CC, Cascades Course at the Homestead, etc.) is a fairly gentle par 4 of less than 400 yards. In the grand scheme of things, it would go largely unnoticed. But, when perhaps the most famous golfer of all time (pre-Tiger Woods) does something newsworthy there it suddenly becomes altogether more interesting.

DRIVE FOR SHOW

Thirty-year-old Arnold Palmer arrived at Cherry Hills CC for the 1960 U.S. Open with a fairly mixed record in the event. Yes, he tied for fifth the year before at Winged Foot GC and finished seventh at Oak Hill CC in 1956, but he also missed three cuts between 1953 and 1957.

Palmer did survive to the weekend in Denver, but mediocre rounds of 72 and 71 put him eight strokes behind halfway leader, Mike Souchak. A third-round 72 bought him one stroke closer to Souchak, but he was still back in 15th place with the likes of Ben Hogan, Sam Snead, Julius Boros, 1955 champion Jack Fleck, the reigning British Open winner Gary

ROCKY MOUNTAIN WAY
Cherry Hills Country Club is situated in suburban Denver, 8 miles south of downtown.

EASY DOES IT
There isn't a great deal here to worry the good golfer. Even the bunker to the left of the fairway has no lip to speak of.

Player, and a 20-year-old amateur by the name of Jack Nicklaus ahead of him. No one gave him a chance.

As he threw down a quick hamburger between going out again, however, Palmer began thinking what he might need to win. He sat talking with his friend Bob Drum of the *Pittsburgh Press*, and *Sports Illustrated* writer Dan Jenkins.

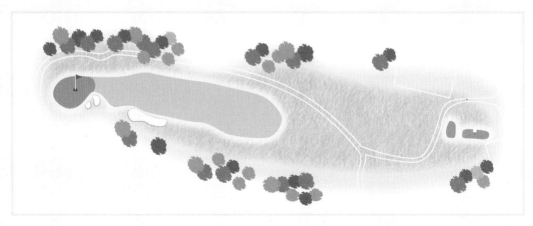

"If I drive the first green and make a birdie, I could shoot a hell of a score," Palmer said. "I might even shoot sixty-five. What would that do for me?"

"Nothing," said Drum. "You're too far back."

"Well, it would give me two-eighty. Doesn't two-eighty always win the U.S. Open?"

Palmer was pumped. After finding the creek to the right of the fairway at the 1st hole in round one and failing to make an impression on the green in the two subsequent rounds, he was determined to make it to the putting surface and, after unleashing a ferocious tee shot, his ball pitched on the front fringe and bounded onto the green. Palmer's ball had traveled roughly 340 yards—a pretty good punt with a 190-cc persimmon-headed driver and soft balata ball.

The crowd went crazy. Palmer, pretty excited himself, knocked his eagle putt well by the hole but managed to make the return for birdie. He then chipped in for a birdie at the 2nd and made a birdie on the 3rd and 4th too. He made par on the 5th then made a birdie on the 6th and 7th. After a bogey at the 8th and par at the 9th, Palmer reached the turn in 30.

Hogan, who had the lead at the 71st hole, found the stream that fronts the green at the 17th, then made a triple-bogey at the last to finish on 284. Nicklaus eagled the 9th to hold the lead briefly, but three-putted the 13th and 14th, missed a short birdie putt at the 16th then made a bogey at the 18th to finish on 2-under 284.

Palmer made pars on both the 17th and 18th, shot 35 on the back for a round of 65 and finished with a four-round total of 4-under 280. And, just like he said, it was good enough to win.

Palmer would record eight top-fives over the next 15 years, a run that included four runner-up finishes and three playoff losses. But 1960 would prove to be the only U.S. Open victory Arnie's Army (which first followed its hero at the 1958 Masters, when soldiers from Camp Gordon were granted free admission to the tournament and began cheering on the former member of the U.S. Coast Guard) would celebrate.

The final-round 65 was perhaps the best known of Palmer's famous charges—a charge no doubt triggered by that mammoth drive at the opening hole.

RECREATING PALMER

◆

At the 2014 BMW Championship, the third of four FedEx Cup playoffs, five PGA Tour players attempted to match Palmer's feat at the 1st hole. Using a replica persimmon driver and balata ball, Rory McIlroy, Zach Johnson, Camilo Villegas, Hunter Mahan and Keegan Bradley attempted to reach the green from the 346-yard tee ... but failed. The closest anyone got was McIlroy, whose best drive went 300 yards.

"The shaft felt whippy, the head felt heavy, and the ball felt like a marshmallow. Palmer's shot was beyond impressive."

Zach Johnson after failing to match Arnold Palmer's 1960 drive on the 1st using the same equipment

1922

18th Royal Birkdale

Location: Southport, Lancashire, England

Distance: 473 yards, par 4

Original course designer: George Lowe (1894)

Subsequent alterations: Fred G. Hawtree & J.H. Taylor (1922), Fred W. Hawtree (1960s), Martin Hawtree (1991)

At the 1971 British Open, four of Royal Birkdale's final six holes played as par 5s—the 13th, 15th, 17th and 18th. The 18th measured 513 yards and played downwind during the final round, making it very reachable in two shots. Indeed, Lee Trevino, who won the tournament on 14-under 278, needed only a 6-iron for his approach. Writer Dan Jenkins thought the venue undistinguished, and labeled the closing hole a "phony par 5." It was still a par 5 for the 1976 British Open, but by the time 1983 rolled around—Royal Birkdale's sixth British Open—it had been converted to a 473-yard par 4, providing a much more challenging finish. Tom Watson won his fifth Claret Jug after striping a drive down the middle, then hitting what he later described as one of the best 2-irons of his life to about 15 feet from the hole. Two putts for a par gave him victory by one stroke over Andy Bean and Hale Irwin, who had completely whiffed a putt at the 14th hole the day before. The 18th has remained a long and demanding par 4 ever since, playing to 473 yards during the course's most recent British Open in 2008.

THE REAL DEAL

Birkdale Golf Club was established in July 1889 by nine plucky enthusiasts who met at the home of one of the founding members to draw up the by-laws and agree on what needed to be done prior to opening day. They decided their nine-hole course in nearby Shaw Hills, for which they paid £5 (about $8) a year to the landowner—a Mr. Weld Blundell—would be ready for October 5, when the treasurer was to supply "whiskey and aerated waters" for the inauguration ceremony.

The Shaw Hills site lasted all of five years, the club deciding to move to the mighty sandhills in Birkdale in 1894 to build its first 18-hole course. George Lowe, an apprentice of Old Tom Morris, who became a respected club-maker, club professional and course architect, was hired to design it. Apparently, it took a while for the members to accept the move was necessary, however. They wondered if golf might actually be a passing fad and speculated that if the River Mersey silted up in Liverpool, 20 miles to the south, ocean-going cruise ships would need to dock in nearby Ainsdale instead, causing land to rise sharply in value.

Even so, the club paid £100 ($150) a year for their new ground and built a clubhouse in 1897. It had to be knocked down in 1903, however, as it was discovered the building had been constructed outside the

OUTSTANDING
Royal Birkdale's white-
washed, art deco clubhouse
opened in 1935 and was a
bold replacement for the
club's original building. It
is an inspiring sight as you
approach the 18th green.

perimeter of the property the club was leasing. A new clubhouse was built near what is now the 4th green.

In 1922, the club attempted to purchase the land on which their course was laid out, but could not afford the £19,000 ($28,500) asking price. Instead, the local authority, Southport Corporation, bought it and not only gave the club a 99-year lease but also encouraged it to develop the links to championship standard. A seven-year plan was instigated and included the construction of a new clubhouse—the eye-catching art deco building that stands behind the 18th green. Fred G. Hawtree, who worked closely with five-time British Open champion J.H. Taylor, was commissioned to make the necessary upgrades to the course.

To avoid blind shots and uneven stances, the duo decided to direct holes through the dunes rather than over the top of them. They leveled playing areas to ensure Birkdale did not penalize players with the unfortunate bounces so common in Scotland.

Fred G.'s son, Fred W., added several hundred yards to the length of the course in the 1960s and also created the short 12th, a wonderful par 3 cut into the dunes on the course's western boundary. Fred W.'s son, Martin, then rebuilt all 18 greens following the 1991 British Open.

In all, Royal Birkdale, which was awarded its "Royal" prefix by King George VI in 1951, has now hosted 25 major international tournaments: nine British Opens, three British Amateur Championships, five Ladies'/Women's British Opens, two Ryder Cups, a Walker Cup, a Curtis Cup, a Senior British Open, a British PGA Championship, a British PGA Matchplay Championship and a Ladies' British Amateur Championship.

It may not be considered the most fun or charming of Britain's historic links courses, but unlike so many others which describe themselves

DYNAMIC DUO
Fred G. Hawtree (left) and
five-time Open champion
J.H. Taylor (right) made
huge changes to Birkdale's
original course, routing
the new holes on flattish
land between the dunes.

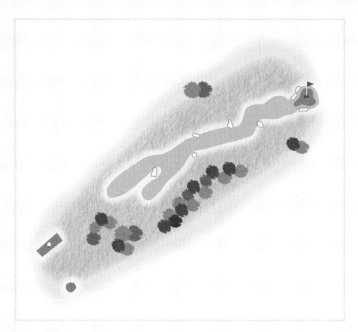

Staggered
The first fairway bunker, in the middle at 228 yards, isn't in play for the pros. Bunkers further up the hole certainly are, though, if they miss the fairway with their drive.

Golf Coast
Southport, located on what marketers like to call "England's Golf Coast," is a 20-mile drive north of Liverpool and home to a number of historic courses.

as "championship" courses, but which probably haven't staged anything more significant than their own club championship, Royal Birkdale is indubitably the genuine article.

Good Sport

The Ryder Cup today is not only extremely competitive, it seems also to be played in the spirit that founder Samuel Ryder always envisaged for the tournament. The teams are extremely eager to beat each other, obviously, and occasionally celebrations do become a little overzealous, but at recent matches, a mutual respect, good etiquette and a welcome degree of sportsmanship have become apparent. This spirit transforms the competition from a tense, occasionally controversial encounter and a win-at-all-costs confrontation into an exhibition of what is right with the game—witness Phil Mickelson's generous acknowledgement of Justin Rose's brilliant putt on the 17th green in their singles match at Medinah in 2012.

It certainly wasn't always like this, however. The matches started out in the right fashion in the late 1920s when a British/Irish side met the Americans (players from the Continent would not be involved until 1979), but it wasn't long before a little antipathy started to appear. Throughout the Ryder Cup's history, numerous have been the petty scuffles between scrappy, even antagonistic, players who knew each other very little and respected each other even less.

It was little more than a decade ago that the U.S. team soured its incredible come-from-behind victory at the Country Club near Boston with its frenzied reaction to Justin Leonard's 45-foot birdie putt on the 17th green that took the U.S. a step closer to an improbable win (see p.63). Eight years before that, the contest at Kiawah Island in South Carolina had been dubbed the "War by the Shore."

The 1990s was right up there, but it was the 1960s that seemed to be the decade when ill will between the teams was at its peak. The Americans had dominated the event for 20 years and many felt they only had to show up to win. They were considerably more affluent than their opponents, who still had no organized professional tour, and they didn't exactly relish coming to Britain with its poor weather, dubious hotels and questionable cuisine (the 1949 team, captained by Ben Hogan, had even taken 600 steaks, 12 sides of ribs, 12 hams and 12 boxes of bacon to Britain to give their meals a boost). Unlike today, when all the players know each other pretty well because they play together so regularly on the PGA Tour, it was really only Tony Jacklin and maybe one or two others on the British team that were familiar with the American superstars. The British team was, by and large, jealous and sceptical of the Americans.

In 1969, friction was in the air as early as the first morning at Birkdale. British captain Eric Brown instructed his players not to look for the American's golf balls in the rough and in the morning foursomes, Scotsman Bernard Gallacher and Englishman Maurice Bembridge jousted with Lee Trevino and Ken Still, the wrangling coming to a head on the 13th tee when, after being asked to move out of Bembridge's peripheral vision, Still melodramatically moved all the players, caddies and officials. At the next hole, Still hit from a bunker, but the ball rebounded off the lip and struck his shoulder. His partner, Trevino, told him to pick it up as the hole had been lost, but Still stood his ground and didn't answer.

The following day, Gallacher and Welshman Brian Huggett met Still and Dave Hill—four of the most irascible players in the game—in a fourball match that very nearly descended into a fist fight. On the first hole, Huggett had to ask Hill to stop moving while he putted and Still was also asked to move. On the 2nd green, Gallacher was about to putt when Still shouted to his caddie not to tend the flag as Gallacher's caddie was supposed to do it. At the 7th, Still putted up close to the hole then walked up to his ball and holed out, thus playing out of turn. While the British pair discussed the incident with officials, Still picked up Gallacher's coin and stormed off the green shouting, "You can have the hole and the cup." The argument continued as the players walked up the 8th fairway and, had Brown and Sam Snead, the U.S. captain, not appeared along with

MAGIC MOMENTS ON THE 18TH

◆

The 18th at Royal Birkdale also saw the unforgettable moment when a 17-year-old Justin Rose holed a 50-yard pitch to tie for fourth at the 1998 British Open. Arnold Palmer also won the first of his two British Opens on the final green at Royal Birkdale, Australian Peter Thomson won two of his five Claret Jugs here, and a brilliant young Englishwoman by the name of Laura Davies won the first of her four major championships here in 1986, aged 23.

Californian professional Melissa "Mo" Martin won the 2014 Ricoh Women's British Open after making an eagle 3 at the 18th, when her 3-wood second shot, pitched 40 yards short of the green, bounded into the putting surface, clattered into the pin and finished 6 feet away. "An absolutely perfect 3-wood. When it was in the air, I said, 'Sit.' And then I said, 'Stop.' And then when it was going toward the hole, I said, 'OK, I don't have anything more to say to that ball.' I actually heard it hit the pin. It's definitely one to remember."

THE CONCESSION
Jack Nicklaus's concession to Tony Jacklin on the 18th green at the 1969 Ryder Cup has to be one of the sport's most magnanimous gestures.

Lord Derby, the President of the British PGA, chances are the exchange would have descended into fisticuffs by the time they'd finished the hole.

The match itself was developing into a real nail-biter. The British had established a 3½–½ lead after the first morning's play, but the Americans had squared the match at 8–8 by the end of the second day. On the final morning, GB & Ireland won the last four singles matches with Jacklin, who had won the British Open at Royal Lytham & St. Annes just two months before, defeating Jack Nicklaus 4&3 to take the home team into a 13–11 lead. In the afternoon, the match remained incredibly tight. Huggett holed a 4-footer on the 18th green in the penultimate singles to halve with Billy Casper, meaning the outcome would be decided by the final match in which Nicklaus had an opportunity to exact his revenge on Jacklin.

Nicklaus, 29 and making his Ryder Cup debut because PGA of America policy stipulated players had to have five years' Tour experience before they could play in the event, was 1-up after 16, but Jacklin holed a 50-foot putt for a 3 on the 17th to square the match going to the last. On the 18th green, Jacklin lagged his first putt to a couple of feet, while Nicklaus ran his first attempt 5 feet by. After bravely holing the return, Nicklaus picked up Jacklin's marker and told him he didn't think he would have missed the putt, but didn't want to give him the chance.

A number of Nicklaus' teammates were unhappy with his decision to give Jacklin his putt, and captain Snead made little secret of how displeased he was. But without Nicklaus' supreme act of sportsmanship and what became known simply as "The Concession," the 1969 Ryder Cup would have been remembered for all the wrong reasons.

BIRTH OF A GENIUS

Spain's Seve Ballesteros played his first British Open at Carnoustie in Scotland in 1975. He was 18 years old and missed the cut by 11 shots. It was an ignominious start, but he qualified for the following year's championship by winning the 1975 Continental Order of Merit.

Royal Birkdale was dry and firm and Seve adapted well, shooting a first-round 69 to tie for the lead. He wasn't expected to hang around the top of the leaderboard for long, but a second 69 gave him a two-shot lead over the United States' Johnny Miller through 36 holes.

Both players shot third-round 73s, and after Miller began the fourth round with a bogey, Ballesteros was three clear.

The wheels came off dramatically thereafter, however. A double-bogey here and a triple-bogey there saw Seve plummet down the leaderboard. On the 17th tee, Miller spoke to him in Spanish, saying he needed to finish strong in order to catch Jack Nicklaus, who had already finished on 3-under 285.

So Ballesteros eagled the 17th. At the par 5 18th, he was just short in two, but would be hard-pressed to make a birdie as two bunkers sat between his ball and the flag. He had two choices—hit an easy pitch over the bunkers and beyond the flag leaving himself a 15- to 20-foot putt, or a devilishly difficult chip shot between the bunkers and risk running into the sand.

We may not have known it at the time, but for a player with Seve's skill, imagination and determination, the decision was simple.

With a delicate flick of the wrists he threaded the ball deftly between the bunkers, leaving himself about 4 feet for a birdie. He holed the putt, tied Nicklaus for second 6 behind Miller, who shot a brilliant 66, and a star was born.

"That shot alone convinced me Seve was a genius."

John Jacobs, acclaimed instructor and two-time European Ryder Cup team Captain

WHIPPERSNAPPER
The 19-year-old Seve Ballesteros couldn't hold off Johnny Miller at Royal Birkdale in 1976, but he certainly did enough to entertain a crowd that would love him until his untimely death 35 years later.

11th Thornhill

Location: Vaughan, Ontario, Canada

Distance: 378 yards, par 4

Original course designer: Stanley Thompson

The 1945 Canadian Open was played at the Stanley Thompson-designed Thornhill CC in suburban Toronto. Though World War II was still in progress and a number of the top North American players were away on duty, the field for the tournament was still quite healthy. Sam Snead was there, as were Harold "Jug" McSpadden, Claude Harmon, Canada's own Stan Leonard, and a man riding rather a hot streak—Byron Nelson.

ALL THE WAY UP TO 11

Nelson, unable to go to war because of a blood disorder, had won an incredible 10 consecutive tournaments, including the previous week's Tam O'Shanter event in Chicago with a score of 19 under par. At Thornhill, he began with rounds of shot 68, 72 and 72 to be near the top of the leaderboard, but he suffered a major scare at the start of final 18 holes. After making par at the 1st, Nelson topped his tee shot at the 2nd into a stream. He dropped then hit his third into the same stream further up the hole. Because it had been so hot in recent weeks, however, the riverbed was mostly dry and Nelson was able to hit his fourth shot safely on to the green, about 10 feet from the hole. He made the putt, and what had seemed like a potential triple-bogey became a bogey 5.

At the short par 4 10th (now the course's 11th hole) which bends sharply from left to right, Nelson found trouble again when attempting to drive the green. He had made three bogeys on the hole to that point, but managed to halt the run of 5s ... by making a 6. As a result, the club renamed the hole Nelson's Folly.

NICE HOLE, EH?
The trees to the right of the fairway are no doubt significantly taller now than they were in 1945, but Byron Nelson's decision to take on the green from the tee was perhaps a little foolhardy.

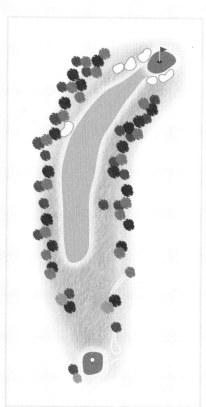

BORDERLINE
Thornhill G&CC is found in the suburb of Thornhill, 21 miles north of downtown Toronto, and 20 miles northeast of Stanley Thompson's finest design, St. George's G&CC.

At some point during the final round, Nelson was also forced to borrow a ball from playing partner Tony Penna. That certainly wouldn't be allowed under today's rules but, largely because of the war, golf balls were not as readily available then as they are now.

After what had been an eventful start to the final round, Nelson managed to steady the ship over the final few holes and eventually ran out a four-shot winner. He had now won 11 tournaments in a row.

Such a run would be inconceivable today, given the number of quality players at every PGA Tour event. Nelson tried for a straight dozen in Memphis two weeks later, but finished fourth.

No matter—over the remainder of 1945, Nelson won another seven times, making 18 official victories in all. In his 12 other tournaments that year, he finished second seven times, and had a third, two fourths, a sixth and a ninth. He won a grand total of $51,500 (about the same as one 20th place finish on the PGA Tour nowadays), and finished the year with a scoring average of 68.34.

SENSATIONAL SEASON

Nelson's 18 wins in 1945 was an incredible achievement, but there are other contenders for golf's greatest season. In 2000, Tiger Woods won the U.S. Open by 15 shots, the British Open by eight, and beat Bob May in a playoff at the PGA Championship. He finished the year with nine PGA Tour victories and a scoring average of 68.17. In 1953, just four years after a car crash nearly killed him (see p.91), Ben Hogan won the Masters, U.S. Open, British Open and twice more in America. Many, though, give the nod to Bobby Jones and his historic 1930 Grand Slam (see p.86).

EVERY ROSE
Byron Nelson had terrible trouble at Thornhill's 11th hole (then the 10th) during the 1945 Canadian Open, playing it in 5 over par for the week.

1924

16th The Olympic Club (Lake)

Location: San Francisco, California

Distance: 670 yards, par 5

Original course designer: Willie Watson, Sam Whiting

Subsequent alterations: Sam Whiting, Robert Trent Jones (1953), Tom Weiskopf (1996), Bill Love (2006, 2011)

The Olympic Club was founded in 1860, making it America's oldest athletic club. Its 5,000 members participate in 19 sports including rugby, soccer and golf. The main clubhouse is located in downtown San Francisco, while the lakeside clubhouse, 10 miles southwest on the southern edge of Lake Merced, is home to the club's three golf courses—Cliffs, Ocean and (the layout for which the club is best known) Lake, which was designed by Scotsman Willie Watson and the club's superintendent Sam Whiting. It opened in 1924 and hosted its first U.S. Open in 1955 and has since staged four more U.S. Opens and three U.S. Amateur Championships. It has been the scene of many memorable and significant moments, never more so than during the 1966 U.S. Open.

PALMER'S REVERSE CHARGE

He wasn't exactly declining fast, but by 1966 Arnold Palmer's best golf was probably behind him. After losing the momentous playoff to Jack Nicklaus at the 1962 U.S. Open (see p.71), the Pennsylvanian had rebounded fast, winning the British Open a few weeks later then the Masters in 1964. He also tied for second at the 1963 U.S. Open in Boston. The Tour victories, though, weren't piling up as they once had.

He looked good in the first half of 1966, however, managing a tie for fourth at the Masters and winning his 46th and 47th Tour events. At the Olympic Club in June, he was seeking his second U.S. Open title (his first

THE BIGGER THEY ARE
Arnie's Army suffered much anguish at the massive par 5 16th (604 yards in 1966, 670 yards for the 2012 U.S. Open) during the 1966 U.S. Open, as it watched its hero Arnold Palmer surrender to Billy Casper.

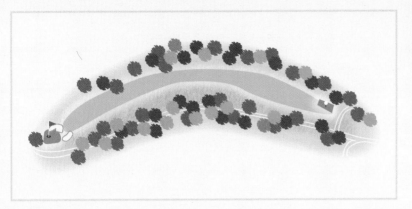

had come in Denver six years previously—see p.116) and, after 63 holes, all bets were off as he had opened up a seven-stroke gap over his nearest pursuer, Billy Casper.

Casper hadn't compiled Palmer's record but, with 29 Tour victories including the 1959 U.S. Open at Winged Foot, he was certainly no slouch.

Surely, though, he had no chance of catching Palmer who, he admitted later, was conscious of Ben Hogan's U.S. Open record of 276, which he had shot at Riviera in 1948.

All Palmer needed was an inward 1-over 36 to shoot 275. He made a bogey on the 10th, but no biggie. He was still six clear, and he remained six in front after a par at the 11th and birdie at the 12th. A bogey at the 13th didn't set off any alarm bells either. Pars for both players at the 14th took Palmer one step closer to a glorious victory.

The first beads of sweat began running down Palmer's forehead at the 15th, where he made a bogey and Casper made a birdie. The gap was suddenly just three. At the par 5 16th, another two-shot swing occured as Casper made a birdie and Palmer a bogey after hitting a wild snap-hook off the tee.

At the 17th, Palmer made another bogey and the lead had vanished altogether. Pars at the 18th saw both players finish on 2-under 278.

After 11 holes of the following day's 18-hole playoff, Palmer was 2 under par and two clear. But then a Casper birdie and Palmer bogey at the 12th leveled the scores. By the 16th tee, Casper was three ahead and then Palmer self-imploded when he made a double-bogey at the par 5, 604 yards long at the time.

Casper would finish with a 69, Palmer a 73.

On the back nine in the final two rounds, Casper had outscored Palmer 66 to 79. Palmer, famous for his charges, had performed the ultimate anti-Palmer.

3rd Philadelphia

Location: Gladwyne, Pennsylvania

Distance: 585 yards, par 5

Original course designer: William Flynn

Subsequent alterations: William Gordon (1956), Ron Forse (1991)

I t may be the 3rd on the Philadelphia Country Club's Spring Mill Course now, but prior to 1957 when the clubhouse was relocated and the course rerouted, this rather docile par 5 was the closing hole. Located 15 miles northwest of downtown Philly in a wonderful stretch of golfing country that's home to numerous other classic layouts—Merion's East and West courses, Philadelphia Cricket Club's 45 holes, Philmont CC, Huntingdon Valley CC, Manufacturers CC, Aronimink GC, Gulph Mills GC, Sunnybrook GC and Green Valley CC—the Spring Mill Course first opened in 1927 and was designed by William Flynn, who worked on the construction crew at Merion and was the club's first superintendent, and who created much of the great golf in and around the City of Brotherly Love.

IN LIKE FLYNN

The Philadelphia Country Club was formed in the town of Bala, Pennsylvania in 1890, primarily so members could ride horses and play polo—hence the club's horse-head logo. Golf was soon added to the menu however and by the middle of the 1920s the club's nine-hole course had become too small and too busy. Land suitable for 18 holes was found 6 miles to the north in Gladwyne, and William Flynn was hired to build a course worthy of hosting the national championship.

Flynn's 558-yard 18th was a three-shot hole with 10 bunkers—four beside the fairway, two more 100 yards further up the hole, one about 30 yards short and left of the green, and three tight to the putting surface. But despite the sand, the hole would be something of a pushover for today's professionals with modern equipment, and nor was it terribly difficult in Flynn's day. It really should be fairly straightforward, provided you avoid the bunkers.

QUAINT
Philadelphia CC is located in the suburb of Gladwyne, half an hour northwest of downtown Philadelphia.

IF ONLY HE KNEW
What might have happened if Sam Snead had heard he needed only a par 5 at this hole to win the 1939 U.S. Open has become one of golf's biggest "what ifs."

SCHOOL'S IN
The City of Brotherly
Love was home to six
architects —William
Flynn, George Crump,
William Fownes, George
Thomas, A.W. Tillinghast
and Hugh Wilson—whose
collective philosophy
became known as the
"Philadelphia School."

SNEAD FAILS TO AVOID THE BUNKERS

Only five men have won golf's professional Grand Slam—Gene Sarazen, Ben Hogan, Gary Player, Jack Nicklaus and Tiger Woods (Bobby Jones won the amateur slam made up of the Amateur Championships and British Opens of both Britain and the U.S.)— winning each of the Masters, U.S. Open, the British Open and the PGA Championship at least once in their career. There are currently 10 players who have won three of the four—Northern Ireland's Rory McIlroy becoming the most recent addition after winning the British Open at Royal Liverpool (Hoylake) in 2014.

As you'd imagine, there are some awfully good golfers on the Three-Legs-of-the-Grand-Slam list, including Phil Mickelson who has six runner-up finishes in the one major he has yet to win—the U.S. Open.

Also on the list is Sam Snead—Slammin' Sam—who won the 1949, 1952 and 1954 Masters, 1946 British Open, and 1942, 1949 and 1951 PGA Championship but who, like Mickelson, always came up short at the U.S. Open (Mickelson does have a few opportunities remaining, of course).

Snead was one of life's natural athletes, tremendously strong and incredibly supple. He owned a deliciously smooth and rhythmic golf swing, developed during childhood when he would practice in his Ashwood, Virginia backyard with "clubs" made of a swamp-maple branch and buggy whip—a horsewhip with a long shaft and short lash. Both were soft and bendy and when swinging Snead would naturally feel some give or "lag" in the club and learn to wait for the club head to catch up with his hands.

With his strength and beautiful tempo (he once said he wanted his swing to feel like honey pouring from a jar), Snead was one of the longest hitters of his day, and he should have made light work of Philadelphia CC's par 5 18th in the final round of the 1939 U.S. Open.

Just 27 years old, Snead had made a fine start to his pro career, finishing second in his U.S. Open debut in 1937, winning the PGA Tour's Vardon Trophy for the year's lowest scoring average in 1938, and winning three tournaments in 1939 before he arrived in Philadelphia for the U.S. Open in June.

An opening 1-under-par 68 on the Thursday gave Snead a one-shot lead over Lawson Little, amateur Bud Ward and a 25-year-old assistant pro from the Philmont CC named Matt Kowal. He maintained the one-stroke advantage with a 2-over 71 in round two.

The final two rounds were played on Saturday. West Virginian Johnny Bulla took the lead with a third-round 68 while Snead, playing with his

BIG HITTER
With seven major championship victories, 82 PGA Tour titles and 165 professional wins, Sam Snead built one of the game's best ever records.

uncle and host professional Ed Dudley, shot 73 to fall back into a tie for second with Wood and Densmore Shute on 5-over 212.

The afternoon's final round went smoothly enough for Snead, who seemed to be cruising. He was 1 over for the first 16 holes, meaning two pars would give him a 72-hole total of 6-over 282—two better than Byron Nelson who had finished strongly with a 68.

Snead made bogey on the 17th, however, and as he walked to the 18th tee he heard a roar from behind and assumed Wood or Bulla, playing in the final group, had made a birdie. There were no scoreboards on the course, so Snead had no idea where he stood. He didn't know Nelson had finished at 8 over, nor did he know Bulla was struggling, but that Wood was still very much in the picture. Without this vital information, Snead believed he would need a birdie 4 and decided to attack the hole.

"When you need only a bogey 6 to tie for the U.S. Open and make an 8, you're ready to take the gas pipe."
Sam Snead, speaking 47 years after his Philadelphia nightmare

But he would have to wait for marshals to clear the 18th fairway. The great Bobby Jones, who had played Pine Valley in the morning before arriving at Philadelphia CC to watch the final round, was there causing great excitement in the gallery.

Snead grew agitated. "I was stewing every second," he said many years later. "I wanted to let off a shotgun blast."

Eventually, he was able to drive but, though he struck his tee shot well, the ball veered left into a bunker. Instead of knocking his second 100 yards safely up the fairway, which he surely would have done had he known a par would have been good enough to win, Snead chose a 2-wood and attempted an overly ambitious shot that didn't come off, the ball squirting into a terrible lie in the left bunker further up the fairway. Again, instead of taking the safe option, Snead took an 8-iron and went for the green. But the ball never cleared the lip. He blasted out again and this time found a bunker to the left of the green.

Only now did someone inform him Nelson had finished at 284. Snead couldn't believe it. "Why the hell didn't someone tell me earlier?" he snapped.

Needing to get up and down to tie Nelson, Snead hit his fifth shot to 40 feet. The putt to tie looked good but drifted left, leaving a 3-footer for double-bogey. Snead was mentally shot and missed, finishing with a triple-bogey 8 and a four-round total of 10-over 286—good only for fifth place. Snead played in a total of 31 U.S. Opens, finishing second or tied second four times.

1928

16th Cypress Point

Location: Monterey Peninsula, California

Distance: 231 yards, par 3

Original course designer: Alister MacKenzie

S eth Raynor devised the first routing at Cypress Point, but died before the course was built. Alister MacKenzie took over and produced a layout that ranks in the top five in the world, no matter whose list you're reading. Both architects wondered if the 16th might not work best as a two-shot hole, thinking the carry over the ocean might be too great for the club's members. It surely would have been a great par 4. But it's done OK as a 3.

BEAUTY AND A BEAST

A combination of three factors make the construction of spectacular golf holes possible. First, though the numbers playing the game in Britain and the U.S. have been declining for a number of years, golf is growing around the globe and, thanks to the economic benefits inherent in building a golf industry or destination, more and more countries are making spectacular land available to developers. Who, for instance, thought a golf course would ever be built in Bulgaria? Well, not only

TOUGH LOVE
It's a daunting carry across the water at Cypress Point's glorious 16th hole. But most golfers would prefer the chance to make a triple-bogey here than a par or birdie anywhere else.

does the former Eastern Bloc country now have six courses, one of them—the Gary Player-designed Thracian Cliffs—has to be seen to be believed. Set on cliffs overlooking the Black Sea 350 miles east of the capital, Sofia, Thracian Cliffs boasts sea views from all 18 holes, a dozen of which might qualify as the course's "signature hole"—an annoying term that began appearing after architect Robert Trent Jones used the phrase "Give your course a signature" in his advertising during the 1960s and which golf courses parade besides images of their most photogenic hole in an effort to make the course look more enticing than it probably is.

Second, machinery used to build golf courses—skid-steer loaders, multi-terrain loaders, hydraulic excavators and compact-wheel loaders with breakout force (the maximum force the arm can apply on a load) of 15,000 pounds or more plus 10,000 pounds of hydraulic lift capacity—is stronger, more sophisticated and altogether more capable than it used to be. Third, because there are so many spectacular holes that golfers want to play, a new course needs to have at least one mesmerizing hole that can appear on the front cover of a magazine if it is to have any hope of attracting golfers in large numbers.

The 16th at Cypress Point on California's Monterey Peninsula may not have been the world's original "signature hole," but for 86 years it has swept aside all wannabe newcomers. Played across 220 yards of rocks and occasionally crashing Pacific Ocean surf, the 16th is a very demanding par 3 that Seth Raynor, the man originally hired to design the course, and MacKenzie who replaced him, actually thought might work better as a short par 4.

"Let's put the green there."
Marion Hollins to Alister MacKenzie (reportedly) after carrying the ocean with her speculative shot

Raynor, the Princeton civil engineering graduate who learned the business of golf course architecture from Charles Blair Macdonald (see p.27), completed the first Cypress Point routing, but died tragically of pneumonia at the age of 51, before construction began. Prior to his being taken ill, Raynor had remarked to Marion Hollins, the 1921 U.S. Women's Amateur champion and founder of the Cypress Point club, that it was a pity the carry over the ocean was too great for a golf hole. Alister MacKenzie, who replaced Raynor just a month after

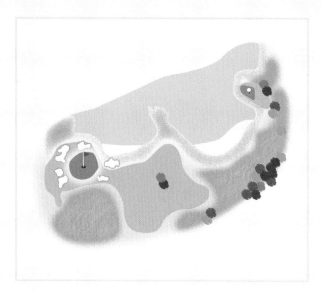

his untimely death, and who by now had designed several of his best courses in England—Alwoodley, Moortown, Sandmoor, Seaton Carew—agreed with Raynor, saying that a two-shot hole would be preferable. But he ultimately bowed to Hollins' insistence that the hole be a heroic par 3 after she teed up a ball and, on her first attempt, knocked it safely across the ocean.

For a while afterwards, MacKenzie probably harbored some concerns about players' ability to hit the shot Hollins had, and that the hole would prove too difficult for club members. To cover his bases, he drew up plans for a 350-yard par 4 with a back tee somewhere between the 15th green and present 16th tee and the fairway on a shelf of land short left of the green, just in case the whole par 3 thing didn't work out.

BITTERSWEET 16

The AT&T National Pebble Beach Pro-Am has been a familiar stop on the PGA Tour for decades, but golfers of a certain vintage remember it as Bing Crosby's tournament, affectionately known as the Clambake. The Broadway and Hollywood star first played his tournament in San Diego in 1937, hoping to bring together low-handicap members of Lakeside GC in Los Angeles, where he was a member and the fifty or so PGA Tour pros who would venture west each winter. In 1947, the event moved north to the Monterey Peninsula where the City of Monterey actually made Crosby an honorary police chief.

The tournament—"part moving cocktail party, part sporting event"—became a great favorite of the pros and celebrities Crosby invited and was played on three courses: Pebble Beach, Monterey Peninsula Country Club (replaced in 1967 by Spyglass Hill) and the extremely exclusive Cypress Point.

The 16th hole was obviously a popular spot for fans, and over the years they got to witness plenty of noteworthy action. In 1947, Crosby himself made a hole-in-one. Six years later, eight-time Tour winner and three-time Ryder Cupper Ed "Porky" Oliver, who was said to have two refrigerators in his car, made a 16 at the 16th after knocking five straight tee balls into the ocean. On entering the clubhouse maybe half an hour

GO FOR IT!
Unless you're a member who plays the hole regularly, or a 30-handicapper utterly convinced you have no chance of making it across, you have to take on the carry at the oceanside 16th.

GOOD COMPANY
Like so many of the world's great golf courses, Cypress Point GC, located on California's Monterey Peninsula, has several fine neighbors. Pebble Beach is 2 miles east along the coast, and Spyglass Hill and Monterey Peninsula CC are also close by.

later, Oliver was handed a message instructing him to call the long-distance operator, number 1-6.

Sometime in the 1960s, Jack Lemmon nearly killed himself by attempting a shot perilously close to the cliff. As he made a practice swing, the actor lost his balance and could well have fallen to his death had Clint Eastwood not been there to grab him. Lemmon, determined to continue, had half a dozen men link arms and hold him while he played the shot. And the 16th is where Groucho Marx finally decided to quit golf after years of trying in vain to break 90. Playing with Ed Sullivan, Marx drilled five balls into the Pacific, then calmly picked up his bag and dropped it into the water.

Fans didn't get to see perhaps the last notable incident at the 16th before the members decided they no longer wanted to host the tournament (new PGA Tour guidelines restricted clubs without minority members from hosting PGA Tour events, and Cypress Point didn't want to change its membership policies), firstly because it happened during a practice round at the 1987 AT&T, and second because the hole was completely lost in fog. England's Howard Clark had never played the hole before, so was a little disappointed to see so much fog. Playing partner Jack Nicklaus had to give him a line, and Clark teed off in the general direction of the green. When he arrived on the other side of the inlet, Clark could not find his ball ... until he looked in the hole and discovered he had made an ace at the most famous par 3 in the world. He was totally euphoric, of course, right up until the moment Jim Nelford and Richard Zokol, who had been playing in the group in front of Clark, told him they had picked his ball up and put it in the hole.

> **"The whole place resembled the crystallization of the dream of an artist who had been drinking gin and sobering up on absinthe."**
>
> O.B. Keeler, *biographer of Bobby Jones*

SO LONG, CYPRESS

✦

Cypress Point was replaced as a venue for the PGA Tour's AT&T National Pebble Beach Pro-Am in 1991, after the club refused to change its membership policies in response to the PGA Tour's new anti-discriminatory guidelines. Sadly, it meant the public could no longer see MacKenzie's design and the amazing 16th hole in particular, a wound tournament organizers made worse when it swapped Cypress for the rather ordinary Poppy Hills, which had opened five years previously. Designed by Robert Trent Jones Jr., Poppy was surrounded completely by forest and is by far the least popular of the tournament's venues. It reopened following a much-needed $12.5 million, 13-month renovation carried out by Jones in April 2014. Poppy Hills is a whole new golf course that will play firm and fast instead of slow and squelchy ... but it's still no Cypress Point.

2nd Royal Pedreña

Location: Pedreña, Spain

Distance: 198 yards, par 3

Original course designer:
H.S. Colt

Real Golf de Pedreña opened in 1928 and, though a members club, was built ostensibly for the golf-loving king, Alfonso XIII. He and his wife, Queen Victoria Eugenie—granddaughter of Queen Victoria of the United Kingdom—spent summers at the residence that became the clubhouse. The course was designed by the great English architect H.S. Colt (Sunningdale New, Royal Portrush, Swinley Forest Muirfield, Wentworth, County Sligo, Kennemer, etc.) who was in his late fifties and had ceased traveling across oceans, leaving the long-haul trips to his partner, Charles Alison (see p.140). It was actually the home of two kings: Alfonso, and Seve Ballesteros, the king of Spanish and European golf.

COLT CLASSIC

WIDE OPEN
It's early in the round for a long iron or hybrid, but Colt gave the amateur golfer a chance of running his tee shot on to the green by leaving the entrance clear.

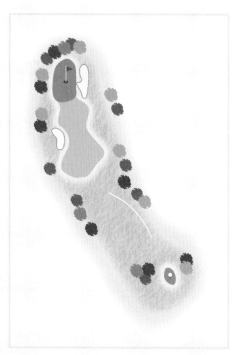

Northern Spain was quite a trip for Englishman Colt, but he had in fact been involved with King Alfonso before—in 1913, when he laid out a course for the King and the Duke of Alba at the Madrid Polo Club (whose original course had been designed by five-time British Open winner J.H. Taylor) on a site adjacent to the royal land at El Pardo, 10 miles northwest of Madrid's city center. There the club became the Real Club de la Puerta de Hierro, a future European Tour venue.

Royal Pedreña sits on a wooded peninsula on the eastern side of the Bay of Santander. With the Cubas River to the south and the Bay of Biscay to the north, it boasts a beautiful location and was awarded its royal status shortly after opening by the King, who became the club's honorary president.

Alfonso wasn't the only king of Pedreña though, as the thee-time Spanish Open venue was also the home course and training ground of a young Severiano Ballesteros. Seve grew up the son of a dairy farmer (just a few cows at the back of the house, along with some chickens, some rabbits and a donkey) in a whitewashed two-storied house close to the southern edge of the course. Though he never had an official handicap, Seve was competing with scratch golfers at the age of 13 and, at some point in his early teens, beat his brother Manuel, a tournament professional, for the first time. In

BEACH BALLS
When Seve wasn't at school, caddying at Real Pedreña or hopping fences to get on to the course, he could probably be found practicing down on the beach. And he would often return as an adult to rekindle his boyhood passion.

March 1974, at the age of 16, he turned professional and, later that year, won his first pro title, the Spanish Under-25 National Championship, which he successfully defended in 1975.

The 2nd at Pedreña is a typically outstanding Colt par 3. It points south toward a small green and the nearby Cubas River, and measures 198 yards from the back tee, making it one of the many holes at Pedreña that helped make Ballesteros such a fine long-iron player (even the best golfers needed a 3-iron or 4-iron to cover 198 yards 35 years ago.) The open entrance to the green allows a ball to roll onto the putting surface.

> **"He also hit balls over the high trees on to the 2nd green—a shot of about 150 yards."**
>
> *Lauren St. John in* Seve: The Biography

NIGHT-TIME SHENANIGANS

In her 1993 Ballesteros biography simply entitled *Seve*, former *Sunday Times* golf correspondent Lauren St. John described the young Spaniard's fondness for a bit of night golf. After faking sleep for hours and waiting for his brother Vicente, with whom he shared a bed, to go to sleep, Seve would steal out the house and, taking his rusty 3-iron club head into which he had inserted his homemade stick shafts, set out for the 2nd hole at Royal Pedreña. Though Seve couldn't see his shots land, he could sense how good each one was by the feel "in the hands and the sand."

After hitting a hundred balls or so, Ballesteros would walk home for a few hours' sleep before returning to the course at dawn to find the balls he had hit earlier in the night. Seve would do this in rain or snow, in pitch dark or illuminated by moonlight.

MODEST
Pedreña is a small finishing village on the north coast of Spain, about 130 miles from the French border, and 280 miles north of Madrid.

1929

10th Kasumigaseki (East)

Location: Saitama Prefecture, Japan

Distance: 177 yards/144 yards, par 3

Original course designer: Kinya Fujita, Shiro Akaboshi

Subsequent alterations: Charles Alison (1931), Tom Fazio (ahead of 2020 Olympics)

It isn't Japan's oldest, but Kasumigaseki is surely the country's foremost golf club, having been the scene of the home country's historic and unexpected victory in the 1957 Canada Cup, and being named, in September 2013, as the host course for the 2020 Olympic Games golf tournament. Kasumigaseki opened in October 1929 and was founded by local landowner Shohei Hocchi. The original course was designed by Kinya Fujita and Shiro Akaboshi, two of Japan's finest amateurs, who invited English architect Charles Alison to take a look.

JAPAN'S FIRST GOLF HOLES

Less than a year after Emperor Meiji came to power in 1867 and begun opening up Japan to foreign trade, thus sparking the country's industrial revolution, young Englishman Arthur Groom disembarked in Kobe intent on building his fortune.

Taken with 3,054-foot Mt. Rokko, which rose nearly vertically above the city, Groom built a cottage near the summit in 1895 and, three years later, began clearing trees and rocks to make space for Japan's first four golf holes. It wasn't until 1901 that Groom and his friends struck their

PROPPED
The 10th hole on the East Course at Kasumigaseki is instantly recognizable for the planks that prop up the black pines close to the water's edge.

first shots, but it only took a year or so for five more to be added. In February 1903, the Kobe Golf Club officially opened and a year later there were 18 holes, designed by two members, Messrs. Adamson and McMurtie, and measuring 3,576 yards. Today the course has grown to 4,049 yards and plays to a par of 61. Because caddies carry four bags at a time, players are limited to 10 clubs each.

THE SEED TAKES ROOT

One or two other courses built by foreigners appeared around that time, but the first course built by Japanese natives for the Japanese was at the Tokyo GC in Komazawa in 1914. The prime mover behind the project was banker Junosuke Inouye, who had been introduced to the game during business trips to New York. The course was laid out by an American named Brady, Captain of the Yoko-

REGAL
Prince Hirohito was a keen golfer. He is seen here at Tokyo GC in Komazawa in August 1926. One wonders if a Japanese pro ever had the nerve to comment on the prince's faulty weight transference.

hama GC. But the club had made the rather imprudent decision to lease rather than purchase the land and, as Tokyo grew, the landowners became increasingly unhappy with the arrangement. Eventually they offered the club the chance to buy, but the cost was prohibitive so the club had to move.

A member named Kohmyo Ohtani, who was educated in Britain where he had developed a good understanding of classic golf architecture, believed Tokyo GC now had a good opportunity to build a world-class course on its new property at Asaka. To plan it, Ohtani chose his favorite British designer—H.S. Colt.

Despite the fact he was now 61 and hadn't travelled overseas for 16 years, Colt agreed, demanding a fee of £1,500 ($2,300) plus travel and living expenses. But shortly before his departure date, Colt decided he didn't like the idea of the three-week voyage, so assigned his partner Charles Alison to the job.

Not surprisingly, the members at Tokyo GC weren't terribly excited with the notion of paying so much money for an architect they weren't familiar with, especially having just shelled out for the new land. We can assume, though, Ohtani was aware Alison had spent most of the 1920s in the U.S., operating as the U.S. branch of the Colt Alison design firm and working on acclaimed courses such as Kirtland Country Club in Ohio, Burning Tree in Maryland, the Country Club of Detroit, Timber Point on Long Island, New York, Sea Island in Georgia, and, most significantly, Pine Valley.

George Crump, Pine Valley's founder, died in 1918 with only 14 holes of his masterpiece in play (see p.107). To complete the remaining four, the club formed an advisory committee of which Alison was part. Colt had previously contributed to the design of the course, but was now confining himself to the U.S. so Alison represented him, completing a five-page report that led to the reconstruction of five greens.

ALISON'S IMPACT

Alison arrived in Tokyo by cruiseliner from California in December 1930, accompanied by his most valued construction supervisor, George Penglase. He was met by Kohmyo Ohtani who showed him the Tokyo club's new 200-acre property, which Alison described as "flat as a pancake" and which was mostly devoid of any interesting features. Alison shut himself away in his hotel room for seven days and emerged with a bold design for the new course, which a huge army of laborers would build by hand (sadly, Alison's design at Tokyo GC, which opened in 1932, lasted only nine years before the military seized control and destroyed the course completely. Ohtani would design the club's third course, at Sayama.)

From Tokyo, Alison moved a short distance west to the Izu Peninsula and designed the highly acclaimed Fuji Course at Kawana for Baron Kishichiro Okura, the son of Japan's wealthiest businessman and also a former Cambridge student.

Alison then returned to the capital and, in January 1931, consulted at

ANCIENT HISTORY
Today, the course at Kobe GC stretches past the 4,000-yard mark. Although a tough walk over mountainous terrain, it is extremely attractive and overlooks the Seto Inland Sea, 265 miles west of Tokyo.

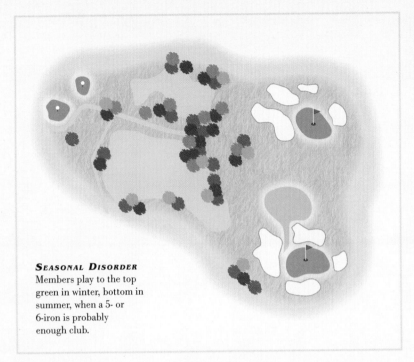

SATELLITE CITY
Kasumigaseki GC is
located in the city of
Kawagoe-Shi in Saitama
Prefecture, a half-hour
train ride north of the
capital Tokyo.

SEASONAL DISORDER
Members play to the top
green in winter, bottom in
summer, when a 5- or
6-iron is probably
enough club.

Kasumigaseki before being invited by a friend of Ohtani's to Kobe, where Alison was asked to transform a gorgeous parcel of land into a Sunningdale-like heathland course.

Unlike the land at Asaka, the site for the Hirono GC (see p.156) was altogether more interesting—full of ravines, ponds, lakes, forest, hills and valleys. Just as he had in Tokyo, Alison repaired to his hotel for seven days, producing the plan for a course which would open in 1932 and which he regarded as one of the best of his career.

TWO GREENS

At Kasumigaseki, which he described as "pleasantly undulating," Alison made changes to only five holes—9th, 10th, 14th, 17th and 18th—making them all a good deal more challenging than they had been. The most notable change probably came at the short 10th, which he turned into a superb par 3, replacing the shallow bunker in front of the green with a 6-foot-deep Alison bunker (see p.157). The hole plays 177 yards across a lake with a handful of huge black pines—two of them propped up by long wooden planks that prevent them from toppling into the water—lining the edge. As with most holes in Japan, there are two greens (144 yards to the second)—one sewn with a cool-season bent grass, the other a warm-season turf—to ensure the members have good putting surfaces throughout the year. While winters aren't desperately cold in and around Saitama, 20 miles north-west of Tokyo, the summers can be extremely hot and humid and, until recently, no one single turf could be maintained to a desirable quality year-round. Kasumigaseki was the first course in Japan to adopt this two-green system, installing its second set in 1937

after Alison and a local botanist had failed to come up with a bent grass that would remain healthy during the summer. With advances in both turf technology and maintenance practices, however, the club is now able to remove the second green, and each hole for the Olympics will feature just one. The changes will be carried out by Tom Fazio, consulting architect at Augusta National and designer of 15 of the top 100 courses in the US, as ranked by *Golf Digest* magazine.

HIGH-SPEED GRASS

✦

Bent grass (genus *Agrostis*), as employed at Kasumigaseki, is a cool-season turf used for lawns and golf greens in northern Europe, the northern U.S. and Japan. Creeping bent grass, which produces horizontal stems called "stolons" that run along the soil's surface, is the most common form of bent turf on golf courses. It is especially suitable for greens as it produces an attractive, deep green color and dense coverage. It can also be mowed extremely short—as low as a tenth of an inch—which allows greenkeepers to produce very smooth, very fast surfaces. The turf used for warm season greens in Japan is invariably Korai *(Zoysia matrella)*, more commonly referred to as Manilagrass, though Bermuda is becoming more popular.

GAME CHANGER

Most Western-hemisphere golfers are aware the Japanese are fanatical about the game, but up until the 1950s, the number of golf courses in Japan barely reached 100. Now, there are well over 2,000. So what happened?

The event that sparked the nation's fervor was the 1957 Canada Cup (now the World Cup of Golf), played on the East Course at Kasumigaseki. Wealthy industrialist John Jay Hopkins, founder of the General Dynamics Corporation, now the U.S.'s fifth-largest defense contractor, came up with the idea of an annual competition played for by two-man teams representing their home country. Just seven countries were represented in 1953—the tournament's first year—while 26 competed in 2013 (in 2009, the World Cup became a biennial event, because of golf's return to the Olympics).

The U.S. team of Sam Snead and Jimmy Demaret began the 1957 tournament as firm favorites, but it was Japan's Torakichi Nakamura and Koichi Ono (a native of China who had become a Japanese citizen in 1955) that prevailed, beating the American pair by nine shots. Nakamura also won the individual event, completing the 72 holes on 14-under-par 274, seven shots clear of Snead.

1931

18th Carnoustie (Championship)

Location: Carnoustie, Tayside, Scotland

Distance: 499 yards, par 4

Original course designer: Allan Robertson

Subsequent alterations: Tom Morris Sr. (1872), James Braid (1926), Braid, James Wright (1930)

I t's an odd name, Carnoustie. Most probably it's a fusion of the Scandinavian words *car* (meaning "rock") and *noust* (meaning "bay"), though locals prefer the altogether more stirring legend of Camus, leader of the Danes. Apparently, this Camus was defeated by the Scots, led by Malcolm II, at the Battle of Barry in 1010. Whichever theory you opt for, no one doubts this former police burgh on the Angus coast, just 9 miles across the Firth of Tay from St. Andrews, is home to one incredibly tough golf course.

CARNOUSTIE CHRONICLE

The more you delve into Carnoustie's past, the more intriguing it becomes. For starters, parish records show that golf was played on the Barry Links as early as 1560. There was no course, just a bunch of merry hackers—among them one Sir Robert Maule, who was described as a "gentleman of comlie behaviour, of hie stature, sanguine in colour both of hyd and haire," and who was "given to leicherie, hawking, hunting and the gawf"—whacking wooden balls with bizarre-looking clubs called "long noses," the heads of which were fashioned from beechwood, holly or apple, and whose shafts were cut from something a little softer like ash or hazel.

Edinburgh author and publisher Robert Chambers laid out a few holes in 1834, but it was St. Andrews club- and ball-maker Allan Robertson who created the first recognized course in 1842—with

CRASH AND BURN
The approach to the 18th green on the Championship Course at Carnoustie must cross the Barry Burn—no biggie for the pros, but a terrifying prospect for amateurs.

assistance from his young apprentice Tom Morris. Robertson laid out only 10 holes, but Morris was back 25 years later to extend the course to 18, the course measuring 4,565 yards. Morris' elder brother George had been appointed greenkeeper the previous year. In 1868, the Dalhousie Golf Club—the first of the six clubs that call Carnoustie home—was founded.

Carnoustie's busy timeline shows how active the town's golf community was in the late 19th century and early 20th, but no year is as significant as 1892 when the town council became the rightful owners of the links, having raised the money (the equivalent of $2,000) to buy the 176 acres during a three-day market held at Dundee's Kinnaird Hall. Items that had been received from golf enthusiasts all around the world were sold during the sale, and cash was donated.

It was also around this period that roughly three hundred young Carnoustie golfers set sail for a new life across the Atlantic. Among them were the Smith brothers—Willie, Alex and Macdonald (Willie would win the U.S. Open in 1899, Alex in 1906 and 1910), and the Maiden brothers—James and Stewart. Both spent time as the professional at East Lake CC in Atlanta, and it was here that Stewart would meet Bobby Jones, whom he would mentor for several years. One chap, destined for South America, overindulged at his going-away party, however, and ended up asleep on the 10th fairway. By the time he woke up, his ship had sailed. To commemorate this sad but slightly amusing tale, the hole was named South America.

In 1926, the committee that had been created to manage the links hired five-time Open Champion James Braid to make improvements to the course, and he really went to town, lengthening it to 6,680 yards, repositioning tees and greens, and adding 60 bunkers.

Carnoustie was now a formidable course, but at the 1930 Scottish Amateur Championship it became apparent that the finishing holes were still a little weak. The 15th measured 339 yards, the 16th 335, the 17th 160 and the 18th 365. All four holes were considered good birdie chances, and if competitors at the following year's British Open were to be adequately tested down the home stretch something needed to happen.

Instead of asking Braid to return, the Chairman of the Golf Course Management Committee, James Wright (see box), made the changes himself, which he did in time for the 1931 British Open. The event, won by Scottish-born Tommy Armour, who had emigrated to the U.S. 10 years before, went so well it was only six years before Carnoustie was hosting its second Open, England's Henry Cotton winning this time with a superb final-round 71 in atrocious weather.

Ben Hogan won the only British Open he ever played in, at Carnoustie in 1953 (see p.148), Gary Player won his second Claret Jug in 1968, and Tom Watson won his first in 1975, beating Australia's Jack Newton in a playoff.

Later that year, however, a local government reorganization saw the Angus District Council, headquartered 15 miles north of Carnoustie in Forfar, take over control of the links. The new operator's park superintendents didn't really appreciate the need for firm, fast conditions at a seaside links however and, thinking golf courses should be green, watered them mercilessly. It was a disaster, the nature of the turf changed, and the heart and soul of the Carnoustie courses were lost at the hands of managers who really had no idea what they were dealing with.

ERR ON THE SIDE OF CAUTION
Probably only those working on a good score, feeling sufficiently pumped up or needing a birdie to win the Open Championship, should contemplate crossing the Barry Burn with their second.

TAY TOWN
Carnoustie is a town of about 12,000 people, located on the Firth of Tay, roughly 15 miles northeast of St. Andrews, as the crow flies.

Thankfully, a new champion of the Carnoustie Links, John Calder, managed to persuade Angus District Council to hand control back to a local links management committee, of which Calder became chairman in 1984. Just like James Wright 50 years before him, Calder was a Captain of the Dalhousie Club and utterly devoted to advancing Carnoustie's position in the game. Besides his determination to put the course back where he believed it belonged, Calder's appointment of John Philp as greenkeeper was instrumental in Carnoustie's return to prominence.

Philp, who came to Carnoustie from St. Andrews where he had been mentored by the legendary Walter Woods, set to work in 1985 and within a few years had succeeded in re-establishing the fine bents and fescues. With the course back to its best, Calder approached the R&A to enquire about hosting the Open. The R&A said no, concerned about roads, lack of hotel space and communications. A couple of years later, Calder went after the Ryder Cup and was turned down again. In 1993 Calder commissioned another feasibility study in the hope of attracting a European Tour event. But there were no gaps on the Tour's schedule. But, happily for Carnoustie, the Scottish Open finished its run at Gleneagles and became available. Calder met with the tournament chairman Allan Callan and made the deal. Carnoustie hosted its first major international event in 20 years in 1995, and the tournament returned the following year.

The feedback from the players was positive, and with plans for a five-star hotel to replace the rather ugly clubhouse behind the 1st tee and 18th green, the R&A was at last convinced Carnoustie was worthy of the Open again.

The 1999 Championship is remembered for two things—how incredibly tough the course played (a result of strong winds, narrow fairways and lush rough caused by a very wet spring), and Jean Van de Velde's capitulation on the 18th hole in the final round (see p.148). Paul Lawrie won the tournament after a three-hole playoff with Justin Leonard and

WRIGHT MAN FOR THE JOB

✦

James Wright was a Carnoustie accountant and former Captain of the Dalhousie Golf Club who, in 1926, as chairman of the links management committee, persuaded James Braid to lengthen and redesign the course Tom Morris Sr. had built 59 years before.

Wright proposed the old 15th become the 16th, and shortened into a long par 3. The old 16th, he said, would become the 17th with a new back tee and new green taken from the neighboring Burnside Course (opened as a nine-holer in 1892 and then known as the "Auxiliary" Course), and a fairway that the winding Barry Burn would turn into a somewhat isolated target. The short 17th was to be abandoned altogether and replaced by the par 3 13th. And the home hole would become a par 5 with two carries over the burn by taking the tee back to the old 17th's tee box.

Greenkeeper Andrew Scott miraculously had Wright's final three holes ready in time for the 1931 British Open. They proved suitably challenging, and have been regarded as just about the most difficult closing trio in the world ever since.

Braid's work at Carnoustie was pivotal, Wright's paramount.

Van de Velde, but his victory, if and when mentioned, is usually attributed to Van de Velde's final-hole meltdown, not his own brilliant closing 67.

Carnoustie staged its seventh Open in 2007 when Padraig Harrington won his first major, beating Sergio Garcia in a playoff.

HOGAN'S ALLEY

Shortly before he left for home at the end of his brief November 1930 trip to Carnoustie to inspect James Wright's new finishing holes, James Braid strolled out to the par 5 6th and suggested three new bunkers, one of them in the middle of the fairway.

The bunker forced players to make an important decision on the tee—drive safely to the right to leave an awkward second, or thread the needle between the sand and Out of Bounds on the left, leaving a much easier approach. At the 1953 British Open—his first and only appearance at the Open—the great Ben Hogan took the narrow line on the 567-yard hole every day, and took advantage with three birdies. He won the Championship by four shots and earned the nickname "the wee ice mon" from the locals, on account of his steely nerve.

The 6th was officially renamed Hogan's Alley at a ceremony during the 2003 Alfred Dunhill Links Championship. Paul Lawrie, the 1999 Open Champion (see below), unveiled a plaque commemorating Hogan's win and his quartet of brave, arrow-straight drives.

MON DIEU!

James Wright turned the 18th from a bland 365-yard par 4 into an exciting 503-yard par 5 with the approach to the green played over a stretch of the Barry Burn. It remained a par 5 until the Open returned to Carnoustie in 1999 when it reverted to a par 4—albeit 487 yards long (in 2007, it played 499 yards.)

Jean Van de Velde, a Frenchman whose one European Tour victory had come six years previously, arrived at the 18th hole on the final day of the 1999 British Open with a three-shot cushion over 1997 champion Justin Leonard and Scotland's Paul Lawrie, who had finished with a 4-under 67. Despite being able to take six and still win, Van de Velde chose not to play safely with a long iron from the tee and treat the hole as a par 5. Instead, he took a driver and pushed his tee shot well to the right. The ball somehow avoided dropping into Barry Burn.

Surely now he would choose the sensible option and hit a short iron safely up the fairway, then a wedge to the green. *Mais, non.* Van de Velde took a 2-iron and went for broke. But he blocked it badly again, and the ball headed for the grandstand on the right. The ball could have lodged somewhere in the stand and he could have got a drop, but it actually careened off the stand backwards and into a horrible lie in the thick rough. Again, a safety-first pitch to the fairway, another to the green and one or two putts would have given Van de Velde the Claret Jug. But he went for the green, the club got snagged in the hay, and the ball flew only 15 yards … straight into the burn.

He now made a good decision at last, opting not to play out of the burn but take a penalty drop short of it. He caught another bad lie though and was able to hit his fifth shot only as far as the bunker to the right of the green.

He then watched as playing partner Craig Parry holed out from the bunker for a birdie 3 to finish on 7-over-par 291. If Van de Velde could emulate the Australian, he would end the drama with a 6 and victory.

He didn't make it, but a decent splash shot left him 5 feet left of the hole and with a putt to make it a three-way playoff.

To his immense credit, Van de Velde rolled in the putt. It was a 7 though and, round in 77, he completed the 72 holes on 6-over 290, the highest "winning" total since Fred Daly's 293 at Royal Liverpool in 1947. The four-hole playoff, involving Lawrie, Leonard and Van de Velde, began on the par 4 15th where Van de Velde's woes continued. A double-bogey 6 put him a shot behind his opponents, and he followed it with a bogey at the par 3 16th. Lawrie and Van de Velde traded birdies at the tough par 4 17th, meaning the Scotsman would take a one-shot lead over both Leonard and Van de Velde into the final hole. There, Lawrie made another superb birdie while the others made 5s. Van de Velde's nightmare was complete.

The only silver lining was that his second-place finish helped Van de Velde win enough money to qualify for the European Ryder Cup team. But at the Country Club in Brookline, Massachusetts, he played only one match—a single against Davis Love, which he lost 6&5. He would win only once again on the European Tour—in Madeira in 2006.

JEAN, QUE DIABLE?
After chunking his third shot into the Barry Burn, Jean van de Velde seriously considered hitting out of the water. He'd made three terrible decisions in short order but, at last, he made a good one and took a drop.

6th Royal Melbourne (West)

Location: Cheltenham, Victoria, Australia

Distance: 439 yards, par 4

Original course designer: Alister MacKenzie

Royal Melbourne is an immense part of Australia's golf story. But its renown extends far wider than the bottom right-hand corner of the world map. Course rankings in golf publications seem heavily biased toward courses in the U.S. and UK, but the West Course at Royal Melbourne is as good as anything in the world's top five. Though half a mile from the coast and with no great views of Port Phillip Bay, the land itself is every bit as good for golf as the British links land. MacKenzie made full use of it, fitting a dozen or more world-class holes in among the random undulations and pockets of vegetation. Only Pine Valley in the U.S. might have as many great holes as Royal Melbourne. And of all the West Course's highlights, the 6th is surely the pick.

DOWN UNDER
Australia's Jason Day, a member of the International Team, plays his approach to the 4th green (the 6th on the West Course) during the 2011 Presidents Cup.

SANDBELT SPLENDOR

Augusta National and Cypress Point were still in his future, but by 1926 Alister MacKenzie had already forged a fine reputation as a golf course architect adapting the knowledge of camouflage he had developed during the Boer War and World War II. In England, he had created Alwoodley, Moortown, Sandmoor, Seaton Carew and others and, for a

time, had formed an alliance with fellow course architects H.S. Colt and Charles Alison. He had also charted the Old Course at St. Andrews producing, in 1924, a famous map, copies of which still hang from the walls in clubhouses and golf geeks' bedrooms around the world.

As a Brit, MacKenzie was well known in the golf-playing colonies, especially Australia. So when the Royal Melbourne Golf Club (the club had been granted the "Royal" status by Queen Victoria in 1895) decided to move from its existing property and build an entirely new course, the members had little hesitation in choosing MacKenzie to design it.

"Royal Melbourne, I think, is the course Augusta wants to be: wide enough for anybody, but brilliantly routed to make use of the topography and bunkered to reward bold play and bold decisions."

Tom Doak, golf course architect

Melbourne GC was formed in the suburb of Caulfield in 1891, and is considered the oldest continuously existing golf club in the country (the Australian GC in Sydney opened in 1882, but did not possess a golf course from 1888 to 1895). Its first course was laid out by two St. Andrews natives, on land that had originally been earmarked for housing. A financial crisis had delayed that project, however, so the club remained at Caulfield longer than expected. In time, though, development did get under way and when new housing began encroaching on the course, the members agreed they needed to move. In 1901, the club relocated a few miles to the south in Sandringham.

It remained there for 29 years before moving south again to a parcel of land in Black Rock it had been eyeing for a while. With the money it raised from the sale of the Sandringham site, the club had the means to hire the very best architect available.

MacKenzie had been recommended to the club president by members of the Royal and Ancient GC. He charged £1,000 ($1,500) for his services and set sail on the SS *Otranto* from Southampton, England on September 26, 1926, arriving at Fremantle (Perth) on October 19. He docked in Melbourne six days later, and walked the land at Black Rock with Royal Melbourne's superintendent Mick Morcom.

Over the next 11 weeks, MacKenzie designed, inspected, redesigned, planned and re-routed 19 courses in Adelaide, Melbourne, Sydney and Brisbane, the most significant work occurring 10 miles south of Melbourne's city center, where he basically invented the Melbourne Sandbelt. There, he had a hand in the development of some of the area's—and the world's—finest golf courses, including Kingston Heath GC, Victoria GC, Metropolitan GC and, of course, Royal Melbourne's West Course (Royal Melbourne earned a commission for introducing MacKenzie to every other club he consulted at, thus recouping much of the £1,000.)

MacKenzie left Australia on December 31 bound for New Zealand, where he inspected a handful of courses in Auckland including Maungakiekie (now Titirangi), which he transformed into another world-class venue. He sailed from Auckland to San Francisco on February 1, 1927, having enjoyed a whirlwind tour that would change the face of golf Down Under forever.

BLACK ROCK BEAUTY

At Black Rock, MacKenzie teamed with the 1924 Australian Amateur champion and Royal Melbourne member Alex Russell, and the club's superintendent Mick Morcum. The land—sandy, undulating and with eucalyptus and ti-tree scattered randomly throughout—was just about perfect for golf and MacKenzie made the best possible use of it, conceiving 18 dramatic holes that adhered to all his course design principles: natural, walkable, thought-provoking, playable for high-handicappers, exacting for scratch golfers, etc.

It's not clear exactly how involved Russell was on the West Course, but by designing the club's similarly excellent East Course (and nearby Yarra Yarra, Lake Karrinyup in Perth and Paraparaumu in New Zealand) following MacKenzie's departure, it's clear he was paying close attention as the Scot went about his business. MacKenzie obviously thought very highly of him, though, as he appointed Russell his partner in Australasia.

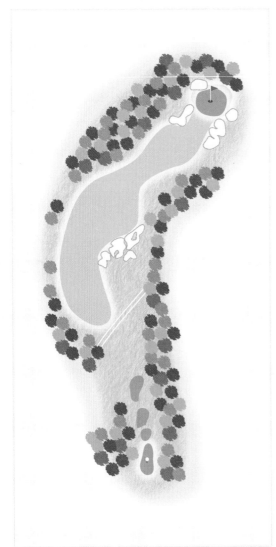

Perhaps even more crucial than having Russell on hand, however, was being able to rely on the construction talents and agronomy expertise of Morcum, whom MacKenzie labeled the best superintendent he ever worked with (Morcom's successor Claude Crockford was also an important figure in the development of Royal Melbourne's greens). One of the best holes on the course is the 176-yard, uphill 5th where the huge fast, green is set on a sandy bank and surrounded by the sort of huge, deep bunkers that give sandbelt courses, and Royal Melbourne in particular, their distinctive look. There is little or no fringe between these beautiful, sand-faced, sharp-edged traps and the putting surface, and it was apparently after watching Morcum build them and the green complex at the 5th that MacKenzie felt comfortable leaving him and Russell in charge while he journeyed on.

It is perhaps the following hole though that best portrays MacKenzie's design philosophy and which invariably appears in many commentators "Best 18 in the World." The par 4 6th begins on a high tee among the ti-tree and falls downhill over a mass of broom and untidy bunkers before bending to the right. The carry over the sand and scrub requires a drive of about 240–250 yards, but once over you are left with a much easier approach to the green than the golfer who bails out left of the bunkers. Not only will that person face a much longer approach, they will also be hampered by the huge bunker that eats into the left side of the green.

The typically vast putting surface tilts sharply from front to back and can be outrageously quick.

In essence, it may be the perfect hole. It is beautiful, which is something everyone likes. You need three fantastically good shots to make a birdie, four good

MACK ATTACK
The impact Alister MacKenzie had on golf in Melbourne, and really the whole of Australia, during his three-month stay in the country at the end of 1926 cannot be overestimated.

"It burns me up that with the billions of dollars spent on course construction in the past 50 years, all the architects together haven't been able to build another Royal Melbourne."
Gene Sarazen

ones to make a par—which the scratch player appreciates. And the high-handicapper can head safely left off the tee, aim short and right of the green with his approach, and pitch on before hopefully two-putting for a 5. So everyone's happy.

EMBARRASSING THE BEST

In one sense, it is a shame Royal Melbourne is in Melbourne. Because it's so far away from the "centers" of the known golf universe and where most of the world's golfers live, and because the Australasian Tour has never been considered as prestigious as the PGA or European Tours, fans eager to play it not only have a hard time getting there, they also see it only rarely on their TV screens.

Ideally, an Australian tournament (specifically the Australian Open, which was first played in 1904 and which Gary Player won seven times, Jack Nicklaus six times, and Greg Norman five times) could be given the Major status it probably deserves, and the West Course could be a regular venue.

As it is, we have seen it just a few times in recent years. In 2013, we got a lucky double dose when it hosted the Australian Masters, won by Adam Scott, and the World Cup of Golf, won by the host nation represented by Scott and Jason Day, the following week. In 2011, the club hosted its second Presidents Cup which the U.S. team won 19–15.

From 2002 to 2005, it hosted an Australasian/European Tour event (Heineken Classic) which Ernie Els won three straight years, and it staged its first Presidents Cup in 1998 when the International team overwhelmed the U.S. side $20^1/_2$–$11^1/_2$.

Before then, Royal Melbourne's appearances on the world stage were even scarcer.

The World Cup of Golf (then called the Canada Cup), first came to Royal Melbourne in 1959—the year a composite course (see box) with a selection of

CLASSIC COMPOSITE

✦

In 1959, when the Canada Cup was played at Royal Melbourne, organizers wanted to avoid having players and galleries cross busy public roads, so only holes from the property's central paddock were used. Twelve holes from the West Course were added to six from the East to create Royal Melbourne's Composite Course. Though the West is certainly worthy of staging any tournament or championship in the game, it is this composite course that has been used for every big event since 1959. That said, it is not the same composition every time. A total of 21 of the 29 holes in the central paddock have been used. The 2011 Presidents Cup course was made up of 11 holes from the West Course and seven from the East, and measured 7,023 yards. The 6th hole played as the 441-yard 4th. it is this composite course that has been used for every big event since 1959, except the 1963 Australian Open (east), and 1983 Australian PGA (East).

"This course is a great big bear trap which is set to grab you if you make a false step."
Sam Snead, 1959 Canada Cup

holes from both courses was first used. Australia won, but the tournament is best remembered these days for the manner in which the U.S.'s Sam Snead made a hash of the 6th hole by putting off the green and into the front bunker. At the World Cup 13 years later, Snead's countryman Tom Weiskopf fared equally badly on the hole. After four-putting, Weiskopf said the 6th was the only green he had ever four-putted after "trying on every putt."

And Els had a run-in with the hole himself during the 2004 Heineken Classic when he took an 8, quickly wiping out his four-shot lead. Els had begun the event with an amazing 12-under-par round of 60, the course record, and was 22 under going into the fourth round. Despite the eight at the 6th and an ugly 74, the South African did manage to hold on for a one-stroke win over Adam Scott.

5th Hirono

Location: Hyogo Prefecture, Japan

Distance: 152 yards, par 3

Original course designer: Charles Alison

"**Whether for a blood match from the back tee, or for a gamble among the portly and venerable, I can name no superior among British inland courses. For variety of scene and of strokes, Hirono is difficult to beat.**"

Charles Alison

Because only three of its male golfers were ranked inside the top 100 in the world at the time of writing, with none higher than Hideki Matsuyama at 20th, and because it can't yet boast a single men's major champion (female golfer Chako Iguchi won the LPGA Championship in 1977), it is easy to forget Japan has the second largest golf industry in the world, with its nearly eight million golfers spending roughly three billion dollars a year. There are nearly 2,500 courses in the Land of the Rising Sun and Hirono, 20 miles northwest of the port city of Kobe, is invariably considered the best of them—and the 5th, Fiord, its most memorable hole.

LOOK FAMILIAR?

The 5th hole is the first of a superb quartet of par 3s. Like two of its fellow short holes, Fiord crosses water, which at first seems unusual for a course designed by a man—Charles Alison—who, as a rule, spoke of water hazards derisively: "Water is a bad feature in that the ball cannot be played from it," Alison said, "and in consequence, it does not test the golfer's skill." He was aware of the need for irrigation water of course and, after having spent well over a month in the country by the time he got to Hirono, he also knew well Japan's affection for ponds and lakes. "Their love of water-hazards, were it not for their self-control,

SHORT HOP
The 5th at Hirono may measure only 152 yards, but it's still a daunting shot across water to a green ringed by deep "Alison" bunkers.

might develop dangerously," he remarked, conscious of the fact architects and developers often relied too heavily on water to the great detriment of the course.

It's probably no coincidence, given how much time he had spent there, but Alison's 5th hole at Hirono bears more than a passing resemblance to the 5th at Pine Valley in New Jersey. Both are par 3s played across a water hazard set well below the tee, the ground on the far side rising sharply to a green protected by sizeable bunkers. The only differences are that Pine Valley's hole is nearly 70 yards longer and the bunkers at Hirono wrap around in front of the green while a run-up shot is possible at Pine Valley, as the sand is found to the sides.

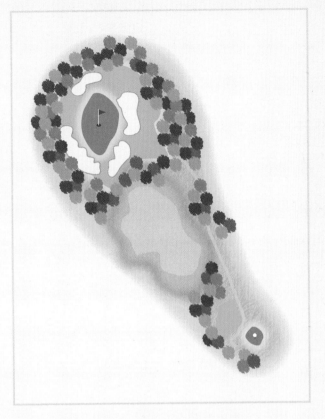

Though Alison's design remains largely intact, Hirono has evolved a good deal in the nearly 85 years since it opened, as Japanese golfers tend to prefer the manicured, garden look over the rugged, natural look that characterized the early course.

Hirono has hosted a number of Japan's most important championships, most recently the 2005 Japan Open won by Shingo Katayama.

ALISONS

Much of Charles Alison's design philosophy was shaped and influenced by his mentor and partner H.S. Colt, who championed strategic design over penal. Like Colt, Alison made his courses playable for everyone, but made sure only the very best players could match par. Alison was the more stringent of the two though, building bunkers from which an easy recovery was rarely possible. Alison liked his bunkers big and deep, and those he built or designed at Tokyo, Kasumigaseki, Kawana, Naruo and Hirono during his three-month stay in the country were so distinct from those they replaced or what could be found elsewhere in the country, Japanese golfers called them Alisons.

SAFE HOME
Your ball needs to carry water, bushes, rough and sand before it finds the safety of the putting surface. Good job it's only a 7- or 8-iron shot.

WORTH THE TREK
Hirono GC is located in Miki-Shi, Hyogo Prefecture, 20 miles northwest of Kobe and 375 miles west of Tokyo.

10th Augusta National

Location: Augusta, Georgia

Distance: 495 yards, par 4

Original course designer: Alister MacKenzie

Subsequent alterations: Perry Maxwell (1930s), Robert Trent Jones (1947), George Cobb (1960s and 1970s), Tom Fazio (late 1990s, early 2000s)

This was the opening hole when the course was established in 1933, and the 1st hole at the first Masters in 1934, when it measured 430 yards (the nines were reversed ahead of the 1935 tournament). It is named after an Asian flowering shrub called *Camellia japonica*, which has white, pink and red flowers and leaves that are used in the production of tea. The plant can be seen down the hole's left side and behind the green. On opening day, the green at Camellia was situated to the right of the huge, irregularly shaped bunker that is now in the middle of the fairway, about 60 yards short of the green. Though wonderfully strategic—players finding the high side of the fairway to the right had a simple approach to the flag while those hitting an easy drive to the left had to come in over the bunker—the hole was deemed a little too easy for the game's best players, so in 1937 Perry Maxwell moved the green forward to where it is now. As a result, the 10th became the toughest hole at the Masters, with a stroke average from the first 78 Masters tournaments of 4.31 (the 10th is one of nine holes that have never played under their par). As for drama, the 10th has seen plenty, the best of it in recent years.

GOOD LOOKING
The glorious view down the hill toward the green at the 10th. It is much better to approach the putting surface from the left half of the fairway— a much flatter lie and you don't have to contend with the bunker to the right of the green.

WATSON'S WEDGE

The 2012 Masters was decided in a playoff between Floridian Bubba Watson (born Gerry Lester Watson Jr.) and South Africa's Louis Oosthuizen, after they had both completed 72 regulations holes on 10-under 278 (Oosthuizen having made an albatross/double-eagle 2 on the par 5 2nd in the final round—the fourth albatross in the tournament's history).

The playoff began at the 18th, where both players made solid par 4s. At the second extra hole, the 10th, both hit poor drives to the right. Though finding the right side of the fairway was the best play when the course opened, and at the first three Augusta National Invitationals (tournament founder Bobby Jones eventually gave in to media pressure to call it the Masters in 1939) when the green was situated to the right of the large fairway bunker, the strategy of the hole had changed when the green moved. Drives headed right tend to stay up on high ground rather than catch the downslope on the left which can give the player an extra 20–30 yards. Oosthuizen's drive was on the fairway, but he had well over 200 yards to the hole off a tricky downhill lie. He caught the ball cleanly, but it came up just short of the green.

Watson, meanwhile, was in the trees. One of the longest hitters on the PGA Tour, he had blown it through the fairway and now appeared to be in a position from which chipping out sideways was his only option. But he had a backswing and, as he was fond of saying, if he had a swing he had a shot. A gap in the trees made getting the ball out and back on to the fairway fairly straightforward, but the view of the green was obscured by tall pines. He had 134 yards to the front, 164 to the hole.

As he set up for the shot, it clearly didn't look as though the left-handed Watson intended chipping out sideways. No, he had something much more elaborate in mind and, with his 52-degree gap wedge, hit a

HUBBA BUBBA
Bubba Watson won his first Green Jacket in 2012, after hitting this amazing shot from the trees to the right of the fairway at the 10th hole, during a playoff with Louis Oosthuizen.

"I'm like Sam Snead. I think about the shot I want to hit, and my body and mind create it. All I'm thinking is, I've got to hook this ball. A lot. I got into that zone where everything went blank."

Bubba Watson on his approach shot to the 10th

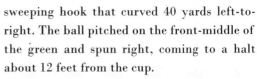

LEFT OF LEFT

✦

In 2011, Northern Ireland's Rory McIlroy had a four-shot lead at the end of three rounds. An outward 37 on the final day wasn't ideal, but as he arrived on the 10th tee he still had a one-shot cushion over the chasing pack.

Because the lead typically changes hands so frequently, and the level of tension and excitement grows so rapidly, they say the Masters doesn't start until the back nine on Sunday. Well, it started and effectively ended for McIlroy in the space of a few minutes on this Sunday, after he hit a freakishly poor tee shot that flew so far left that the ball ended up left of the trees on the left, between two of the club's cabins 50 yards left of the fairway. Did I mention it went left?

McIlroy eventually made a triple-bogey 7 and continued to unravel, bogeying the 11th and taking 5 at the par 3 12th. He was home in 43, and wound up in a tie for 15th.

sweeping hook that curved 40 yards left-to-right. The ball pitched on the front-middle of the green and spun right, coming to a halt about 12 feet from the cup.

It was the sort of shot that defies physics, and one that only a very select group of players could conceive, let alone execute. How could he create so much hook spin with so lofted a club? How, after hooking so much, could the ball actually have any backspin on it?

Oosthuizen chipped a little strong and missed his par putt, leaving Watson with two easy putts for the victory. Watson won his second Masters in 2014.

HOCH HICCUP

More memorable (though not always positive) moments that have occurred at the 10th include Scott Hoch's missed 2-foot putt on the first playoff hole in 1989. Hoch would have won had he holed it, but he let Nick Faldo back in and the Englishman won his first Masters with a birdie on the next hole (Faldo would win his second the following year, beating Ray Floyd in another playoff at the 11th.)

In 2013, Adam Scott became the first Australian to win the Masters when he made a superb birdie at this hole (second extra hole) in steady rain, beating Argentina's Angel Cabrera.

Ben Crenshaw holed a 60-foot putt across the green here en route to his first Masters victory in 1984.

REBOUND
Rory McIlroy proved what an immense talent he is by winning multiple majors since collapsing at the 2011 Masters, a catastrophe that could have wrecked him mentally.

(He would win again in 1995, four days after carrying the coffin at the funeral of his longtime teacher Harvey Penick.)

The 10th was also the scene, in 2014, of the only known incident of streaking (though technically it wasn't streaking as the only clothing the person removed was her shoes) at Augusta National, which takes a pretty dim view of anything that tarnishes its clean-cut image (CBS commentator Jack Whitaker was banned from working at the Masters for five years after calling the gallery a "mob" in 1966, and in 1994 Gary McCord was banned when he said the greens were so fast they were "smoothed with bikini wax." He has not worked at Augusta since.)

GEORGIA STATE OF MIND

Augusta National GC is located in the city of Augusta, Georgia, 150 miles east of Atlanta. South Carolina lies just across the Savannah River from downtown Augusta.

15th Augusta National

Location: Augusta, Georgia

Distance: 530 yards, par 5

Original course designer: Alister MacKenzie

Subsequent alterations: Perry Maxwell (1930s), Robert Trent Jones (1947), George Cobb (1960s and 1970s), Tom Fazio (late 1990s, early 2000s)

TRICK SHOT
The ideal approach shot at the 15th comes in high to clear the pond, has little or no backspin so it doesn't suck back into the water, and doesn't bound over the green into the pond in front of the 16th tee.

This was the 6th hole when the Alister MacKenzie/Bobby Jones-designed course opened officially in January 1933. A short, downhill par 5, it is now the 15th and frequently the scene of unforgettable drama at the Masters Tournament each year. The hole is called Fire Thorn after the large evergreen shrub that can be found to the left of the fairway (*Pyracantha* is a member of the rose family and produces white flowers and red berries, and can reach 20 feet in height.) MacKenzie's original hole measured 485 yards, bent a little from left to right, and was always meant to be reachable with two well-struck shots.

PERILOUS POND

The thin creek that ran in front of the green in the hole's first incarnation gave players pause before deciding whether to go for it or not (this creek, which also appeared short of the 2nd green and in front of the 1st and 17th tees, ran throughout much of the property but was largely taken out before the course opened. It was removed entirely in 1951). The creek is now a pond, of course—the expansion thought to have

SLIPPERY SLOPE
Some years the strip of grass between the pond and green is shaved low meaning balls that catch the front of the green usually roll back into the water.

occurred in 1961—and the hole 530 yards long following a 2006 renovation. The mound that stood to the right of the 1932 green was replaced by a bunker in 1957.

Players who get a good tee shot away have little trouble clearing the pond with their second, but those whose drives leak left behind a copse of pines, or right into the second cut (Augusta's fairways are maintained at $^3/_8$ of an inch, while the second-cut is an inch taller) may be forced to lay up. The pitch to the green, played from a downhill lie, is a nasty little shot, however, as the 78 yards of grass between the pond and the putting surface are usually trimmed low, meaning balls loaded with backspin can easily zip back off the green and trundle back into the water. Those fearful of the water and who therefore pitch too strong, go over the shallow green and face a delicate little chip back.

Despite these challenges, the 15th has actually been the easiest hole at the Masters. In 2014, it was the 16th most difficult, with a scoring average of 4.75, but its cumulative average over the first 78 Masters Tournaments (1934–2014) was 4.78, making it very slightly easier than the dogleg left 13th and downhill 2nd.

SHOT HEARD AROUND THE WORLD

The inaugural Masters Tournament was held in 1934 and won by Horton Smith, a native of Missouri, who shot 4-under 284 to win by one stroke from Craig Wood. The following year, Wood looked certain to go one better after birdieing the 72nd hole to complete four rounds on 6-under 282.

According to a report in the *Atlanta Journal* by Oscar Bane Keeler (O.B. to his friends), when Walter Hagen heard the applause for Wood's

RARE BIRD
Not many people saw the albatross Gene Sarazen made (seen here playing at home in Florida) at the 15th during the 1935 Augusta Invitational. But everybody's heard about it.

birdie he looked over at playing partner Gene Sarazen, who had hooked his drive well left, and said, "Well, Gene, that looks as if it's all over."

"Oh I don't know," Sarazen replied. "They might go in from anywhere."

Sarazen, born Eugenio Saraceni and known as The Squire for his dapper plus fours, made par at the 14th and asked his lanky caddie, nicknamed Stovepipe, what he needed to win.

"Oh, you need four threes Mr. Gene," was the response.

The New Yorker hit a good drive down the par 5 15th, leaving himself about 235 yards across the creek to the hole. He struck the ball firmly and watched as it cleared the water, pitched on the bank in front of the green, jumped onto the putting surface ... and rolled smoothly into the hole for an albatross/double-eagle 2. With one swing Sarazen had caught Wood on 6 under par. Hagen just smiled and shook his head.

In his book *A Golf Story: Bobby Jones, Augusta National and the Masters Tournament*, Charles Price wrote the gallery that witnessed the shot numbered about 12, one of whom was Bobby Jones, who had strolled down to the 15th to watch his two contemporaries in action—Jones was now largely retired from competitive golf, having won his Grand Slam five years before. He did play in the Augusta National Invitation Tournament 11 times between 1935 and 1948, and had finished tied for 25th before heading out to watch Sarazen and Hagen.

Sarazen made three pars to finish to tie with Wood on 282. The following day, the pair met in a 36-hole playoff, which Sarazen won 144 (level-par) to 149.

Only golf historians can tell you what happened after Sarazen's miraculous shot at the 15th, and about the resulting playoff. But while Wood is largely forgotten (you'll be glad to know he did eventually win the Masters—in 1941, shortly before he also won the U.S. Open), Sarazen's second to the 15th became known as the "Shot Heard round the World."

By winning the second Masters, Sarazen claimed his seventh and final major championship and completed the Grand Slam, having won the U.S. Open in 1922 and 1932, the British Open in 1932 and the PGA Championship in 1922, 1923 and 1933. (It should be noted, however,

Sarazen would not have regarded his accomplishment as a Grand Slam. The Bridge term, meaning a contract to win all 13 tricks, was first applied to golf by O.B. Keeler, following Bobby Jones' feat of winning the Amateur and Open Championships of the U.S. and Britain in 1930. But it wasn't until the early 1960s that the concept of the modern-day professional Grand Slam was introduced. Arnold Palmer,

talking with his friend and writer Bob Drum about Jones' Grand Slam while en route to the 1960 British Open at St. Andrews, said that the concept had more or less disappeared and that adding the British Open and PGA Championship titles to the Masters and U.S. Open he had already won that year could constitute a modern Grand Slam. Palmer recounts in his biography, *A Golfer's Life*, that he stopped off in Ireland before the Open to play in the Canada Cup alongside Sam Snead, and that Drum began spreading the word about Palmer's Grand Slam theory to the British and Irish press.)

"Had I not gone on to win, it would have been a double eagle without feathers."

Gene Sarazen speaking 60 years after he hit his famous shot on the 15th

ROUSING A SLEEPING BEAR

His number of career victories in the professional major championships had been stuck on 17 since winning the PGA Championship at Oak Hill CC in 1980. He hadn't won on the PGA Tour since his own Memorial Tournament at Muirfield Village in 1984. He had missed three cuts in seven tournaments to begin the 1986 season, so when a 46-year-old Jack Nicklaus arrived at Augusta National in April for the Masters, a tournament he hadn't won since 1975, it's not surprising very few people fancied his chances.

Tom McCollister, in the *Atlanta Journal-Constitution*, assessed every player ahead of the first round and virtually wrote Nicklaus off, saying he hadn't played well for a while and that basically he was done.

Nicklaus' friend, John Montgomery, stuck the article to the fridge door, knowing Nicklaus would see it several times

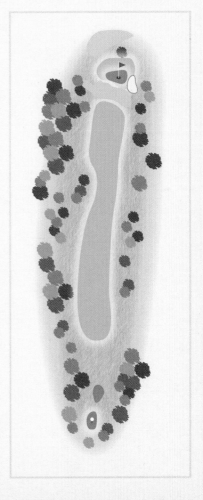

NEXT EXIT
As you exit Interstate 20 and turn on to Washington Road with its typical selection of suburban fast food restaurants, motels, and malls there is no indication whatsoever you are about to pass one of the world's most exclusive golf clubs.

TIGHT LINE
As the collection of pines jutting into the left side of the fairway has grown over time, so too has its influence. And with a strip of rough down the right, finding the fairway has become increasingly important.

Jack Nicklaus's son Jackie caddied for his father at the 1986 Masters and got a front-row seat for what was probably the most exciting nine holes of golf ever played.

each day. "He's a refrigerator freak," Montgomery told *Golf Digest* magazine in 2006. "He's there constantly out of habit."

Putting the story on the fridge door was a move obviously designed to motivate the Golden Bear (or "Olden Bear" as some in the press were calling him), but apparently it didn't work—during the first round at least. A 2-over 74, during which he hit the ball as well as he had all year, put Nicklaus in a tie for 25th, six behind co-leaders Ken Green and Bill Kratzert.

A 71 on the Friday pushed Nicklaus eight spots up the leaderboard into a tie or 17th, still six behind the leader, Seve Ballesteros. The way he was hitting the ball gave Nicklaus some encouragement, though.

"They were the two best rounds I'd played all year," he said, 20 years later. But though he'd struck the ball beautifully, his large-headed MacGregor Response ZT putter was letting him down badly. In the first round, Nicklaus had had 11 putts inside 15 feet, and made just one. A day later, he put it inside 15 feet 12 times and made four.

Saturday's 69 took Nicklaus to 2 under par and into a tie for ninth, four back of Greg Norman and three behind Nick Price, who shot a new course record 63.

Going into the final 18 holes, Nicklaus thought a 65 would be good enough to win. He birdied the par 5 2nd, but bogeyed the short 4th and began with five 4s. At the 8th he got lucky after a wayward drive to the right, his ball finding a good lie and, with a gap in the trees ahead of him, he was able to hit a 3-wood just short of the green. He got out safely with a par, but still had a dozen players in front of him. At the 9th he made his second birdie of the round, reaching the turn in 35. He headed to the 10th tee at 3 under par.

> **"I knew that if I could make a putt, I could scare somebody."**
>
> *Jack Nicklaus on his comeback effort at the 1986 Masters*

Long, snaking birdie putts at the 10th and 11th both went down, so as he strode to the 12th tee, Nicklaus was just two off the lead. He pulled his tee shot badly, though, and made a bogey.

At the 13th, he hit a superb 3-iron onto the green and made birdie. He then made par at the 14th and hit a good drive down the 15th.

Kite and Ballesteros still held onto the lead, Ballesteros making his second eagle of the round at the 13th. The Spaniard appeared to be in the driving seat.

As he assessed his second to the 15th, Nicklaus asked his son Jackie, who was caddying for him that week, how far a 3 might go—an eagle 3, not a 3-iron. From a little over 200 yards, he hit a 4-iron that came in high, landed softly and spun left, finishing about 12 feet from the hole. He made the putt, then hit another sensational iron shot at the short 16th, adding another birdie.

HISTORY MAKERS
A plaque showing Masters Tournaments winners from 1969 to 1984—including the fourth and fifth of Jack Nicklaus' record six victories. Seve Ballesteros's two wins are recorded here also.

The delightful clubhouse at Augusta National was built in 1854 and was the home of indigo plantation owner Dennis Redmond. The Champions Locker Room, where Masters winners now share a small space, is on the second floor.

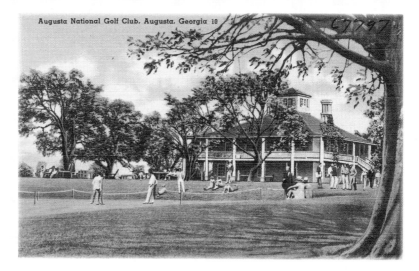

Augusta National Golf Club, Augusta, Georgia 10

Ballesteros, meanwhile, was in the middle of the 15th fairway with 198 yards remaining. At first he thought a 5-iron was the right club, but after waiting several minutes for Tom Watson and Tommy Nakajima to clear the green, he changed to a 4-iron.

Somewhere in the middle of his downswing, Ballesteros eased up, perhaps subconsciously thinking he had too much club. The blade struck the ground a little behind the ball, which ducked low and left into the pond. It was a horrible shot, and a number of people in the crowd cheered, no doubt excited at the increasing likelihood of a Nicklaus victory. Seve was crushed, and though he did win another British Open—at Royal Lytham & St. Annes in 1988—some said he wasn't quite the same player again, at Augusta especially.

At the 17th, Nicklaus coaxed a 12-footer down the hill into the hole for another birdie and, at 9-under, he led for the first time. A par at the last, after hitting his approach putt from 40 feet short of the hole to within a few inches, saw him home in 30 and on top of the leaderboard at 9-under 279.

With Ballesteros out of the picture, Kite and Norman both had chances to tie but came up just short. Nicklaus had won a sixth Green Jacket.

It's hard to pick just one shot from that amazing day that sums up the quality of Nicklaus' back nine. The holed putts at the 10th, 11th and 17th were all pretty special, as was the tremendous lag putt at the 18th. His second to the 13th was spectacular and the near ace at the 16th another crucial moment. But perhaps none were better than the approach to the 15th.

"I loved the way that shot set up, because I could go right at the pin," Nicklaus said years later. "At Augusta you always have to protect one side of the hole—there's danger if you miss it to the left or right, depending on where the hole is. On 15 that day, I had a lot of confidence standing over the ball. I chose a 4-iron and hit the ball solid, very high."

The 15th was pivotal. Not only did Nicklaus make an eagle to jump within two of Ballesteros, it was where Seve came to grief hitting a shot that would haunt him for years.

TIGER DROPS A BOMBSHELL

The 15th was front and center again at the 2013 Masters when four-time champion Tiger Woods took a dubious drop following a bizarre and very unfortunate incident when his third shot hit the flagstick and ricocheted back into the water. Woods dropped and proceeded to get up and down for what he, and everyone else, assumed was a bogey. He signed for a 71. Later though, he said on camera that he had knowingly dropped 2 yards further back from the spot where he had played the original shot—a violation of Rule 26-1a, which states if you choose to return to the original spot you must play a ball "as nearly as possible at the spot from which the original ball was last played."

No one made much of it that eve-ning, but a TV viewer (who happened to be Champions Tour player David Eger, who had worked as the USGA's Senior Director of Rules and Competition from 1992 to 1995) called in to question

"I could see that the fairway was spotless the first time he played the shot and there was that divot hole, maybe 3 or 4 feet in front of where he played after the drop."

David Eger's account of Woods' illegal drop

what had happened. As a result, Woods was summoned to the club early Saturday morning to explain. It became clear his drop was indeed illegal, which meant he was assessed a two-shot penalty and had there-fore signed for the wrong score—something that would have led to auto-matic disqualification before April 2011 when the USGA and R&A revised Decision 33–7/4.5 to allow a committee to waive disqualification if it felt the player was "not aware he had breached a Rule because of facts he did not know and could not reasonably have discovered prior to returning his scorecard."

Fred Ridley, Chairman of the Masters Competition Committee, decided to grant Woods that waiver. Plenty of people in the media argued Woods should have done what they said was the honorable thing and disqualified himself. He saw no reason to, however, and carded a third-round 70 then another 70 on the final day to finish the tournament at 5 under par and tied for fourth.

17th Augusta National

Location: Augusta, Georgia

Distance: 440 yards, par 4

Original course designer: Alister MacKenzie

Subsequent alterations: Perry Maxwell (1930s), Robert Trent Jones (1947), George Cobb (1960s and 1970s), Tom Fazio (late 1990s, early 2000s)

The 17th goes by Nandina, commonly known as Heavenly Bamboo, which is odd given that it isn't a bamboo at all but an evergreen shrub with creamy-white flowers and poisonous, bright red berries. The hole moves slightly uphill, bends subtly to the left and, for many years, was known best not for the Nandina that grows close to the members' tee but the towering loblolly pine that stood just to the left of the fairway, about halfway up the hole (see Eisenhower Tree). Like virtually every other hole at Augusta, the 17th is very different now to how it looked originally. Augusta National is constantly tweaking its holes, and the 17th has certainly seen its share of alterations.

MAXWELL'S MISTAKE?
The nature of the 17th hole has altered a great deal since 1933. Two front bunkers now make a run-up shot impractical.

RANKLED ROBERTS

Alister MacKenzie, the architect course-owner Bobby Jones chose to assist him with the design, envisioned a bunkerless hole of 400 yards. He modeled the wide, shallow green on the 14th green at St. Andrews, with the left side sloping off to the left, meaning that to get the ball close to the hole a run-up shot would work best. For some reason, though, the club rejected the original plan and had Perry Maxwell, a former design partner of MacKenzie's, modify the hole. Maxwell not only added three bunkers in front of the green—one right, two left—he also raised the left side of the putting surface. The changes meant approach shots now needed to come in high, pitch and stop rather than run along the ground.

The strategy for playing MacKenzie's 17th was lost, and club chairman, the iron-willed Clifford Roberts who was never afraid to do whatever he thought was in the best interests of the club, wasn't happy.

> **"This is supposed to be a run-up hole. You have changed the character of the hole by inviting players to pitch it to the green."**
>
> *Clifford Roberts remarking upon*
> *Maxwell's changes to hole 17*

Considering how opposed Roberts was to Maxwell's modifications, it seems strange he would allow him to make them. One assumes he knew what Maxwell planned before he started work. It's odder still perhaps that the bunkers and new green remained in place. Architect George Cobb did remove one bunker from the left side in 1967, the year he also added a spectator mound to the left of the green, but the two others are still there.

In 1999, the hole was lengthened by 25 yards and pines added down the left side, beyond the Eisenhower Tree. And in 2005 the tee was pushed back again, making the hole 440 yards. More mature pines were planted down the left, making the 17th one of the narrowest drives on the course. One wonders what MacKenzie would make of the hole today.

EISENHOWER TREE

President Dwight Eisenhower, an avid golfer and Augusta National member from 1948 to 1969, had a habit of hitting a loblolly pine to the left of the 17th fairway so often he lobbied to have it taken down during a club meeting in 1956. The members, led by Clifford Roberts, rejected the president's appeal, however.

FRIENDLY
FOURBALL
President Dwight Eisenhower (second from left) was a golf fanatic and Augusta National member. His playing companions for this 1953 round were (from left) Byron Nelson, Ben Hogan, and club chairman Clifford Roberts.

The tree, just a 210-yard shot from the Masters tee-markers, grew to a height of about 70 feet and was thought to be 100–125 years old. For 40 years or more, Ike's Tree was an iconic landmark on a course full of them, and it was a great shame when, in February 2014, the club was forced to remove it after it sustained fatal damage during an ice storm.

Besides Eisenhower, one or two other golfers were inconvenienced by the pine. The 1973 Masters champion Tommy Aaron once hit a drive into the tree and, when he arrived at the base of the trunk, neither he nor any of the patrons nearby could find it. Aaron had to return to the tee and hit another drive. The following day, he hit left on the 17th again and, as he neared the tree, his ball from the previous round fell to the ground. Jack Nicklaus wasn't buying it. "I'm not sure I believe it," he said.

Aaron insisted it was his ball, though. "I know it was mine because it had a marking on it and it was a Pinnacle," he said in 2013. "I know Nicklaus didn't believe it, but I've got a witness—my caddie, Rhett Sinclair."

In the third round of the 2011 Masters, Tiger Woods' drive came to rest on pine straw beneath the tree, the lowest branches of which prevented the four-time Masters winner from addressing the ball conventionally. Crouching low, Woods was unable to maintain good balance on the straw and slipped as he played his second shot, causing damage to his left knee and left Achilles tendon. The shot actually turned out quite well though, reaching the front bunker 200 yards ahead. He made his par 4, and the following day shot 67 to finish tied fourth.

But the pain in his Achilles tendon flared up two weeks later at the Players Championship, from which he had to withdraw after nine holes. He wouldn't play again until August.

What a Stupid I am

Tiger Woods, President Eisenhower and Tommy Aaron certainly aren't the only players for whom the 17th was a major stumbling block. No doubt Roberto De Vicenzo has a fairly negative view of the hole too. That said, the Argentinian actually played it very well in the final round of the 1968 Masters, making a birdie 3. It was what happened afterwards that grieves him so.

Playing with Aaron, De Vicenzo was locked in a back-nine battle for the Green Jacket with Bob Goalby, two groups behind. He made a birdie at the 15th then the 17th, but finished with a bogey 5 on the uphill 18th for a 65 and a 72-hole total of 14-under 276.

Or so he, and everyone else, thought. After De Vicenzo signed his card then walked away from the scoring table, Aaron noticed a discrepancy. The 18 hole scores on the reigning Open champion's card added up to 66, not 65. Aaron had put his playing partner down for a 4 on the 17th.

Under the rules of the game, anyone signing for a score lower than that he actually makes is disqualified. Sign for a score higher than you make though and the higher score stands. There was no penalty and he wasn't disqualified, De Vicenzo had just signed for more strokes than he actually hit. The Masters Tournament Committee repaired to one of the cottages besides the 10th fairway to deliberate.

Goalby, meanwhile, shot 4 under par from the 13th to the 15th and finished with a 6-under 66 to complete the four rounds on 11-under 277. He assumed he had tied with De Vicenzo.

But the decision was made that De Vicenzo's final round score would be 66 and his four-round total 278, one behind Goalby. Through no fault of his own (well, he could have checked his card a little better) and because of Aaron's unfortunate and, it's safe to say, unpremeditated mistake, De Vicenzo missed out on the opportunity to win his second major.

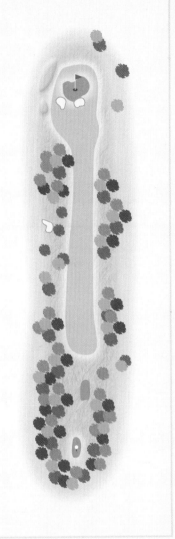

IRON OUT THE KINKS
In its last few years, the Eisenhower Tree made the 17th a slight right-to-left dogleg. But with the tree gone, the hole is more or less straight. At least, it was for the 2014 Masters.

"It's a shame. He should've checked his scorecard."

Tommy Aaron's less-than-sympathetic response to De Vicenzo's error

1936

10th Colonial

Location: Fort Worth, Texas

Distance: 408 yards, par 4

Original course designer: John Bredemus

Subsequent alterations: Perry Maxwell (1940), Keith Foster (2008)

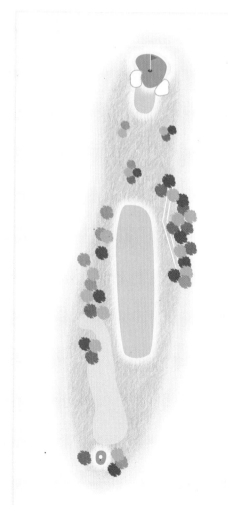

Colonial Country Club was founded by Marvin Leonard, a Fort Worth businessman known as The Merchant, who had a reputation for not stopping until he got exactly what he wanted. He took up golf at the age of 32 and soon became a fan of the bent grass greens he played in the northern states. Determined to introduce bent grass to Texas, where bumpy Bermuda surfaces were the norm, he offered to install two new greens at River Crest GC, where he was a member, at his own expense. But the club president, tired of Leonard's eccentricities, told him to go and build his own course. So he did. Designed largely by John Bredemus, with input from Perry Maxwell, it opened in January 1936 and hosted the U.S. Open in 1941 (won by Craig Wood) before becoming a regular stop on the PGA Tour. Its most celebrated day, however, would come 67 years after opening when a Scandinavian lady came to visit.

HIT IT LIKE A GIRL

In 1938, Mildred Didrikson Zaharias (better known as Babe Zaharias) played in the Los Angeles Open against the guys. A former Olympic athlete (she won two gold medals and one silver at the 1932 Games) who had excelled at virtually every sport she ever tried, and who took up golf at the age of 24, Zaharias had been denied amateur status owing to her athletic record, so thought she'd try her hand against the male pros. She shot 81, 84 and missed the cut. But seven years later she was back, having legitimately qualified for the tournament. This time

SMOOTH THE WAY
A mid-length par 4 with an uncomplicated tee shot was just the sort of hole Annika Sörenstam needed to ease her into the 2003 Colonial tournament.

WHERE THE WEST BEGINS
Colonial CC is located 4 miles southwest of downtown Fort Worth, Texas, and 40 miles west of Dallas.

she did make the 36-hole cut, but shot 79 in the third round to miss the
54-hole cut they used in those days. In the next two weeks, she also
played in the Phoenix Open and Tucson Open, making the cut both
times and finishing 33rd and 42nd, respectively.

Zaharias was a phenomenon, a one-off and, though a handful of
other female golfers—Mickey Wright, Kathy Whitworth, Nancy Lopez,
Laura Davies—might conceivably have made a PGA Tour cut after her,
none tried. In 2003, however, 58 years after Zaharias had teed it up with
the men, Swedish star Annika Sörenstam received an invitation from
the tournament sponsors to play at Colonial.

Sörenstam, then 32, accepted, despite the obvious potential draw-
backs. Some called it a cheap publicity stunt, some said she would be
jeopardizing the reputation of the Ladies Professional Golfers' Association (LPGA) Tour, some said she had more to lose than gain, and one
well-known player said she had no business being there and that he
would pull out of the tournament if they were drawn together.

Sörenstam was certainly aware of the controversy her appearance
was causing, but was determined to prove she was worthy of the invite.
She had won 43 events on the LPGA Tour prior to Colonial, including
four majors. In 2001, she shot a 59 at Moon Valley CC in Phoenix. Clearly,
she was the best female golfer in the world, and her appearance at
Colonial was generating a great deal of interest.

Media representatives from all over the world were there, and thousands of people ringed the 10th tee to watch her opening shot, craning
over the ropes, hanging out of the clubhouse windows and balancing in
the trees. The buzz was substantial as the crowd waited for Sörenstam to
be announced, the applause loud and spontaneous when she was called

to the tee, the silence deafening as she put her ball on a peg and prepared to hit. It's no wonder she felt more nervous than she ever had before.

Thanks to the hundreds of thousands of practice balls she had hit in her life, she eased into autopilot and struck a 243-yard 4-wood (a club she normally hit 220–225 yards) straight down the middle. Her legs buckled as she feigned a collapse, and the crowds loved her for it. The steeliest of players whose on-course demeanor usually betrayed little or no emotion was suddenly playing to the gallery.

"Annika, you da man!"

Gallery member as Sörenstam is announced on the tee

If any PGA Tour course was going to suit Sörenstam, it was Colonial. At 7,080 yards it was considerably longer than any course on the LPGA Tour, but one of a small number of PGA Tour venues that didn't require 300-yard-plus drives off every tee. At Colonial, strategy, accuracy and sagacity would work better than the bomb-and-gouge approach encouraged by so many other Tour courses.

GIRL POWER
Sweden's Annika Sörenstam may not have made the cut at the Colonial (then sponsored by Bank of America) in 2003, but she certainly impressed and inspired a lot of people.

At the 10th (her first), Sörenstam knocked a 9-iron to 17 feet and two-putted for a par. The relief was evident, but she remained calm and composed the whole way round, acknowledging the support of the crowd and engaging with her playing partners—Aaron Barber and Dean Wilson. She made a birdie at the fourth hole to move to 1 under par, and didn't make a bogey until her 14th where she three-putted from about 60 feet. She missed just one fairway all day, and actually had a birdie putt on all 18 holes.

Wilson said Sörenstam hit the ball like a machine and added he had stopped watching and that he had never played with anyone who hadn't missed a shot. Sadly though, Sörenstam's putting let her down. Had she taken the Tour average 28 or 29 putts, she would likely have shot in the mid sixties. As it was, her 37 putts gave her a 1-over 71 that put her in a tie for 73rd at the end of day one. She had missed out on her goal of shooting an even-par round, but she did have the consolation of beating 25 men.

That Sörenstam shot 74 the following day and missed the cut by four shots mattered not a jot. Yes, it would have been fantastic had she hung on to the weekend, but she was satisfied she had done enough and she certainly hadn't embarrassed herself or the Tour she came from. The following week, the Swede won on the LPGA Tour, and the week after that she added the LPGA Championship—her fifth major. It wasn't long before she had her sixth, winning the Women's British Open at Royal Lytham in August. Sörenstam finished her career with 93 professional victories worldwide, including 10 major championships.

MORE TO COME?
After an amazing junior career, everyone assumed Michelle Wie would dominate the LPGA Tour. Four Tour victories in six years suggest that hasn't happened ... yet. Still only 25, she has plenty of time to create her legend.

FOLLOWING ANNIKA

✦

Two months after Sörenstam played at Colonial, a teaching pro from Connecticut named Suzy Whaley became the next woman to play on the PGA Tour when she took on the fellas at the Greater Hartford Open. She had qualified by winning the previous year's Connecticut PGA Section Championship. She too received warm support from the crowd but, like Sörenstam, missed the cut after rounds of 75 and 78. The only other woman to play a PGA Tour event this century was actually a girl—Michelle Wie (pictured below), who was invited to her first Sony Open in Hawaii in 2004, at the age of 14. She shot a 68 in the second round, but missed the cut by a shot. She played three more Sony Opens and three other PGA Tour events missing the weekend each time.

18th Turnberry (Ailsa)

Location: Turnberry, Ayrshire, Scotland

Distance: 461 yards, par 4

Original course designer: Willie Fernie

Subsequent alterations: James Braid (1923), C.K. Hutchison (1938), Phillip Mackenzie Ross (1951), Martin Ebert, Tom Mackenzie (2009)

The Marquess of Ailsa, a member of the board of the South-Western Railway company, saw the potential for a golf course on his property linked to a railway line and had Willie Fernie, the professional at Royal Troon, lay out Turnberry's first holes, which opened in July 1901 (called Course 1, it was a highly acclaimed links that measured well over 6,000 yards. Course 2 was completed in 1909). The railway, an extension of the Glasgow–Ayr line which ran between Ayr and Girvan, followed five years later, and then the famous, whitewashed hotel which overlooks the links, and which was built by the railway company, opened in May 1906. In 1917, the land was appropriated by the Royal Flying Corps, which built an aerodrome that served as an air gunnery school during World War I. It closed in 1918. Five years later, James Braid restored Course 2 and, in 1926, Course 1 was also refurbished.

RAF TURNBERRY

After the refurbishment, Course 1 became the Ailsa Course, Course 2 the Arran. In 1938, Major C.K. Hutchison redesigned the Ailsa, but his work did not last long as the world went to war for a second time. Turnberry was taken over in 1942 by the Royal Air Force, which built three concrete runways over the courses—though how much of them were affected and which parts isn't exactly clear. Over 1,200 men were stationed at RAF Turnberry, the pilots trained in torpedo bombing.

Following World War II, it was feared the courses would never be rebuilt, but the chairman of British Transport Hotels—a subsidiary of the British Railways Board that now owned Turnberry—had prominent seed company Sutton & Sons plough the land to create ridges, hillocks, depressions and mounds. Philip Mackenzie Ross was then engaged to redesign the Ailsa where, it is thought, he stuck closely to Hutchison's routing. Even so, Ross did build entirely new holes and deserves most of the credit for the course, which reopened in 1951. Martin Ebert and Tom Mackenzie added some length, some bunkers and shifted a couple of fairways prior to the 2009 British Open, the course's fourth Open and another humdinger.

THE DUEL IN THE SUN

Twenty-six years after Mackenzie Ross' redesign of the Ailsa was complete, the course hosted its first British Open. It measured 6,875 yards and, thanks to a dry spell, the fairways were baked hard and running fast. The first-round leader was America's John Schroeder, who had earned his only PGA Tour victory in 1973. Round in 4-under 66, the 32-year-old had a one-stroke lead over England's Martin Foster.

Though the very top of the leaderboard might have had the galleries scratching their heads, somewhat more familiar names weren't very far behind. Lee Trevino, Jack Nicklaus and Tom Watson each shot 68, and a shot behind them were the previous year's leading lights Johnny Miller and Seve Ballesteros.

It was another largely unknown American that stole the lead after 36 holes, however, Roger Maltbie shooting a 66 to go with an opening 71. At 3 under, he was a shot clear of the fearsome threesome of Americans who had been joined by Hubert Green, winner of the U.S. Open at Southern Hills in Oklahoma just a month before. Tied for sixth was American Mark Hayes who shot a 7-under 63—two shots better than the previous record low at the British Open.

Nicklaus and Watson were paired together for the third round. At 37 and with 14 major wins, Nicklaus was the game's best player and had been for more than a decade. Naturally he was favored to establish his dominance and take control of the tournament.

Sure enough, he shot a superb 5-under 65 to complete three rounds in 7-under 203. But Watson who had beaten Nicklaus by two to win the Masters earlier that year, matched him stroke for stroke, recording a 65 of his own. With a round to go, the two held a three-stroke advantage over Ben Crenshaw.

On a gloriously hot and sunny day, Nicklaus and Watson squared off again, trading birdies and leaving the rest of the field choking on their dust. Nicklaus started stronger, going 3-up through four holes. If that sounds like a matchplay score, well that's pretty much what this contest amounted to. At the end of the day, Green, who finished third, would say he had won the "other tournament."

Watson was back on level terms after a birdie at the 8th, however, then at the 9th the players had to take evasive action when the galleries, overcome with excitement, spilled on to the fairway. It was 15 minutes before another shot was played, Watson missing the green and taking a bogey to be out in 34, one behind Nicklaus.

Nicklaus birdied the 12th and was 2-up again. But Watson wouldn't go away, making a birdie at the 13th to claw a shot back. Still one behind

after 14, Watson pulled his tee shot at the par 3 15th, the ball finishing a few feet to the left of the green, but 60 feet from the hole. He took his putter and though the ball bobbled on the rough grass before reaching the putting surface, it ran smoothly across the width of the green and into the hole for a birdie 2 to tie.

On the 16th tee, Watson looked at Nicklaus and said, "This is what it's all about, isn't it?" "You bet it is," replied Nicklaus. How cool is that? The game's two best players, two single-minded competitors locking horns but able to stand back for a moment and appreciate just how momentous an occasion this was.

At the par 5 17th, Watson was on in two after a well-struck 3-iron, Nicklaus short and right of the green. He chipped up to about three and a half feet, before Watson two-putted for another birdie. Nicklaus needed to hole his putt to remain level with Watson at 11 under, but pulled it left, the ball not even touching the hole. Now up by one, Watson played conservatively down the dogleg left 18th, hitting a

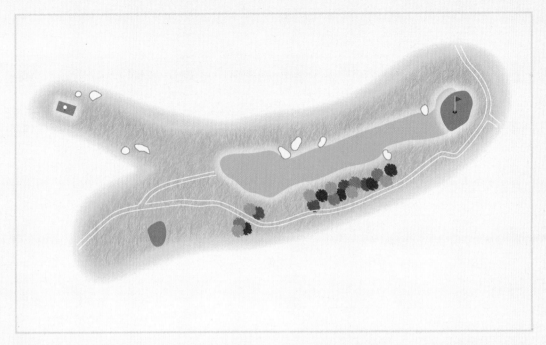

1-iron to the left half of the fairway. Nicklaus took a driver, hoping to gain whatever advantage he could. He pushed the shot into the rough on the right, however, and with his ball sitting down close to a gorse bush, he appeared to have blown his chances of winning a third Claret Jug.

Watson approached the green first, striping a majestic 7-iron that came to an abrupt halt just a couple of feet from the hole—surely the hammer blow. Nicklaus' backswing was impeded by the gorse bush, but he swung his 8-iron so hard he smashed the ball out of its grassy lie and managed to get it all the way to the green—35 feet right of the hole.

Of course, he holed the putt.

But with the crowd still murmuring with delight, Watson stepped up and briskly knocked in his putt for a second consecutive 65, a total of 268, and his second Open title.

The contest between Nicklaus and Watson at Turnberry in 1977 became known as the "Duel in the Sun" (now the name of the 18th hole). Golf had never before seen two such enthralling days. Those who saw it will tell you it hasn't since.

DRAW THE LINE
There are two teeing grounds at the 18th. For visitors, the hole plays fairly straight, but for championships the back tee is used turning the hole into a right-to-left dogleg and making a draw of the tee ideal.

RUGGED
Turnberry is located on the South Ayrshire coast, 20 miles south of Prestwick and 24 miles from Troon.

"I gave you my best shot, but it wasn't good enough."

Jack Nicklaus to Tom Watson as they walked off the 18th green

WATSON'S WOE

Tom Watson, now 59 with five Open titles and one replaced hip (left), was back at Turnberry in 2009 for his 33rd British Open appearance. An opening 65 put him in a tie for second, then a second-round 70 gave him a share of the halfway lead with fellow American Steve Marino.

Marino struggled to a 76 on the Saturday, but Watson kept steady with a 71 that gave him a one-stroke lead going into the final round.

Could he become the oldest winner of the Open, indeed any major? Julius Boros was 48 years, 4 months and 18 days old when he won the 1968 USPGA Championship at Pecan Valley in San Antonio, Texas. The oldest winner of the Open was Tom Morris Sr., who won his fourth Championship Belt in 1867 at the age of 46 years, 3 months and 10 days.

Watson was 1 over for the day when he boarded the 18th tee. America's Stewart Cink had closed with a 69 to finish 72 holes on 2-under 278, and all Watson needed to beat it was a par 4. He found the fairway safely from the tee and, with a little helping breeze felt all he needed for his 180-yard second was a 9-iron. But he changed his mind, eventually deciding on one more club.

He struck the 8-iron beautifully and, with the ball halfway to the hole, said, "I like it." It pitched on the front of the green but, instead of

No Cigar
In 2009, Tom Watson came excruciatingly close to winning his second Turnberry Open and record-equaling sixth overall. But Stewart Cink (in green) outlasted him in a four-hole playoff.

checking up and leaving an easy two putts for victory, the ball bounced hard and ran past the flag and over the green, rolling down a slope then nestling against 2-inch-tall grass about 30 feet from the hole.

He now had a choice—putt or chip. Watson had always said your worst putt is better than your worst chip so, adhering to his own advice it seemed, he took out the putter and struck the ball a little more cleanly than he had anticipated perhaps. The ball rolled 6 feet past the hole, leaving just the sort of putt Watson had often had problems with during his impressive career.

Just as it had been watching Watson on the same green 32 years before, the crowd was gripped with tension and excitement, unable to settle knowing that if Watson holed his putt they would be telling the story of how they were there for the rest of their lives.

Sadly, Watson hit an awful putt, the ball coming up short and right of the cup. The bogey put him on the same score as Cink. A four-hole playoff would be needed to separate the two. The only fans in the gallery not wanting Watson to win were probably Cink's family—no reflection on the easy-going Georgian, just a gauge of how much everyone wanted Watson to create history.

But he didn't have it. Watson was clearly spent, emotionally and physically. He shot 4 over for the four extra holes, finishing six behind Cink, who birdied the 17th and 18th to win his first major championship. Watson had been the most significant part of what was probably the greatest ever British Open, at Turnberry in 1977. In 2009 he was part of its biggest anticlimax. "It would have been a hell of a story, wouldn't it?" Watson remarked.

STORMIN' NORMAN

✦

Turnberry's two other Opens didn't quite live up to the excitement of 1977 and 2009, but they certainly had their moments. Zimbabwe's Nick Price won in 1994, holing a 50-foot eagle putt at the 71st hole en route to a one-shot win over Sweden's Jesper Parnevik. And in 1986, Australia's Greg Norman won the first of his two Open titles after shooting an incredible 63 in strong winds in the second round. It would have been 62 had he not three-putted the 18th green.

7th Torrey Pines (South)

Location: La Jolla, California

Distance: 462 yards, par 4

Original course designer: William F. Bell

Subsequent alterations: Billy Casper and David Rainville (1973), Rees Jones (2001)

Built on spectacular cliffs high above the Pacific Ocean 15 miles north of downtown San Diego (on the former site of Camp Callan, a U.S. Army anti-aircraft training center used during World War II), Torrey Pines South was designed by William F. Bell operating under the name William P. Bell and Son out of respect for his father, who died two years before the City of San Diego gave William F. the go-ahead to start building. Bell couldn't make the best use of the site, however, as all the best land on the cliffs was owned by the State of California. Rees Jones completed an extensive remodel in 2001, adding over 500 yards. It is one of only two municipally owned courses to have hosted the U.S. Open (Bethpage Black in New York is the other. Chambers Bay near Seattle will make it three in 2015).

> "I'm going to play in the U.S. Open, and I'm going to win."
>
> *Tiger Woods to his doctor after being advised to withdraw from the 2008 U.S. Open.*

BEWARE THE INJURED GOLFER

After arthroscopic surgery to repair damaged cartilage in his troublesome left knee in April 2008, Tiger Woods needed to adhere closely to his rehabilitation program if he was to be ready in time for June's U.S. Open. Not altogether surprisingly, he pushed a little hard and suffered two stress fractures in his left tibia. His doctor strongly recommended he withdraw.

Woods wasn't having it. It was the U.S. Open and he loved Torrey Pines, having won six PGA Tour events there in his career. And he got off

HIGH TOP
The 7th hole on the South Course at Torrey Pines bends slightly to the right and finishes on a green perched high above the canyon that cuts into the course from the coast.

to a good start, shooting 72, 68 to easily make the cut. A 70 on Saturday, with two eagles in his last six holes, moved him to the top of the leaderboard on 3-under 210.

Woods had entered the final round of a major with the lead, or a share of it, 13 times before, and had won every time. But he double-bogeyed the 1st for the third time that week, and with a bogey at the 2nd, he fell out of the lead—now a shot behind Westwood and two behind Rocco Mediate. By the turn, Westwood was in front, at 2 under par. Woods birdied the 9th and the 11th to get to 2 under, but bogeyed the 13th and 15th.

It was Mediate who was playing the steadiest, though, a group in front of Woods and Westwood. The 45-year-old Pennsylvanian was round in 71 for a four-round total of 1-under 283.

Woods and Westwood needed to birdie the last to tie.

The Englishman's birdie putt from 15 feet slipped by, but Woods' 12-footer bounced its way to the hole over the scuffed-up *Poa annua* surface, caught the right edge and dropped in.

After 10 holes of Monday's 18-hole playoff (the U.S. Open remains the only tournament with an 18-hole playoff—all other events have changed to sudden death or a three/four-hole aggregate), Woods held a three-shot lead at even-par. But Mediate fought back gamely, making a birdie at the 13th, 14th and 15th to take a one-stroke cushion to the 16th tee. He took it to the 18th tee too, but could manage only a par on the par 5 closing hole while Woods birdied. Both were round in even-par 71, meaning sudden death extra holes.

They began at the 462-yard, dogleg right 7th where Woods found the fairway but Mediate went well left. Mediate struggled thereafter, eventually holing out for 5. Woods' solid par 4 was good enough for his 14th major victory.

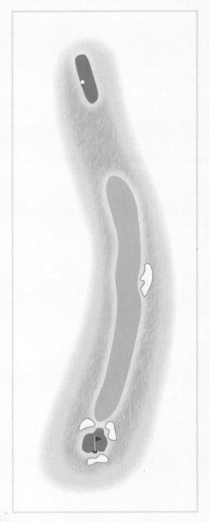

FADE AWAY
With its gentle bend to the right, the 7th sets up perfectly for a power fade. (Just aim at the bunker on the left.)

HEAR ME ROAR
Tiger Woods' fighting spirit shone, as it so often has through his illustrious career, when he battled severe pain in his left leg, to win at Torrey Pines.

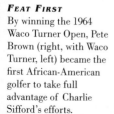

1970

18th Falconhead

Location: Burneyville, Oklahoma

Distance: 287 yards, par 4

Original course designer: Robert Dunning

Subsequent alterations: Robert Trent Jones (1970)

NB: Waco Turner sold his course in 1969. In 1970, new owners hired Robert Trent Jones to redesign it. The 18th is now a 287-yard par 4, and the development called Falconhead Resort.

Despite our love for the game, we need to recognize golf is often far from the accessible, inclusive, tolerant collective it should be. Disappointingly, people have used golf as a means to distance themselves from certain parts of society, be it through economic, gender or racially based motives. Some high-profile British golf clubs continue to exclude women (though the R&A importantly voted to become a mixed-membership club in September 2014), and in the U.S. the PGA of America included a "Caucasians only" clause in its constitution from 1934 to 1961. But it wasn't until three years after the ban was lifted that an African-American man finally won on the PGA Tour—at Turner's Lodge, now Falconhead.

BROWN'S HISTORIC VICTORY

Until November 1961—the point at which the PGA of America reluctantly removed its noxious white-only clause, after Stanley Mosk, California's Attorney General, had stopped the organization from holding its tournaments on the state's public courses unless it dropped the restriction—black professionals had very few opportunities to make a living from the game of golf. The United Golf Association (UGA), formed in 1926, did offer them a place to compete, but the purses were low: usually $500 for the winner.

Mosk demonstrated how Charlie Sifford, who had beaten some of the Tour's biggest names at the 1957 Long Beach Open (not sanctioned by the PGA), was being denied certain civil liberties. The PGA eventually awarded Sifford full membership in 1964, but by that time he was long past his prime. He did win twice—the 1967 Greater Hartford Open and Los Angeles Open two years later—but he wasn't the first black man to win on the PGA Tour.

FEAT FIRST
By winning the 1964 Waco Turner Open, Pete Brown (right, with Waco Turner, left) became the first African-American golfer to take full advantage of Charlie Sifford's efforts.

That distinction belongs to Pete Brown, a then-29-year-old from Mississippi who won the 1964 Waco Turner Open in Burneyville, Oklahoma. The tournament was founded by oil millionaire Waco Turner, a shameless eccentric who built his own course, Turner's Lodge, in 1954, after being run out of Dornick Hills CC in Ardmore, Oklahoma. During his tournament (which ran from 1961 to 1964), Turner would walk around the course handing out cash to anyone he saw playing a good shot, and he was reported to have carried two revolvers in case the black players experienced any hostility.

Brown and Sifford entered the final round a shot behind third-round leader Dudley Wysong. Sifford and Wysong faltered however, allowing Brown to pull away. But Dan Sikes had finished with a 67 to complete four rounds on 281. Brown needed to par the 232-yard 18th for 8-under 280.

His 2-iron tee shot found the left rough, but he hit an excellent flop shot to 3 feet.

He rolled in the putt to make history—though the significance of the stroke would not sink in until a few hours later. Brown would take six years to win again—at the San Diego Open in a playoff with reigning Open Champion Tony Jacklin.

In May 2014, a sculpture by Mario Chiodo titled *The DNA of the Golf Swing*, showing 13 African-American golfers, went on display at the World Golf Hall of Fame (WGHOF) in St. Augustine, Florida, as part of an exhibition named "Honoring the Legacy: A Tribute to African-Americans in Golf."

The golfers depicted were John Shippen, Bill Spiller, Joe Louis (former heavyweight boxing champion and a fine golfer who supported several black professionals financially), Ted Rhodes, Charlie Sifford (also awarded an honorary doctorate by St. Andrews University in 2006 and the Presidential Medal of Freedom in 2014), Ann Gregory, Bill Powell, Althea Gibson, Lee Elder (the first African-American to play the Masters), Calvin Peete, Bill Dickey and, of course, Pete Brown.

There's also space for a certain Tiger Woods.

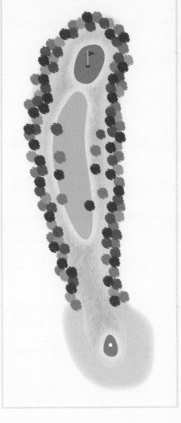

EXTENSIONS
When Robert Trent Jones redesigned the course in 1970, he pushed the tee at the 18th back into the lake, turning a 232-yard par 3 into a short par 4.

LITTLE COURSE ON THE PRAIRIE
The Falconhead Resort is situated 2 miles north of the Red River, and 105 miles north of Dallas.

"In essence, I owe my entire career to them and their pioneering efforts."

Tiger Woods on the African-American golfers who came before him and just wanted to test their games against the best

9th Colonial

Location: Cordova, Tennessee

Distance: 405 yards, par 4

Original course designer: Joe Finger

AL'S WELL THAT ENDS WELL
If you needed to make a birdie 3 to be the first man on the PGA Tour to go below 60, you couldn't ask for much more than this gentle 405-yarder.

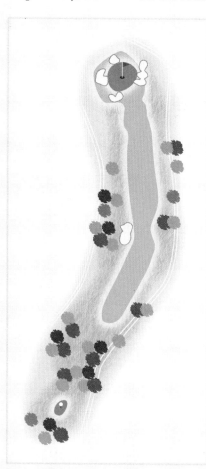

In the second round of the 1977 Danny Thomas Memphis Classic at Colonial CC in Cordova, Tennessee, Al Geiberger shot 59. The 1976 PGA champion and nine-time PGA Tour winner was the first man to go under 60 on the PGA Tour, and he did so with one eagle and 11 birdies, the last of them on the 405-yard 9th—his last hole of the day.

GEIBERGER'S GLORY

Geiberger had shot an opening 72 on the 7,193-yard Joe Finger-designed South Course, and began the second round on the 10th hole. He birdied the 10th and 12th (his first and third) but was still 2 under for the round after five holes, and therefore giving little indication of what was in store.

But then he made four birdies in a row from the 15th, shooting 6-under-par 30 for the front nine. Then he eagled the par 5 10th to go 8 under for the round.

Birdies followed at the 2nd and 3rd (his 11th and 12th), and now he was 10 under. Two more at the 6th and 7th were followed by a par at the 8th, meaning he had to make a birdie 3 at the 405-yard 9th to shoot 13 under and become the first man on the PGA Tour, or indeed any of the major professional tours, to break the 60 barrier.

His drive split the fairway and left about 125 yards to the green with the hole cut right in the middle.

He hit a nice approach, the ball spinning to a halt about 9 feet left of the cup. The putt was fairly level, but broke slightly from left to right.

THE OTHER CCC
This Colonial Country Club (not the one in Fort Worth, Texas that hosts the PGA Tour's Colonial tournament) is found in Cordova, Tennessee, 25 miles east of Memphis.

He buried it and leaped into the air with the gallery going berserk. Two days later, he won the tournament … just. He had shot another mediocre 72 in the third round and, after a 2-over 38 on the front nine on Sunday, found himself two strokes behind Gary Player going into the final nine holes. He retrieved some of that Friday form, however, and shot a back nine 32, finishing with a 2-under 70 and a four-round total of 15-under 273—two better than Player and Jerry McGee.

WOW RYO

The lowest round ever recorded at a tournament on one of the world's major professional golf tours (bear in mind there is no definition for what constitutes a "major professional tour"—some might only regard the PGA and European Tours as "major") is the 12-under 58 shot by 18-year-old Ryo Ishikawa in the final round of the 2010 Crowns tournament on the Japan Golf Tour. The Wago Course at Nagoya GC measured only 6,545 yards, but still, 12 birdies and no bogeys is pretty impressive. Perhaps the most impressive round ever though (there's no way of measuring it for certain) is the 16-under 55 that 26-year-old Australian pro Rhein Gibson shot at the 6,698-yard River Oaks course in Edmond, Oklahoma in May 2012. Gibson, who played college golf at Oklahoma Christian University, carded two eagles, 12 birdies and four pars.

APING AL

✦

In the 37 years since Geiberger shot his incredible 59, only four PGA Tour players have matched it—Chip Beck at the 1991 Las Vegas International, David Duval at the 1999 Bob Hope Chrysler Classic, Paul Goydos at the 2010 John Deere Classic and Stuart Appleby at the 2010 Greenbrier Classic. Fourteen rounds of 60 have been recorded on the European Tour, but no one has yet managed the magical 59. The first man to shoot 59 at a national open was Gary Player at the 1974 Brazilian Open at Gavea GCC in Rio.

ON THE BALL
Geiberger used the same ball (a Hogan model) for all 18 holes of his momentous round, and after donated it to the World Golf Hall of Fame.

"I am trying to think myself what happened. I just kind of got hot I guess and every putt I hit went in."

Rhein Gibson after his amazing round of 55

1975 | 1st The Woodlands (Oaks)

Location: The Woodlands, Texas

Distance: 499 yards, par 5

Original course designer: Joe Lee/Robert von Hagge

Subsequent alterations: Jay Morrish (1999)

The manner in which we play the game, the clothes we wear, the time it takes to complete a round, the nature of the courses we design and build, and the typical golfer's demographic, have all been influenced over the last 600 years or so by numerous social, cultural, economic and environmental factors. Something else that has played a crucial role in shaping the game is the tool we use to play it. Metal-headed woods were a major innovation and first used for victory at a top professional tournament at the Woodlands in 1981.

METAL HEAD

Developments in golf equipment technology over time have made the game both easier and more affordable, allowing millions of people who would otherwise have been priced out to participate. In the 17th, 18th and first half of the 19th centuries, only rich folk could afford featheries, which took a day to make and as much as five shillings (40 cents) to buy. So when Dr. Robert Patterson discovered that gutta-percha (see p.47) was perfect for a golf ball, a whole new section of society was able to take up the game.

Hickory shafts gave way to steel in the 1930s, enabling golfers to become far more consistent ball-strikers. And mechanical engineer Karsten Solheim, founder of Karsten Manufacturing and the Ping brand, had a huge impact by incorporating perimeter-weighting into his irons, thus making the sweet spot bigger than it was on blades, and introducing investment-casting to club head production, resulting in heads that were more consistent than forged heads and which were a lot easier and cheaper to make.

> **"I remember my first shot with the club on the range at a tournament in 1979. The ball took off like a flyer from out of a shallow divot. I immediately put it in my bag."**
>
> *Ron Streck, an early fan of the metal wood*

Another of the great advances was the introduction of metal-headed woods. Persimmon was the popular choice for driver heads from the early 1900s to the mid 1980s, after which metal began taking over (though many players were slow to switch—the last full-time PGA Tour player to use wood was Bob Estes at the 2001 WGC Accenture Match play in Australia).

Metal woods were first used in the late 19th century, but didn't become popular. A Yugoslavian physicist named John Zebelean experimented with a hollow metal head in 1972, but again it didn't take off as

Zebelean was more interested in the science than forming a company and mass-producing his club.

In 1979, Gary Adams, a golf-supply company salesman, noticed the two-piece balls he was selling performed well with irons but not woods, so he began tinkering with metal heads. He took a trunk full of prototypes to the PGA Merchandise Show in Orlando, Florida, and though many were skeptical he was sufficiently encouraged to take out a $24,000 loan and found a new company he called TaylorMade. It had one product and three staff. Sales in 1979 reached $47,000 (Adams sold the company to Salomon in 1984, and sales reached $1 billion in 2006.)

Initially, PGA Tour players dismissed metal drivers as driving range practice aids, but a few adopted them. One was Ron Streck, who became the first player to win on the Tour using a metal-headed driver at the 1981 Houston Open played at The Woodlands (now the Oaks Course). Streck had been using a 10-degree TaylorMade Original One for two years, driving the ball appreciably further and straighter.

In the third round of the 1981 Houston Open, Streck reached the green at the par 5 1st in two shots (both hit with the driver)—something only a few other players could match. He made a birdie and, buoyed by his good start, went on to shoot 62 and build a three-stroke lead. Heavy overnight rain meant the fourth round was cancelled, so Streck was declared the winner.

WOODLANDS
The Woodlands is a 44-square-mile master-planned community 28 miles north of Houston, Texas. It was established in 1974 and currently has a population of close to 110,000.

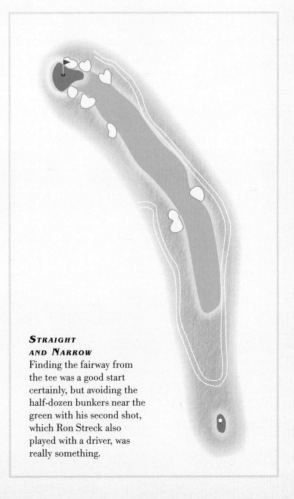

STRAIGHT AND NARROW
Finding the fairway from the tee was a good start certainly, but avoiding the half-dozen bunkers near the green with his second shot, which Ron Streck also played with a driver, was really something.

18th Glen Abbey

Location: Oakville, Ontario, Canada

Distance: 524 yards, par 5

Original course designer: Jack Nicklaus

G len Abbey opened in 1976 and was designed by Jack Nicklaus on the site of an existing course named the Upper Canada Country Club (UCCC), which was laid out by Howard Watson, a former employee of the great Canadian architect Stanley Thompson. Watson's course had opened in 1965 but, despite being over 6,800 yards long, was not considered strong enough a test for the best golfers in North America. That was a problem for the Royal Canadian Golf Association (RCGA, now Golf Canada) who wanted to identify a permanent home for the Canadian Open. The RCGA partnered with developer Rod McIsaac to overhaul the course that would host the Open. Meanwhile, McIsaac would sell the surrounding real estate. The course they had Nicklaus design would host more Canadian Opens than any other, and be the site of one of the greatest golf shots ever hit.

> **"Humans can't do that kind of stuff."**
>
> *PGA Tour Player Steve Flesch commenting on Woods' shot*

SOLO NICKLAUS

Nicklaus, just 12 years into his professional playing career, had completed a handful of courses as a designer, including Harbour Town and Muirfield Village. But he had always worked alongside a more experienced architect—Pete Dye at Harbour Town, Desmond Muirhead at Muirfield Village. Glen Abbey would be the first course at which he could rely solely on his own ideas. It would also be, he said, the first course built with the "spectator in mind." It is not one of the most memorable

HEAD FOR DRY LAND Despite the water and three sizable bunkers, the 18th green is a big target for a player hitting a wedge third shot. For someone firing over the water from a bunker 216 yards away, however, it must seem remote.

courses in his 300-strong portfolio perhaps (his design company boasts nearer to 400 projects), but it does possess a handful of excellent holes on the back nine where the Golden Bear took advantage of the valley surrounding Sixteen Mile Creek.

The fact the RCGA purchased the course from Rod McIsaac for $3 million in 1981 accounts for the 26 Canadian Opens Glen Abbey has hosted since 1977 (most recently in 2013, when Brandt Snedeker won by three shots), but you can't argue with the list of players that have won there—Lee Trevino, Greg Norman, Curtis Strange, Nick Price, Mark O'Meara, Vijay Singh and Tiger Woods among others.

GOLDEN GLEN
Glen Abbey GC and the Canadian Golf Hall of Fame are located in the Toronto suburb of Oakville, 25 miles southwest of downtown.

SHOT OF THE WEEK? YEAR? DECADE? ENTIRE HISTORY OF GOLF?

Though a good test, it's doubtful many golf fans could tell you anything about Glen Abbey except that it was where Tiger Woods hit one of his greatest ever shots, during the 2000 Canadian Open.

The winner of the U.S. Open by 15 shots three months earlier, and the British Open by eight in July, Woods was locked in a two-man tussle with New Zealand's Grant Waite, who was just a shot behind and perfectly positioned in the middle of the fairway.

Trying to become the first man since Lee Trevino in 1971 to win the Triple Crown of the British Open, U.S. Open and Canadian Open in the same year, Woods had pushed his drive into a fairway bunker. With Waite likely to make a birdie, if not an eagle, Woods knew he needed something special to avoid a playoff.

His ball was lying nicely in the sand, but he had 218 yards to the hole, about a hundred of which were across water.

Apparently without even considering the option to aim left, lay up and leave himself a pitch and a putt for birdie, the 24-year-old Woods took dead aim with a 6-iron and hit the ball so perfectly it carried everything in front of him and actually flew too far, coming to rest in the back fringe about 18 feet beyond the hole. With two putts, Woods matched Waite's birdie to finish one clear and win his ninth tournament of the year and 24th of his career.

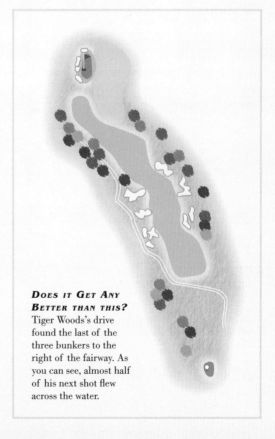

DOES IT GET ANY BETTER THAN THIS?
Tiger Woods's drive found the last of the three bunkers to the right of the fairway. As you can see, almost half of his next shot flew across the water.

10th The Belfry (Brabazon)

Location: Wishaw, Warwickshire, England

Distance: 311 yards, par 4

Original course designers: Dave Thomas, Peter Alliss

DRAMA QUEEN
The short par 4 10th is one of the Belfry's best holes—a risk/reward beauty that has made heroes of golfers gutsy enough to take on the green from the tee and reach the putting surface.

Between 1985 and 2002, the Belfry, near Sutton Coldfield in Warwickshire, England, hosted the Ryder Cup four times, Europe winning in 1985 and 2002, the U.S. in 1993 and the two sides finishing in a tie in 1989 (Europe retained the cup it had won at Muirfield Village in 1987). The Belfry was chosen as the venue not for the quality or charm of its course(s) necessarily, but because the Professional Golfers Association, a co-founder of the Ryder Cup, had been headquartered there since 1977 when the resort's first two layouts—the Brabazon and the Derby, both named for presidents of the PGA—were opened (PGA National, the third course, opened in 1997).

ILL-SUITED SITE

The land on which architects Dave Thomas and Peter Alliss were commissioned to build the Brabazon Course was uninspiring to say the least. Given flat, featureless arable land with heavy clay soil, Thomas, a four-time Ryder Cup player who also represented Wales eleven times at the World Cup of Golf, really had to extend his imagination to come up

with something worthy of a club championship let alone the Ryder Cup.

The two best holes he devised were undoubtedly the 473-yard closing hole, which features two water carries and a three-tiered green, and the wonderfully tempting short par 4 10th, which measures 311 yards from the back tee. A narrow green lies to the right of an equally slender stream, which separates the putting surface from the fairway. The bold can take on the green, a power fade being the ideal shot. The less intrepid (more sensible?) aim for the fairway with a mid-iron, then hit a wedge onto the green.

Made for Each Other

A year after the Brabazon Course opened, the 10th hole measured 280 yards and, considering even the longest hitters on the PGA and European Tours were averaging 272–273 yards off the tee at the time, it was considered out of reach with the game-standard persimmon-headed drivers and wound balata balls.

At the 1978 Hennessy Cup, a team event contested between Great Britain & Ireland, and Continental Europe, Spain's Seve Ballesteros arrived at the 10th tee 1 down in his singles match against England's Nick Faldo, who knocked a safe long-iron down the fairway. Seve needed a spark to get him going so took out the driver and aimed directly for the flag.

With an almighty rip, he sent the ball high and, after clearing the water, it pitched on

FAMILY ESTATE
An 1818 rendering of Moxhull Park by John Preston Neale. The estate's stables became the Belfry Hotel in the 1960s.

the front of the green and came to rest just 10 feet from the hole. TV cameras captured the moment, boosting Ballesteros' and the hole's fame in an instant. Seve missed the eagle effort, but tapped in for a birdie to win the hole. He would take the match 2&1.

Seven years later, having won the English Open at the Belfry in 1979, Ballesteros was back in Warwickshire for the Ryder Cup. In the first morning's foursomes, he partnered fellow Spaniard Manuel Piñero, and the pair arrived on the 10th tee 2-up against Curtis Strange and Mark O'Meara.

Being a foursomes match, taking on the green certainly wasn't the prudent play. However, Ballesteros had agreed with European captain Tony Jacklin that, if they were up in the match, going for the green would be a risk worth taking. This time, the ball clipped some leaves left of the green, but came down safely in the back-left corner, albeit 75 feet from the hole. Again, TV viewers saw the whole thing.

Piñero putted up and Ballesteros made the birdie—good enough for a win. The Spaniards claimed the match 2&1 and, though it was the only point the Europeans won that first morning, Seve's flair ignited his teammates who, two days later, would lift the Ryder Cup for the first time in 28 years, winning the matches 16½–11½.

"We always considered the 10th to be a match-play hole. You wouldn't mess around with it in stroke play, because you could easily make a 10."

Dave Thomas, course designer

Interviewed by the BBC on the edge of the 18th green moments after Scotland's Sam Torrance had holed the match-winning putt, a visibly elated Seve Ballesteros said he felt like he had won another British Open. That 1985 victory triggered an incredible run of success for the European Team, which has now won nine of the 14 Ryder Cups since 1985, with one tie (1989). The Europeans won for the first time in America two years after the Belfry breakthrough, when Ballesteros secured the point that ensured victory at Muirfield Village in Ohio. In 2014, Europe made it three wins in a row when it recorded an impressive $16^{1}/_{2}$–$11^{1}/_{2}$ victory over a team captained by Tom Watson, who had last captained the U.S. side that prevailed at the Belfry in 1993.

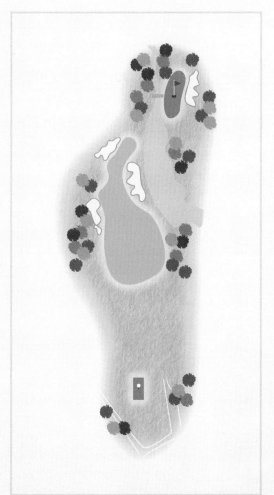

CHOOSE YOUR CHALLENGE
The 10th at the Belfry is tough if you take on the narrow green from the tee, but the easy way out is to hit a mid-iron into that fat part of the fairway and a wedge to the green.

MIDLANDS
You'll find the Belfry outside the village of Wishaw, 10 miles northeast of Birmingham city center.

1980

17th TPC Sawgrass (Stadium)

Location: Ponte Vedra Beach, Florida

Distance: 137 yards, par 3

Original course designer: Pete Dye

Subsequent alterations: Pete Dye (2006)

Whether you think it innovative and thrilling or cheap and gimmicky, you can't deny the island green 17th on the Stadium Course at TPC Sawgrass causes a good deal of discussion. This notorious par 3 measures only 137 yards from the tournament tees and rarely plays anything more than a 9-iron for the game's top professionals. The green is just 3,912 square feet in size—pretty small for a modern tournament green. But, of course, any professional worth his million-dollar endorsement contract should hit a green that's almost 21 square yards with a 9-iron—a club they normally expect to hit within 10–15 feet of the hole.

> "I've always thought that that hole is too gimmicky for the 17th hole of a championship. I think it would be a fantastic 8th hole, but not the 17th hole of your round or the 71st hole of a tournament."
>
> *Tiger Woods, 2008*

SERENE GREEN
On a quiet, misty morning, with the water as flat as a mill pond, the 17th hole seems positively tranquil. In the heat of battle though, as the Players Championship comes down to the wire, it is a cauldron of tension.

SWAMP THING

The Stadium Course was designed by Pete Dye, an often-provocative architect who tends to create love-them-or-hate-them courses, but it was his wife Alice—the winner of the 1978 and 1979 U.S. Senior Women's Amateur Championships, and the first woman President of the American Association of Golf Course Architects (ASGCA)—who suggested the moat.

TPC Sawgrass opened in 1980, and is the permanent home of the PGA Tour's Players Championship, which the Tour likes to think of as the "Fifth Major." The fifth major issue comes up every year—the split between those that think it worthy of the name and those who laugh at such talk seems to be about 50–50. Importantly, while the pros never disparage any event that pays its winner over $1.7 million, most seem willing to admit four majors is plenty.

It was then-PGA-Tour-commissioner Deane Beman who conceived the course, wanting to build a stadium venue that the PGA Tour owned and on which it could stage its flagship event. The Tournament Players Championship (TPC) was first played in 1974 at Atlanta Athletic Club and visited a variety of venues before moving to Sawgrass Country Club in 1977. Beman liked it so much he wanted it to be the tournament's home, thinking a permanent venue would give the

event greater identity, and that the Tour could develop it and set it up exactly as it pleased.

But the property owner turned Beman down, forcing him to look elsewhere. Word got out and numerous developers and landowners approached Beman, offering him the land on which to build, in many cases for free. They knew the TV exposure the tournament received would increase the value of the surrounding property considerably. One such offer came from the brothers Jerome and Paul Fletcher, who owned 5,300 acres in Ponte Vedra Beach, Florida—half a mile from the Atlantic and 25 miles southeast of Jacksonville. Defaulting on their loan, the Fletchers offered Beman 415 acres for just $1. The bank that owned the mortgage didn't think much of the deal at first, but was persuaded by Beman to accept it after the commissioner convinced executives the TPC would soon become the PGA Tour's most prestigious event.

Covered in oak, pine, magnolia, palm and sweetgum trees, and lying just about at sea level with ponds, lagoons, lakes and ditches strewn across the property, it would be an incredibly difficult site to turn into a golf course. In addition, although there was plenty of sand which the architect needs to build a well-draining course, it was found in pockets rather than seams (which is more usual), further complicating the design and construction of the course, which would surely cost a fortune. Given that PGA Tour members insisted Beman not use one cent of the Tour's assets, the commissioner had to exercise all his powers of persuasion, determination and innovation to proceed with his master plan.

He was convinced this was the place. To pay for construction he enlisted 50 local businessmen who each paid $20,000 to become founding members, and 3,000 local associate members who paid $25 each. To design the course, he hired Pete Dye, an insurance salesman turned golf course architect who had worked with Jack Nicklaus on the design of Harbour Town Golf Links on Hilton Head Island, South Carolina, which opened in 1969 and was one of Beman's favorite courses from his playing days.

Beman liked Harbour Town's quirks, so regarded Dye as the ideal man to build something new and original, a prototype almost for the sort of stadium courses he envisioned.

DYED IN THE WOOL
Pete Dye was 54 years old when he began work on the Stadium Course at TPC Sawgrass.

WATERSIDE
TPC Sawgrass is found
between the Intracoastal
Waterway and the Atlantic
Ocean, 4.5 miles south of
Ponte Vedra Beach, Florida,
and 25 miles southeast
of Jacksonville.

A HOLE SHORT

As construction of the course continued, however,
Dye became increasingly concerned he only had 17
holes. The original 17th was to be a short par 3 with a
pond short and right of the green—but the ground
the construction crew dug up to form the pond was so
rich in high-quality sand, they kept digging and
digging. Not much was left of this corner of the property when, one day, Dye brought Alice to have a look.

Pete and Alice were familiar with Robert Trent
Jones' island green at Ponte Vedra Inn, a couple of
miles north, and Alice wondered if something similar
might work here. A narrow path could connect the
mainland with the back of
the green. At first, Dye,
thinking the hole too easy, sloped the back of
the putting surface toward the water, but Alice
persuaded him to flatten it, saying amateur
golfers might never finish the hole. To add a
little extra challenge, Dye lowered the front
left and back right portions of the green, and
added a small pot bunker at the front.

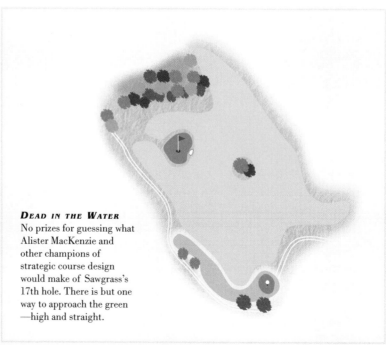

DEAD IN THE WATER
No prizes for guessing what
Alister MacKenzie and
other champions of
strategic course design
would make of Sawgrass's
17th hole. There is but one
way to approach the green
—high and straight.

It's interesting to think that what was a make-up-the-numbers hole, one that wasn't part of the course's original design and that required an extra pair of eyes to find, has become one of the most famous in the world.

It's Not How...

In the first round of the 1999 Players, two-time champion (1984, 1996) Fred Couples arrived on the 17th tee on 5 over par. His tee shot fell into the water short, meaning he was now staring at a round in the eighties. Without changing clubs, he wasted little time in re-teeing and put what looked like the same lazy, rhythmic swing on the ball. Only this time, it flew straight into the hole without bouncing, giving Couples a par 3. Instead of making a double-bogey or worse, and missing the cut the next day, Couples salvaged a 77 then shot 4 under over the next three days to finish in a tie for fourth.

It wasn't the first time Couples had holed out from the teeing ground, how-ever. In the final round two years earlier, and with the hole playing 140 yards into a left-to-right wind, Couples hit a 7-iron to the front center of the green and watched as the ball pitched, spun right and trundled slowly down the slope into the hole.

Other notable feats on the hole include Paul Azinger's four consecu-tive deuces in 1987 and Tiger Woods' birdie during the third round in 2001, when his tee shot found the back edge of the green and he was faced with a downhill, twice-breaking 60-footer. The ball followed the S-shape route to the hole as planned, the ball dropping into the cup at the perfect speed.

Pump It Up!
A birdie at the 17th in the final round of the 1996 Players Championship helped Fred Couples to an 8-under 64 and a four-stroke victory.

1991

18th Kiawah Island (Ocean)

Location: Kiawah Island, South Carolina

Distance: 501 yards, par 4

Original course designer: Pete Dye

Subsequent alterations: Pete Dye (1997, 2002, 2003, 2011)

Pete Dye has a reputation for designing golf courses that are often quirky, frequently controversial and occasionally downright odd, but always extremely challenging. The Ocean Course at the Kiawah Island Golf Resort, which hosted the 1991 Ryder Cup just a couple of months after opening and 18 months after the first few holes were virtually wiped out by Hurricane Hugo, was quintessential Dye. Yes, there were tees, fairways and greens, but somehow it just didn't look like any other course. The bunkers were huge sandy waste areas—30 acres of them. And thanks to Dye's wife, Alice, who often contributed to her husband's designs (see p.200), the fairways were raised 6 feet so golfers could see the ocean but also have to battle the random and often strong winds on the South Carolina coast, where there is no prevailing wind pattern. Some thought the Ocean Course was a little over the top even for Dye. One newspaper columnist in the U.S. called it "Looney Dunes" and "Masochist Marsh," before adding it was "the most ridiculous creation to date by Pete Dye." He concluded by saying he'd rather play through an Iraqi minefield. Sure enough, the players at the Ryder Cup didn't really know what to make of it. Nick Faldo said that after mishitting a shot even slightly you wouldn't make a bogey or even a double, you "just put your ball in your pocket and moved on." Kooky or not, Kiawah threw up a fierce and compelling contest. The drama was non-stop, and after three days the result came down to the very last shot on the last hole …

THE IRRESISTIBLE FORCE VERSUS THE IMMOVABLE OBJECT

The bitter recriminations and hostile accusations that swirled about at the Ryder Cup matches at Royal Birkdale in 1969 (see p.118) were pretty unsavory, but child's play compared with some of the vitriol that passed between the two teams in 1991, a contest that became known as the "War by the Shore." It didn't help that in Bernard Gallacher (Europe) and Dave Stockton (U.S.), the clash featured two fiercely proud and patriotic captains who, they would probably agree, weren't slow to hold a grudge or offer an opinion.

And though many of Europe's top golfers now live and play in America, where they are good friends with the U.S. players they come up against at the Ryder Cup, the situation was different in 1991 when the sides were very distant both physically and psychologically. Only a handful of players on the 1991 European team competed regularly in

FINE FINALE
The 18th on the Ocean
Course is a great closing
hole that finishes next to
the Atlantic. Relatively
conventional compared
with some of the more
theatrical holes that
precede it, it was
nevertheless the scene
of intense drama at
the end of the 1991
Ryder Cup.

the U.S., and when they came it was only for a tournament or two—never enough time to form genuine friendships with the American players, even if they had wanted to. Wales' Ian Woosnam was the world number one and current Masters champion, Seve Ballesteros was a double Masters winner and five-time major champion, Nick Faldo had won two Green Jackets and two Claret Jugs, Bernhard Langer had won the Masters six years previously, and 25-year-old José Maria Olazabal had already played on two Ryder Cup teams and won the NEC World Series of Golf, a prominent tournament on the PGA Tour, by an amazing 12 strokes the previous year.

These five were very familiar to the Americans, as were Ryder Cup veterans Mark James and Sam Torrance, who had played a total of nine Ryder Cups between them. The five rookies—Colin Montgomerie, David Gilford, David Feherty, Steven Richardson and Paul Broadhurst—were virtually unknown in the U.S., however. Montgomerie had attended university (Houston Baptist) in America, but hadn't yet played a professional event there. Feherty and Richardson both played in the PGA Championship in Indiana six weeks before the Ryder Cup (Richardson finishing tied for fifth, Feherty tied for seventh). And Broadhurst had made his PGA Tour debut at the B.C. Open in New York the week before moving on to Kiawah Island. Gilford had never played in America, which meant the five rookies had collectively played three professional tournaments on U.S. soil.

The "Us versus Them" mentality was obviously still evident, and the mood between the two camps wasn't helped any when, at the gala dinner on the Wednesday of tournament week, the hosts showed a video of

Ryder Cup history in which only American players were mentioned or seen hitting shots. European Tour Executive Director Ken Schofield was so incensed he was ready to walk on to the stage and show his dissatisfaction. Thankfully some of the European players were able to persuade him not to.

"My memory of the dinner is of a guy coming up on the stage and asking all of us to pray for American birdies. But for me it went in one ear and out the other. Come to think of it, shouldn't asking God for help have made them liable to a two-shot penalty?"

Europe's Mark James invoking Rule 8-1b—"During a stipulated round, a player may not ask for advice from anyone other than his partner or either of their caddies."

Then there was the local radio station's "Wake the Enemy" campaign, which involved the station host calling members of the European team at five or six in the morning.

The tension only got worse when play actually started. On the first morning, the Spanish pairing of Ballesteros and Olazabal, which was already established as one of the Ryder Cup's greatest teams with $6^1/2$ points from eight matches in the previous two encounters, played Paul Azinger and Chip Beck in a foursomes match that turned ugly on the 10th tee, when the Spaniards accused the Americans of having broken a rule (though they were careful not to say the U.S. pair had cheated). In foursomes, each pair must declare the ball they intend to use for the entire round, but on the 7th hole, Azinger and Beck switched, thinking Azinger's 100-compression ball would be better-suited to the wind conditions than Beck's 90-compression ball, which they had used up to that point. Such a small difference in the balls' characteristics is unlikely to have made an appreciable difference in the outcome of the hole, but rules are rules.

The players, captains and referees debated the issue for several minutes and, though strong emotions were very clearly on display, the players thankfully avoided trading blows.

Fuelled by disdain for their opponents, Ballesteros and Olazabal went on a mission on the back nine and produced some scintillating golf. Beck later said they played like they were possessed. The Spaniards won the match 2&1.

The Americans were out in front at the end of day one though, $4^1/2$–$3^1/2$. After eight more matches on a similarly fraught day two, the Europeans drew level at 8–8.

EASY MAJORS

✦

Rory McIlroy won the 2012 PGA Championship at Kiawah Island— his second major championship victory—by eight strokes. It was the same margin by which he had captured his first, the previous year's U.S. Open. Seven clear as he stood on the 18th tee, McIlroy told his caddie he was going to win this by eight and, sure enough, he put another stroke between him and England's David Lynn in second by pouring in a 25-foot putt for birdie.

The 12 singles matches remained but only 11 were played as Steve Pate had to withdraw on the Sunday morning with bruised ribs, a result of the limousine he was in crashing on its way to the gala dinner four days before. Pate had been drawn to play Ballesteros, Europe's most feared player. Because he withdrew on the morning of the match, he was awarded half a point, which is probably half a point more than he would have won had he played Ballesteros. Gallacher was very suspicious, especially as Pate had played the day before.

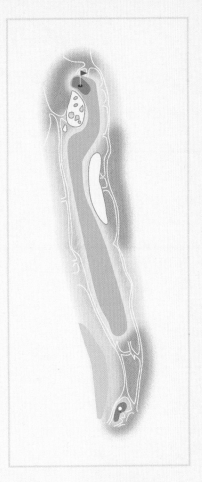

Ballesteros was moved in the order to play Wayne Levi, and Gallacher chose David Gilford to sit out.

It was a day of pulsating drama, Europe winning the first two matches, America matches 4&5.

As the afternoon progressed, the score remained nail-bitingly close and it became clear everything would hinge on the final match—the U.S.'s Hale Irwin against Germany's Bernhard Langer. Two more resolute, more tenacious players you couldn't wish to have on your team.

Irwin was 2-up after 14 holes, but had been battling his swing all week. Over the remaining holes he was really just hanging on as best he could. Langer, who had spent nearly his entire career dealing with the yips and developing any number of solutions, won the 15th with a par then calmly holed a 6-footer at the 16th for a half, the putter clasped firmly against the inside of his left forearm with his right hand—a rather bizarre-looking grip he had introduced at the Lancôme Trophy in September 1988.

At the 197-yard 17th, Irwin needed a wood to clear the water and found the front of the green. But his first putt was too strong, and he missed the return. Langer, meanwhile, rolled in his 4-footer for a 3. They were now tied heading to the last.

The U.S. led the matches 14–13 which meant Langer needed to win the 18th to get the point Europe needed to tie the match and retain the cup. The Bavarian had a 6-foot putt for a 4 and the win. After deciding with his caddie Pete Coleman that a spike-mark would deflect his ball, he decided to hit the putt straight. But he watched in anguish as it broke right and slid by the hole.

There are plenty of candidates, but Langer's putt must rank as the single most pressure-packed moment in the history of the game.

ISLAND COMMUNITY
The Ocean Course lies at the eastern end of Kiawah island, a barrier island on the South Carolina coast with an area of 13 square miles, and a permanent population of just over 1,000. The city of Charleston is 15 miles north.

10th Mission Hills (World Cup Course)

Location: Shenzhen, Guangdong, China

Distance: 417 yards, par 4

Original course designer: Jack Nicklaus

The notion that golf, or something similar, was exported to Europe from China during the Middle Ages perhaps isn't as preposterous as it sounds. The Chinese played a game called *chuiwan*, which differed from golf in significant ways, but did at least involve hitting a ball with a club toward some sort of target. Popularity of *chuiwan* died out during the Qing Dynasty (1644–1911) and historical evidence of it is limited, which partly explains perhaps why golf was viewed with such skepticism when it finally re-emerged in 1984, when Hong Kong developer Henry Fok hired Arnold Palmer to design the Zhongshan Hot Spring course in Guangdong Province. Mao Tse-Tung had allowed a little wiggle room three decades after banning the "sport of millionaires." And though hardline communists still regarded it as far too bourgeois, golf became increasingly popular, even if it was only wealthy businessmen and government officials that could afford to play. Progress was slow at first, the one course in 1984 growing to 176 by 2004, according to Government statistics. But, ironically, since the Government put a stop to the development of new courses in 2004, their number has more than trebled, local officials sidestepping restrictions by calling new courses "leisure facilities."

LABOR OF LOVE
A par 4 at the relatively straightforward 10th hole —the fifth extra hole of the playoff—was good enough for the U.S.'s Davis Love to beat Japan's Hisayuki Sasaki and claim individual honors at the 1995 World Cup of Golf.

BOOMTOWN(S)

Journalist and author Dan Washburn, a native of Georgia who lived in China from 2002–2012, says that if a golf course designer or construction company wasn't working in China in the early 2000s, they probably weren't working at all. Despite the 2004 government legislation banning course development, Washburn says construction continued at a breakneck pace for several years afterward and that only very recently has it slowed.

The Global Financial Crisis of 2007–2009 hit the U.S. golf industry hard, and because there were way too many courses for a dwindling number of golfers, course owners had no choice but to shut down. In China, however, there was growing interest in the sport as a handful of professionals, led by Wen-Chong Liang and Zhang Lianwei, found success on the European Tour, and the economic benefits associated with golf became increasingly evident. The 1995 World Cup of Golf at Mission Hills in Shenzhen also contributed.

Nowhere says "China Golf Boom" quite like Mission Hills Shenzhen, 30 miles north of Hong Kong. Established in 1992 and developed by Mission Hills Group Limited, a Hong Kong-based development company founded by entrepreneur David Chu (and now run by Chu's son Ken), the company's Shenzhen/Dongguan property now covers roughly 10 square miles and offers hotel guests, club members and property residents 12 golf courses each designed by a well-known figure in the game. (An outrageous 36 courses were planned for Mission Hills' second development on the island of Hainan. So far 10 have been built.) The first phase involved seven courses, the other five added shortly before the government-imposed ban on construction and completed simultaneously in little more than a year—a result of abundant, inexpensive labor.

The course that set the ball rolling was designed by Jack Nicklaus, and opened in time to host the 1995 World Cup of Golf (hence the name)—China's first large-scale international tournament. Considering they'd won the three previous years, it was no surprise the American duo of Davis Love and Fred Couples won, shooting a combined 33-under 543—14 strokes better than second-placed Australia. The individual event was more closely contested after Love and Japan's Hisayuki Sasaki finished level on 21-under 267. The tie was eventually broken at the 10th, the fifth extra hole, when Sasaki made a bogey to Love's par.

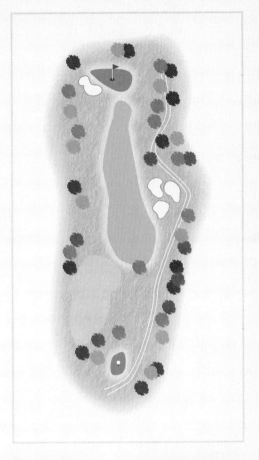

HOLLOW HAZARDS
Though water and sand are certainly very evident on the 10th hole, none of it should really come into play for the top professional.

FANTASY ISLAND
The incredible Mission Hills Resort/city/complex/ is located 17 miles north of Shenzhen in southeastern China, and about 45 miles north of Hong Kong.

"When we first started, there were less than 10,000 golfers in all of China, so it was a very scary proposition to build a golf club. But we wanted to create a platform to complement the economic boom of China. Mission Hills was made to do business networking."

Tenniel Chu, Mission Hills' executive director

16th Bandon Dunes

Location: Bandon, Oregon

Distance: 363 yards, par 4

Original course designer: David McLay Kidd

It might not have hosted any major professional events—just the odd local pro-am, a few Pacific Northwest Golf Association tournaments, a collegiate event or two, the 2006 Curtis Cup and the first three editions of the World Speed Golf Championship, but Bandon Dunes Golf Resort is now a huge part of golf in America.

IT'LL NEVER WORK

In 1971, Mike Keiser, his wife Lindy and a college friend formed a greetings card company—Recycled Paper Greetings—that was the first in the industry to use 100 percent recycled paper. They found a young and talented illustrator named Sandra Boynton, who was looking for a publisher. America loved her whimsical drawings and, within seven years, the company's sales had soared to over $100 million.

Keiser was a golf nut who loved classic, natural layouts. In 1985, he built a low-key nine-holer he called Dunes Club on 90 acres at the southern tip of Lake Michigan. As Boynton's cards kept selling, and the cash kept rolling in, Keiser began to dream bigger. He began looking for coastal sites on the East Coast but found nothing suitable, so shifted his search to California. Howard McKee, an architect friend of Keiser's who lived in Portland, suggested he look on the Oregon coast. Skeptical at first, Keiser agreed and in 1989, after taking a phone call from a realtor who mentioned a 1,200-acre site on the southern Oregon coast with "huge, rolling sand dunes and Scottish broom" he was on a plane. The land was ideal for the sort of golf Keiser loved. He paid $2.5 million for it, cash.

Immediately, Keiser's friends and family called him a fool, saying no one would travel that far to play golf. Bandon had no airport and the nearest, 30 miles away in North Bend (now the Southwest Oregon Regional Airport), wasn't exactly humming with activity. The drive north from San Francisco was eight and a half hours, while those coming from Portland would need four and a half hours. Keiser's course would be somewhat isolated. And when he hired an anonymous Scotsman to design it, the naysayers thought he had lost the last of his marbles.

"I'll keep building golf courses until I die."

Mike Keiser giving hope to every golfer who loves the courses he builds. (In December 2014, Keiser chose Kidd to design the second course at Sand Valley in Wisconsin. Coore and Crenshaw had already been retained to build the property's first course. It would be the first time since Bandon Dunes that Keiser and Kidd would work together.)

David Kidd wasn't just unknown in the U.S., though—few people had heard of him in his native Britain. He had begun his career doing small restoration and renovation jobs for Howard Swan in England, then moved back to Scotland where he joined his father Jimmy, a greatly admired greenkeeper and agronomist, at the Gleneagles Hotel (venue of numerous Scottish Opens and the 2014 Ryder Cup). Guinness, Gleneagles' owner, wanted to build Gleneagles-style golf resorts around the world under the name Gleneagles Golf Developments. David was to be the in-house course architect and development expert.

The resorts never really happened, but the design and development group made its expertise available for hire. David's first job was a course in Nepal, of all places—the very enjoyable Gokarna Forest, 10 miles outside Kathmandu.

Keiser could have had his pick of the world's golf course architects to build his course. He could afford any one of them, and his property was the sort of site any architect would be eager to work on. Sand is the architect's best friend as it can be shaped and moved to create interesting landforms, and enables a course to drain much better than a course built on heavy clay soil.

But Keiser didn't want a big-name architect calling the shots. He did want a little Scottish authenticity, however. So he had the Kidds come to Oregon.

CLIFFTOP CLIMAX
David Kidd took his time deciding how he was going to use this fabulous stretch of clifftop. A short par 4 with the sandy ridge running diagonally across the fairway and a green set on the cliff's edge was a fantastic option.

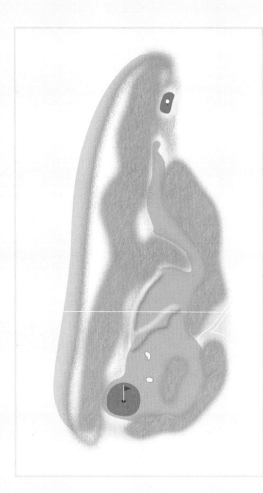

CHOICES, CHOICES
The 16th gives you two clear
options: play an easy shot to
the lower fairway, but face a
tougher approach up and
over the ridge, or carry the
ridge and have an easy
pitch in.

Jimmy and David first visited Bandon in the summer of 1994. The site, though full of sand and possessing fantastic views up and down the Oregon coast, was absolutely covered in gorse, a thorny evergreen shrub closely related to broom, with a yellow flower. It looks beautiful in small clumps and actually smells delightful. But it can quickly get out of control.

Over the next three years, the Kidds returned often, staying in a cheap Bandon motel as they cleared the site. David was clearly excited at the opportunity to design a course on what appeared to be genuine sand dunes (hard to tell exactly what they might look like under all the gorse), but he wasn't unaware it would be hundreds of miles from a decent-sized city and that he was working for "some rich dude from Chicago no one in the golf world knew."

When the gorse was finally gone in 1997, Kidd began designing and building. The cliff top where the 16th would go was a wonderful spot for a golf hole, but there was some debate over what sort of hole it should be.

One day, with Keiser back in Chicago, Kidd built a short par 4, intersected by a ridge of bunkers and rough ground. It looked great to him, but he had no idea what his boss would make of the split fairway idea. Keiser returned to Bandon with Mike Davis—then the championship director for the U.S. Open, and now the USGA's executive director. Keiser knew his course couldn't host a U.S. Open—it was too short and too remote—but Davis was a friend whose opinion he valued.

Keiser took Davis out to the 16th tee. Kidd, meanwhile, stood at the opposite end of the hole watching and wondering what his boss and the USGA man were thinking. Kidd hoped they would all meet halfway down the hole and exchange high-fives, at which point Keiser would tell him how great the hole was. Instead, after several minutes, Keiser and Davis just walked away.

Kidd was convinced Keiser didn't like it, and that he would soon be fired. Keiser was clearly stringing Kidd along though. Inexperienced (in his late twenties) but headstrong and a little stubborn, Kidd needed to be reminded it was Keiser who was signing the checks. After making his young designer agonize just long enough, Keiser admitted how much he liked it.

The course opened in May 1999, and though Keiser suspected it would attract 10,000 rounds in its first year, it actually recorded 23,000.

WEST COAST
The Bandon Dunes Golf Resort sits on cliffs high above the Oregon coastline, 240 miles south of Portland. Bandon itself is 7 miles south, over the Coquille River.

Obviously on to a winner, Keiser purchased more land to the north of the original course and hired Tom Doak to build a second, Pacific Dunes, which opened in 2001. A third, Bandon Trails, designed by Bill Coore and Ben Crenshaw, opened in 2005, then a fourth, Old Macdonald (see p.15) where Doak and Jim Urbina created a superb tribute to C.B. Macdonald, came along in 2010. Coore's 13-hole par 3 course, Bandon Preserve, was added in 2012, and a 2$^{1}/_{2}$-acre putting green called the Punchbowl opened in May 2014.

Bandon Dunes Golf Resort is immensely successful, and it's hard to imagine that 20 years ago the land on which it sits was just a sea of gorse in a faraway corner or America. It's still rather remote, of course, but now a total of 125,000 rounds are played there every year. Keiser built it and they most certainly did come. There are numerous outstanding holes throughout the resort's 3,000 acres, but David Kidd's 16th on the eponymous Bandon Dunes remains one of the best.

OLD MACDONALD
Like the 16th on Bandon Dunes, the 7th on the Tom Doak/Jim Urbina-designed, C.B. Macdonald-inspired Old Macdonald finishes on a green overlooking the ocean.

2000 2nd Fancourt (Links)

Location: George, Western Cape, South Africa

Distance: 216 yards, par 3

Original course designer: Gary Player

The Links at Fancourt is one of three Gary Player-designed courses at the lavish resort outside of George, 270 miles east of Cape Town (Outeniqua and Montagu are the other courses. There was a fourth, Bramble Hill, but that closed). It opened in 2000 to great acclaim and has upheld its reputation since, being named the best course in the country by *Golf Digest* SA in 2014, and 34th best in the world by the U.S. edition of the magazine.

FAUX LINKS, REAL CHALLENGE

The 350-acre Fancourt resort is owned by German billionaire Hasso Plattner, who cofounded software giant SAP in 1972. The Fancourt Estate had been there for over a hundred years, but the resort didn't open until 1991. Plattner bought it three years later, after the original development company collapsed. In 1998, Plattner acquired additional land to the south of the original property and worked with South Africa's greatest ever golfer, Gary Player, to produce a course reminiscent of a British links.

Indeed, Player's design team, headed by Phil Jacobs, traveled to Britain and Ireland to take notes. Unlike genuine links courses that were

FAUX LINKS
Purist links fans might baulk at the rather lush turf, the water hazards and the cart paths, but no one can deny Gary Player and Phil Jacobs came up with a number of really good holes on the Links at Fancourt.

simply laid out, rather than built, next to a sea or ocean on wind-blown sand dunes with little natural vegetation save for hardy bent and fescue grasses, and various scrub bushes such as gorse and broom, the Links at Fancourt is what has come to be known as a "faux links." It might have the outward appearance of the genuine article (revetted pot bunkers, sandy banks, few, if any, trees), but it was actually constructed on a flat, disused airfield 5 miles north of the Indian Ocean coastline. Well over 700,000 cubic yards of soil and sand were dumped on the site before being pushed around to form dunes, ridges, humps and hollows.

A REAL PLAYER
South Africa's greatest ever golfer Gary Player became a prolific course designer after reducing his playing schedule. His company has been involved in over 300 projects in 35 countries.

The 2nd hole at the Links at Fancourt, named Lang Drop, is a downhill par 3 whose green is defended by six bunkers. It measured 231 yards for the 2003 Presidents Cup (see box).

FIT TO BE TIED

At the end of 1993, eight of the top 20 players in the world were from countries outside the U.S. and Europe. Australia's Greg Norman was a global icon, Zimbabwe's Nick Price was getting there, and Fiji's Vijay Singh, South Africa's Ernie Els and Australia's Steve Elkington were all emerging fast—Japan's Masashi Ozaki, meanwhile, was a household name in his native land. This group of international stars was backed up by several more top players that had won big tournaments around the world—David Frost, Mark McNulty, Rodger Davis, Peter Senior, Frank Nobilo, Tony Johnstone, Craig Parry, etc.

By contrast, there were just five Europeans in the top 20. It was time for a team competition involving the U.S.—by far the most prominent golfing country in the world—and players from what was referred to as the "Rest of the World" (not sure Norman, Price, etc., realized they grew up in the Rest of the World). An announcement was made early in 1994 that a biennial team match modeled on the Ryder Cup, which had been played in alternate years since 1927 (see p.63), would debut later that year at the Robert Trent Jones GC in Gainesville, Virginia—35 miles east of Washington, DC.

Run by the PGA Tour, the competition would be called the Presidents Cup and honor U.S. Presidents

MEASURING UP

✦

The course was stretched to 7,489 yards for the 2003 Presidents Cup, but the standard championship length is 6,930 yards. In 2005, the course hosted the inaugural Women's World Cup of Golf, won by Japan represented by Rui Kitada and Ai Miyazato, and the South African Open won by Retief Goosen (actually part of the 2006 European Tour season). In 2012, the European Tour returned, staging the Volvo Golf Champions event won by Branden Grace in a playoff with Goosen and Ernie Els.

GARDEN ROUTE BEAUTY
The Links at Fancourt is located just outside the town of George in Eastern Cape, 200 miles west of Port Elizabeth and 270 miles east of Cape Town.

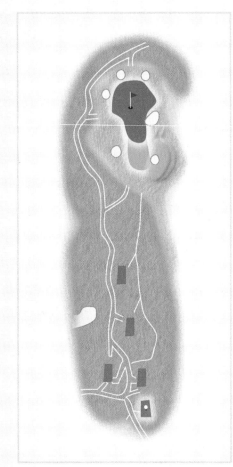

GONE GREEN
With the magnificent Outeniqua Mountains in the background, trees and wetlands to the right, and a sea of wispy grass and brush between the tee and green, the putting surface at this downhill par 3 can seem an elusive target.

and leaders of countries represented by players in the event (Australia's John Howard in 1998, South Africa's Thabo Mbeke in 2002, Canada's Stephen Harper in 2007 and Australia's Julia Gillard in 2011.)

The venue for the matches would alternate between the U.S. and a golf-playing country outside the U.S. and Europe (although the first two events were played in Virginia). The event would be played in even-numbered years, although the terrorist attacks of September 11, 2001, caused the 2001 Ryder Cup to be postponed until 2002, meaning the Presidents Cup moved to the odds.

It began as a three-day tournament, but that was changed to four days in 2000. Likewise, the format has been tweaked at various points but does include foursomes, fourballs and singles matches, the main difference between the two team competitions now being the participation of all 12 players on each side in the first day's foursomes and second day fourballs at the Presidents Cup. On the third day, five foursomes are played in the morning followed by five afternoon fourballs. Twelve singles conclude the tournament on the final day. A total of 34 matches are therefore played at the Presidents Cup, compared with the Ryder Cup's 28.

The captains for the first Presidents Cup were Hale Irwin—the only playing captain in the matches so far—and Australia's David Graham. The tournament was greatly anticipated, but would suffer a major blow just prior to the start when Greg Norman, the player whose influence had contributed so much to the event's very existence, was forced to pull out owing to what his doctor described as a "gastrointestinal condition." Norman was replaced by fellow Aussie Bradley Hughes.

The U.S. side, which included a 24-year-old Phil Mickelson, and the former world number one Fred Couples, won that first encounter 20–12. Two years later, at the Robert Trent Jones GC again, the U.S. successfully defended the cup but were hard pushed by the Internationals, who went down by just one point.

In 1998, the matches moved overseas for the first time—to Royal Melbourne GC (see p.150) in Australia, where a formidable International team that included Norman, Price, Singh, Elkington, Nobilo and a young Stuart Appleby beat a shell-shocked U.S. side $20^{1}/_{2}$–$11^{1}/_{2}$,Norman beating a 22-year-old Tiger Woods in the singles 1-up.

The U.S. exacted ruthless revenge in 2000 when it won $21^{1}/_{2}$–$10^{1}/_{2}$, meaning that when the teams arrived at Fancourt for the 2003 edition, the match score stood at 3–1 in favor of the U.S.

The Internationals entered the final day with a three-point lead, but won the singles $7^{1}/_{2}$–$4^{1}/_{2}$ to tie the scores at 17–17. Each team was required to select one player to play off for the cup. The U.S.'s captain JackNicklaus chose Tiger Woods while International captain Gary Player selected Ernie Els.

The pair halved the first two holes, then came to the par 3 2nd. After each player had played two shots, Woods was left with a tricky, left-to-right-bending 12-footer, while Els had about half that distance. In near darkness, Woods holed his putt and Els followed him in.

But it had become too dark to continue, even if Els wanted it to. Nicklaus, Player and their teams deliberated for several minutes, eventually deciding to call it a tie and share the cup for six months each.

"Both Gary and I feel in our hearts, and I think both teams feel, that sharing the Presidents Cup was the right thing to do, and we stand by it."

Jack Nicklaus after deciding with International Captain Gary Player to call a tie at the 2003 Presidents Cup

PRESIDENTS CUP
Jack Nicklaus (left), Gary Player (right), and Thabo Mbeki, President of South Africa (middle), hold the Presidents Cup aloft following the dramatic tie in 2003.

18th Trump National Los Angeles

Location: Palos Verdes, California

Distance: 512 yards, par 4

Original course designer: Pete Dye

Subsequent alterations: Jim Fazio (2003)

"If I'm ever in California for an earthquake, this is where I want to be standing."

Trump on the rebuilt 18th hole at his course in Los Angeles

LOCATION, LOCATION, LOCATION
Whatever you want to say about Donald Trump's methods and manner, and forgetting Jim Fazio's somewhat over-the-top design for a moment, you can't argue with Trump National Los Angeles's setting.

On June 2 1999, the 18th hole at the soon-to-be-opened Ocean Trails Golf Course in Palos Verdes, California, 30 miles south of downtown Los Angeles, lurched downward and slid 50 feet toward the Pacific. Fragile cliffs and a leaking sewer pipe were blamed for the incident on headland that had shifted significantly on three prior occasions—referred to by geologists as Landslides A, B and C.

BUY LOW, REBUILD HIGH

The Zuckerman family, which owned the land and had hired Pete Dye to design the golf course, had spent $126 million on construction, but were covered by insurance payments that enabled them to attempt a rebuild. While golfers paid $99 to play the 15 holes that weren't affected, engineers filled the crevice at the 18th with well over a million cubic yards of earth. It cost the Zuckermans $20 million or thereabouts, and after three years of legal wrangles and continued financial complications, the work stopped.

In November 2002, Donald Trump stepped in and purchased 215 acres for $27 million—something of a steal for oceanfront property in southern California—keen to succeed where the Zuckermans had failed.

Trump had entered the world of luxury golf development three years before when he built his first Trump-branded course in West Palm Beach, Florida. There, the billionaire developer had engaged Jim Fazio, brother of the better-known Tom Fazio, to design the course and it was he that Trump turned to again to remodel Dye's original holes.

To be honest, Ocean Trails was never going to be Dye's best. Sure, the location of the property was exceptional, but the Zuckermans had given Dye too small a piece of it to build a really great course. It was short, cramped and riddled with faux mounds and blind shots.

Before Fazio could get to work, the 18th needed to be put back, as it were. It cost 61 million to restore and stabilize the cliff using 116 1-inch-thick steel tubes and a geosynthetic material used in the construction of dams.

With the 18th playable again, and after Fazio had widened the fairways (thanks to Trump's decision to sacrifice home sites for extra space), eliminated the blind shots and added three rather extravagant (unnecessary?) waterfalls, the course reopened as the 7,242-yard Trump National Los Angeles in January 2006, with a peak green fee of $280 (expensive, certainly, but not altogether unexpected after Trump spent a total of $264 million building the course). The salvaged 18th hole is now a daunting 512-yard par 4 with a split-level fairway and 14 bunkers—one about 100 yards long.

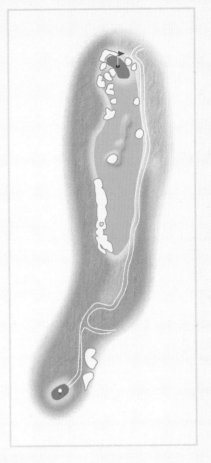

TRUMP: HELPING SAVE GOLF ONE LUXURY COURSE AT A TIME?

Whatever your opinion of Trump, whether you admire the acumen or abhor the arrogance, you can't deny he has an impressive portfolio of golf courses—the best of them quite possibly the Martin Hawtree-designed (with early input from Tom Fazio II—Jim's son, Tom's nephew) Trump International, Scotland, near Aberdeen, which opened in 2012. There are now 17 venues in Trump's collection, including the site of the 2022 PGA Championship—Trump National in Bedminster, New Jersey.

Trump insists the strategy of buying financially stressed courses and turning them into playgrounds for the ultra-rich with exorbitant green fees or joining/initiation fees is somehow good for the game.

SANDBLAST
With 13 conventionally sized bunkers, a 75-yard-long bunker to the left of a split-level fairway, and fabulous views over the Pacific, the 18th provides a typically dramatic finish.

CALI COAST
Thirty miles south of downtown Los Angeles, California, Trump National sits on cliffs overlooking the Pacific at the edge of the Palos Verdes Peninsula.

Further Reading

Bahto, George. *The Evangelist of Golf: The Story of Charles Blair Macdonald.* Chelsea: Clock Tower Press, 2002.

Barrett, David. *Miracle at Merion: The Inspiring Story of Ben Hogan's Amazing Comeback and Victory at the 1950 U.S. Open.* New York: Skyhorse Publishing, 2010.

Callow, Nick. *The Ryder Cup: The Complete History of Golf's Greatest Competition.* London: Carlton Books, 2014.

Campbell, Michael and George Peper. *True Links: An Illustrated Guide to the Glories of the World's 246 Links Courses.* New York: Artisan, 2010.

Cook, Kevin. *Tommy's Honor: The Story of Old Tom Morris and Young Tom Morris, Golf's Founding Father and Son.* New York: Gotham, 2008.

Corcoran, Michael. *Duel in the Sun: Tom Watson and Jack Nicklaus in the Battle of Turnberry.* New York: Simon & Schuster, 2002.

Doak, Tom. *The Anatomy of a Golf Course: The Art of Golf Architecture,* USA: Burford Books, 1998.

Dodson, James. *American Triumvirate: Sam Snead, Byron Nelson, Ben Hogan, and the Modern Age of Golf,* New York: Alfred A. Knopf, 2012.

Frost, Mark. *The Greatest Game Ever Played: Vardon, Ouimet and the Birth of Modern Golf.* London: Little, Brown, 2002.

Frost, Mark. *The Grand Slam: Bobby Jones, America, and the Story of Golf.* London: Time Warner, 2004.

Goodwin, Stephen. *Dream Golf: The Making of Bandon Dunes.* Chapel Hill: Algonquin Books, 2006, revised and expanded 2010.

Hansen, James R. *A Difficult Par: Robert Trent Jones Sr. and the Making of Modern Golf.* New York: Gotham, 2014.

Huber, Jim. *Four Days in July: Tom Watson, the 2009 Open Championship, and a Tournament for the Ages.* New York: Thomas Dunne Books, 2011.

Jenkins, Dan. *Jenkins at the Majors: Sixty Years of the World's Best Golf Writing, from Hogan to Tiger.* New York: Anchor, 2010.

Jones, Robert T. Jr. and O.B. Keeler. *Down the Fairway.* New York: British American Publishing, 1927 reprinted in 1995.

Klein, Bradley. *Discovering Donald Ross: The Architect and his Golf Courses,* Chelsea: Sleeping Bear Press, 2001.

Lord, Henry. *St. Andrews: The Home of Golf.* London: Corinthian Books, 2010.

MacKenzie, Alister. *The Spirit of St. Andrews.* Chelsea: Sleeping Bear Press, 1995, reprinted in 1998.

MacPherson, Scott. *St. Andrews— The Evolution of the Old Course: The Impact on Golf of Time, Tradition and Technology.* London: Hazard, 2007.

Nicklaus, Jack. *My Story.* New York: Simon & Schuster, 1997.

O'Connor, Ian. *Arnie and Jack: Palmer, Nicklaus and Golf's Greatest Rivalry.* New York: Houghton Mifflin Company, 2008.

Owen, David. *The Making of the Masters: Clifford Roberts, Augusta National and Golf's Most Prestigious Tournament.* New York: Simon & Schuster, 1999.

Palmer, Arnold. *A Golfer's Life.* New York: Ballantine Books, 1999.

Pugh, Peter and Henry Lord. *Masters of Design: The Golf Courses of Colt, MacKenzie, Alison and Morrison.* London: Icon Books, 2009.

Ross, Donald. *Golf Has Never Failed Me: The Lost Commentaries of Legendary Golf Architect Donald J. Ross,* Wiley, 1996.

Sampson, Curt. *The War by the Shore: The Incomparable Drama of the 1991 Ryder Cup.* New York: Gotham, 2012.

Sampson, Curt. *The Masters: Golf, Money and Power in Augusta, Georgia.* New York: Villard, 1998.

Shackelford, Geoff. *Alister MacKenzie's Cypress Point Club.* Chelsea: Sleeping Bear Press, 2000.

Steele, Donald. *Classic Golf Links of England, Scotland, Wales and Ireland.* London: Pelican Publishing, 1993.

St John, Lauren. *Seve: Ryder Cup Hero.* New York: Rutledge Hill Press, 1997.

Washburn, Dan. *The Forbidden Game: Golf and the Chinese Dream,* London: Oneworld Publications, 2014.

Wexler, Daniel. *The Missing Links: America's Greatest Lost Golf Courses & Holes.* London: John Wiley & Sons, 2000.

Whitten, Ron and Geoffrey Cornish. *The Architects of Golf: A Survey of Golf Course Design from Its Beginnings to the Present, With an Encyclopedic Listing of Golf Architects and Their Courses.* London: Harper Collins, 1993.

Wind, Herbert Warren. *Following Through,* London: Ticknor & Fields, 1985, reprinted in 1995.

USEFUL WEBSITES:

✦

The Royal and Ancient Golf Club www.randa.org

The British Open www.opengolf.com

St. Andrews Links www.standrews.com

United States Golf Association www.usga.org

U.S. Open Championship www.usopen.com

The Masters Professional Golfers Association www.pga.info

PGA of America www.pga.com

Today's Golfer & Golf World (UK) www.todaysgolfer.co.uk

Golf Digest magazine (US) www.golfdigest.com

Golf magazine (US) www.golf.com

British Golf Museum www.britishgolfmuseum.co.uk

USGA Museum www.usgamuseum.com

The Ryder Cup www.rydercup.com

The Presidents Cup www.presidentscup.com

Alister MacKenzie Society www.alistermackenzie.co.uk

The Colt Association (H.S. Colt) www.coltassociation.co.uk

Golf Club Atlas www.golfclubatlas.com

European Tour www.europeantour.com

PGA Tour www.pgatour.com

The World Golf Hall of Fame www.worldgolfhalloffame.org

2016 Olympics Golf
www.rio2016.com/en/the-games/olympic/sports/golf

Index

A

Aaron, Tommy 172, 173
Abbott, Peggy 64–5
Adams, Gary 191
Alfonso XIII, king of Spain 136
Alison, Charles 14, 107, 136,
    138–9, 151, 156–7
Alps 15
Anderson, Jamie 32
Anderson, Tom 23
Appleby, Stuart 189, 215
Armour, Tommy 70–1, 16
Askernish, 16th 44–7
Atkinson, Tim 45
Atlantic City, 10th 54–5
Augusta National 7, 52
    10th 158–161
    15th 6, 162–9
    17th 170–3
Ayton, David Sr. 19
Azinger, Paul
    78–9, 201, 204

B

Bahto, George 40–1
Baker, H.H. 83–4
Ballesteros, Seve
    16, 20–1, 56–9, 122–3, 136–7,
    167–9, 179, 195–7,
    203, 204, 205
Baltusrol (Lower), 4th 110–3
Bandon Dunes 15
    16th 208–9
Banks, Charles 27, 42, 43
Barnes, Brian 52
Barnes, Jim 61, 77
Beck, Chip 189, 204
The Belfry (Brabazon), 10th
    194–7
Bell, William F. 184

Beman, Deane 198–9
Bembridge, Maurice
    52, 53, 121
bent grass 142
Biarritz Le Phare, 3rd 38–43
birdie (term) 54–5
blind holes 14
Boros, Julius 116, 182
Bradshaw, Harry 37
Braid, James 33, 34, 52, 144,
    145, 146, 147, 148, 178
Bredemus, John 174
British Open, origins 30–3
Broadhurst, Paul 203
Brown, Eric 121
Brown, George 30
Brown, Pete 186–7
Bulla, Johnny 130, 131
Burns, Jimmy 195

C

Cabrera, Angel 71, 72, 160
Calder, John 147
Campbell, Willie 60
Carnoustie (Championship),
    18th 144–9
Carr, Simon 102, 103
Casper, Billy 52, 122, 127
Chambers, Robert 144
Cherry Hills, 1st 114–17
Chicago Golf Club 25, 27, 43
Chiodo, Mario 187
Cink, Stewart 182, 183
Clarke, Darren 36
Cobb, George 171
Colonial, Cordova, Tennessee,
    9th 188–9
Colonial, Fort Worth,
    Texas, 10th 174–7
Colt, H.S. 27, 43, 47, 50, 56,
    101, 106–7, 109, 136,
    139–40, 151
Coore, Bill 43, 80–1, 211
The Country Club, 17th 60–3

Couples, Fred 201, 207, 214
Crafter, Neil 13
Creamer, Paula 73
Crenshaw, Ben 36, 43, 59,
    80–1, 160, 180, 211
Crockford, Claude 153
Crosby, Bing 91, 134
Crump, George
    55, 101–7, 140
Culver, Dr. Leroy 76
Cypress Point, 16th 132–35

D

Darwin, Bernard 10, 36, 109
Dason, Peter 17
Davies, Laura 121, 175
Davis, Mike 89, 210
De Vicenzo, Roberto 173
Dedman, Robert 80
Demaret, Jimmy 91, 142
Doak, Tom 15, 43, 45–6, 54,
    86, 151, 211
Drum, Bob 116, 117, 165
Dunn, Tom 38
Dunn, Willie 38
Dutra, Olin 82, 85, 96
Duval, David 63, 78–9, 189
Dye, Alice 198, 200, 202
Dye, Pete 192, 198, 199–201,
    202, 216

E

Eastwood, Clint 135
Ebert, Martin
    34, 44, 45–6, 178
Egan, Chandler 65, 66
Eger, David 169
Eglinton, Archibald
    Montgomerie, 13th Earl 29
    18 hole courses 28–9
Eisenhower, Dwight 171
Elkington, Steve 213, 215
Els, Ernie 52, 59, 72,
    155, 213, 215

F

Fairlie, Colonel James 29, 30
Falconhead, 18th 186–7
Faldo, Nick 52, 59, 160, 195, 202, 203
Fancourt (Links), 2nd 212–15
Farrell, Johnny 50, 111
Fazio, George 85, 93, 94
Fazio, Jim 217
Fazio, Tom, II 217
Feherty, David 203
Fernie, Willie 34, 178
Finger, Joe 188
Fletcher, Jerome and Paul 199
Flynn, William 54, 60, 96, 101, 110, 114–16, 128
Fort Augustus GC, Scotland 47
Foulis, James 115
Fownes, Henry C. 68–9, 101
Fownes, William C. 69–70
Franz, Kyle 81
Furgol, Ed 77, 110

G

Gallacher, Bernard 52, 97, 121, 202, 205
Geiberger, Al 188–9
Gilford, David 203, 205
Ginson, Rhein 189
Glen Abbey, 18th 192–3
Glen Echo, 16th 64–7
Govan, Jim 105
Graham, Allan 9
Graham, David 86, 96, 214
Grand Slam (term) 87
Green, Hubert 179
greens, top dressing 32
Groom, Arthur 138–9
gutta percha 47

H

Hagen, Bobby 59
Hagen, Walter 11, 36, 50, 52, 61, 71, 77, 163–4
Hanse, Gil 67
Haskell ball 69
Hawtree, Fred G. 119
Hawtree, Fred W. 119
Hawtree, Martin 8, 16, 18, 51, 119
Herron, Tim 79
Hill, Dave 121
Hilton, Harold 33, 52
Hilton, Howard 49
Hirono, 5th 156–7
Hoch, Scott 160
Hogan, Ben 71, 77, 85, 91–6, 113, 116, 117, 121, 125, 127, 129, 146, 148
Hollins, Marion 133, 134
Homans, Eugene 86–8
Hopkins, John Jay 142
Huggett, Brian 52, 121, 122
Hunter, Charles 32–3, 34
Hunter, George 110
Hunter, Ramsay 36
Hunter, Willie 8
Hutchinson, Horace 23, 109
Hutchison, Major Cecil 23, 178

I

Inouye, Junosuke 139
Irvine, Gordon 45
Irwin, Hale 57, 58, 59, 118, 205, 214
Ishikawa, Ryo 189

J

Jacklin, Tony 121, 122, 187
Jacobs, Phil 212
James, Mark 57, 203
Jenkins, Dan 116, 118
Jimenez, Miguel Angel 21

Jones, Bobby 8–11, 59, 86–9, 112, 115, 125, 129, 131, 145, 159, 162, 164, 165, 170
Jones, Rees 43, 133, 136, 170
Jones, Robert Trent 101, 112–3, 126, 133, 170
Jones, Robert Trent Jr. 136

K

Kasumigaseki (East), 10th 138–43
Keeler, O.B. 87, 163, 165
Keiser, Mike 208–9, 210–11
Kiawah Island (Ocean), 18th 202–5
kick plates 24
Kidd, David 43, 208, 209–11
Kidd, Tom 32
Kingarrock GC, Cupar, Fife 47
Kirk, Bob 31
Kirkaldy, Andrew 50

L

Lamb, Henry 36
Lambert, Albert 65
Langer, Bernhard 203, 205
Lawrie, Paul 147, 148
Lees, Peter 108
Lemmon, Jack 135
Leonard, Justin 63, 120, 147, 148, 149
Lerna, Tony 79
The Lido, 18th 108–9
Locke, Bobby 37
Loeffler, Emil "Dutch" 70
Longmuir, Bill 57
Love, Davis, III 77, 149, 207
Lowe, George 56, 118
Lyon, George 66, 67

M

Macdonald, C.B. 15, 24, 25–6, 38–42, 41, 43, 84, 85, 86, 101, 108, 114, 115

MacGregor, Colin 45

MacKenzie, Alister 8, 18, 109, 132, 133, 134, 150-3, 158, 162

Mackenzie, Tom 178

McCord, Gary 161

McCulloch, Jack 23

McDermott, John 54, 61

McGrew, Colonel George 65

McIlroy, Rory 117, 129, 160, 204

McIsaac, Rod 192, 193

Macpherson, Scott 16

Magrum, Lloyd 93

Mahan, Hunter 51, 117

Mangrum, Lloyd 85, 94–5

Maples, Frank 78

Marino, Steve 182

Martin, Bob 20

Martin, H.B. 55

Martin, Melissa "Mo" 121

Marx, Groucho 135

Mary, Queen of Scots 49

Matthew, Catriona 59

Maule, Sir Robert 144

Maxwell, Perry 101, 158, 170, 174

Maxwell, Robert 50

Mediate, Rocco 185

Merion (East)
11th 82–9
18th 90–7

metal-headed woods 190–1

Mickelson, Phil 51, 52, 78–9, 86, 120, 129, 180, 214

Middlecoff, Cary 77, 95

Miller, Johnny 71, 123

Mission Hills (World Cup Course), 10th 206–7

Mogford, Paul 13

Montague, Russell 46

Montgomerie, Colin 34, 63, 72, 203

Morcum, Mick 152, 153

Morris, Tom Jr. 25, 30–2

Morris, Tom Sr. 14, 17, 22, 25, 29–30, 32–3, 44–5, 49, 76, 144, 147, 182

Morrison, Wayne 114, 115

Mosk, Stanley 186

Muirfield 29
18th 48–53

Musselburgh Old Links 47, 49

N

Nakajima, Tsuneyuki (Tommy) 20, 168

Nakamura, Torakichi 142

National Golf Links of America (NGLA) 26, 38, 39

Nelson, Byron 77, 91, 124–5, 131

Nelson, Larry 72

Nicklaus, Jack
as course designer 67, 77, 192–3, 199, 207
as player 20, 36, 52, 53, 57, 59, 72–3, 77, 86, 96, 116, 117, 122 –3, 126, 129, 135, 154, 165–9, 172, 179–81, 180, 215

Nicklaus, Jack, II 77

Nisbet-Hamilton, John 22

Nobilo, Frank 213, 215

Norman, Greg 67, 154, 166, 168, 183, 193, 213, 214, 215

North Berwick, 15th 22–7

O

Oakley, Annie 75

Oakley, Dr. R.A. 115

Oakmont, 18th 68–73

Ohtani, Kohmyo 139, 140, 141

Olazabal, José Maria 63, 203, 204

Olmstead, Frederick 75

The Olympic Club (Lake), 16th 126–7

Olympic Games 64–7

O'Meara, Mark 193, 196

Ono, Koichi 142

Oosthuizen, Louis 159, 160

Ouimet, Francis 61–3, 62, 111

P

Padgett, Don 80

Padgham, Alf 52

Palmer, Arnold 52, 54, 56, 72–3, 79, 112–13, 114, 116–7, 126–7, 165, 206

Park, Willie 30

Park, Willie Jr. 30, 34, 54, 102

Parnevik, Jesper 34

Parry, Craig 149, 213

Paterson, Rev. Robert 47

Penglase, George 140

Pennink, Frank 36

Perry, Alf 52

Peskin, Hy 95–6

Philadelphia, 3rd 126–131

Philp, John 137

Pine Valley, 13th 98–107

Pinehurst (No. 2), 17th 74–81

Piper, Dr. C.V. 115

Plattner, Hasso 212

Player, Gary 52, 67, 116, 129, 133, 146, 154, 189, 212–13

Plenderleith, David 49

Presidents Cup, origins 213–15

Prestwick
1st 28–33
17th 14–15

Price, Nick 59, 166, 183, 193, 213, 215

Purves, Dr. Laidlaw 36

R

Ramsay, John 13

Ratho Farm, 8th 12–13

Rawlins, Horace 61

Ray, Ted 52, 61–2

Raynor, Seth 15, 26–7, 42, 43, 108, 133, 134

Redans 22–7
Reid, Alex 12, 13
Reid, John 54
Reverse Redans 24
Richardson, Steven 203
Roberts, Clifford 167
Robertson, Allan 17, 20, 30, 144–5
Rose, Justin 86, 96, 97, 120, 121
Ross, Donald 76–8, 77, 112
Ross, Philip Mackenzie 178
Royal Birkdale, 18th 118–23
Royal Lytham & St. Annes 11
  16th 56–9
Royal Melbourne, 6th 150–5
Royal Pedreña, 2nd 136–7
Royal St. George's 66–7
  5th 36–7
Royal Troon, 8th 34–5
Ruddy, Pat 15
Russell, Alex 148
Ryder Cup, origins 120–22

S

Sarazen, Gene 6, 35, 70, 71, 82, 96, 129, 153, 164–5
Sayers, Ben Jr. 23
Schlee, John 71
Scott, Adam 51, 59, 154–5, 160
Scott, Andrew 147
Sharp, Frederick 47
Sheehan, Patty 73
Sickle, Gary Van 42
Sifford, Charlie 186, 187
Silva, Brian 43
Simpson, Archie 19
Simpson, Tom 50–1
Singh, Vijay 79, 193, 213, 215
Smith, Abner 55
Smith, Alex 61, 145
Smith, Horton 77, 163
Smith, Macdonald 61, 145

Snead, Sam 71, 77, 91, 92, 116, 122, 124, 128–31, 142, 155, 165
Solheim, Karsten 190
Sörenstam, Annika 175–7
St. Andrews, Old Course 42
  11th 8–11
  17th 6, 16–21
Steel, Donald 36, 45
Steinhauer, Sherri 59
Stewart, Payne 63, 78–9
Strange, Curtis 77, 193, 196
Stranz, Mike 15
Strath, Andrew 30
Strath, Davie 22, 31, 32
Strath, George 34
Streck, Ron 190, 191
Street, Howard 106
Sullivan, Ed 135

T

Taylor, J.H. 61, 119, 136
Thomas, Dave 194–5
Thomson, Peter 19, 79, 121
Thornhill, 11th 124–5
Tillinghast, A.W. 55, 101, 104–7, 110, 180
Tissies, Herman 34
Toomey, Howard 115
Torrance, Sam 196, 203
Torrey Pines (South), 7th 184–5
TPC Sawgrass (Stadium), 17th 198–201
Travis, Walter 77, 101, 104
Trevino, Lee 52, 85–6, 96, 121, 179, 193
Trump, Donald 216–17
Trump National Los Angeles, 18th 216–17
Tucker, John 76
Tufts, James W. 74–7
Turnberry (Ailsa), 18th 178–83
Turner, Waco 186–7
Tway, Bob 200

U

Urbina, Jim 15, 211

V

Van de Velde, Jean 147–9
Vardon, Harry 52, 61–2
Villegas, Camilo 117

W

Walker, George 8
Ward, Bud 130
Washburn, Dan 206
Watson, Bubba 159
Watson, Howard 192
Watson, Tom 21, 52, 72, 118, 146, 168, 179–83, 197
Westwood, Lee 96–7, 185
Whaley, Suzy 177
Whigham, H.J. 38, 84, 85, 86
Whitaker, Jack 161
Whyte-Melville, Major John 23
Wie, Michelle 177
Willis, Grinnell 106
Willson, Robert 76
Wilson, Alan 106
Wilson, Hugh 85, 86, 90, 96, 101, 106, 115
Wind, Herbert Warren 71, 88
Wood, Craig 163, 174
Woodlands (Oaks), 1st 190–1
woods, metal-headed 190–1
Woods, Tiger 32, 34, 51, 79, 89, 125, 129, 169, 172, 184–5, 187, 193, 201, 215
Woosnam, Ian 203
Wright, James 144, 147, 148

Y

Yale 26, 27, 42

Z

Zaharias, Mildred Didrikson "Babe" 174–5
Zebelean, John 190

Credits

5 © yykkaa | Shutterstock

6, 23, 71, 89 © Library of Congress | public domain

7 © Alessandro Colle | Shutterstock

8 © Julietphotography | Shutterstock

9, 14, 16, 28, 35, 37, 60, 137, 182, 194, 196, 209 © David Cannon | Getty Images

10 © Kirby | Getty Images

12 © Ratho Farm

18 © Alan Stewart | Creative Commons

20 © Peter Dazeley | Getty Images

21 © Terry Kettlewell | Shutterstock

22 © Mark Alexander | Courtesy of North Berwick GC

27 © Joseph W. Bausch

29 © Hulton Archive | Getty Images

30 © Jeff McBride | Getty Images

31 © PBWPIX | Alamy

39 Courtesy of Ransomes Jacobsen Ltd

40 © Topical Press Agency | Getty Images

42 © MikeSweeneyMV | Creative Commons

44 © Martin Ebert

46 middle © Darin Bunch (GolfGetaways); bottom © Pvt Pauline | Creative Commons

48 © karenfoleyphotography | Shutterstock

51 © Jim Hunter | Shutterstock

53 © Bob Thomas | Getty Images

54 © Atlantic City CC

56 © Wojciech Migda | Creative Commons

58, 114, 144, 149, 166 © Phil Sheldon/Popperfoto | Getty Images

64 © Jack Curran | Courtesy of Glen Echo CC

68 © Bettmann/Corbis

69 © Fred Vuich /Sports Illustrated | Getty Images

72 © Robert Huntzinger | Getty Images

74 © Craig Jones | Getty Images

76 © Mike Renlund

77 © Michelle Donahue HIllison | Shutterstock

78 © Ed Balaun | Creative Commons

80 © Ross Kinnaird | Getty Images

82 © Drew Hallowell | Getty Images

86 © Adam Hunger/Reuters/Corbis

87, 145, 161 © Augusta National Archive | Getty Images

88 © Heritage Images | Getty Images

92 © Jimhealy24 | Creative Commons

97 © Al Tielemans | Getty Images

103 © The Life Picture Collection | Getty Images

105, 113 © Richard Meek | Getty Images

111, 138, 156, 203 © David Alexander | Getty Images

115 From the Library of Dr. Michael J. Hurdzan

119 top © Ben Queenborough | Alamy; bottom © Hawtree Ltd

122 © The Concession Residences, Sarasota, FL.

123 © Bob Thomas | Getty Images

126 © Sean Ogle | breakingeighty.com

129 © Philadelphia CC

130 © Everett Collection | Mary Evans

132 © Billy Satterfield

139 © Underwood Archives | Getty Images

143 © Augusta National | Getty Images

150 © Chris Condon | Getty Images

153 © Bettmann | Corbis Images

155 top © Quinn Rooney | Getty Images; bottom © Barry Salmons | Shutterstock

159 © Timothy A. Clary| Getty Images

160 © David W. Leindecker | Shutterstock

162 © Danny E. Hooks | Shutterstock

163 © Rob Carr | Getty Images

167 © photogolfer | Shutterstock

175 © Scott Halleran | Getty Images

179 © Richard Heathcote | Getty Images

180 © Brian Morgan | Getty Images

184 © Stephen Dunn | Getty Images

186 © Daily Ardmoreite

185 © Andy Dean Photography | Shutterstock

189 © Sports Illustrated | Getty Images

192 © Kevan Ashworth | Courtesy of Glen Abbey GC

198 © Craig ONeal | Creative Commons

199 © Kohler Co.

201 © J.D. Cuban | Getty Images

206 © Mission Hills GC

211 © Ryan Healy

212 © Phil Inglis | Getty Images

213 © Lady 11390 | Creative Commons

215 © Stuart Franklin | Getty Images

216 corner © Everett Collection | Shutterstock; bottom © Michael-John Wolfe | Shutterstock

All other images in the public domain.

Every effort has been made to credit copyright holders of the images used in this book. We apologize in advance for any unintentional omissions or errors and will be pleased to insert the appropriate acknowledgement to any companies or individuals in any subsequent edition of the work.